COLD WAR AT SEA

AN ILLUSTRATED HISTORY

COLD WAR AT SEA

AN ILLUSTRATED HISTORY

Kit and Carolyn Bonner

MBI Publishing Company

First published in 2000 by MBI Publishing Company, 729 Prospect Avenue, PO Box 1, Osceola, WI 54020-0001 USA

MBI Publishing Company books are also available at discounts in bulk quantity for industrial or sales-promotional use. For details write to Special Sales Manager at Motorbooks International Wholesalers & Distributors, 729 Prospect Avenue, PO Box 1, Osceola, WI 54020-0001 USA.

Library of Congress Cataloging-in-Publication Data
Bonner, Kit.
    Cold War at sea / Kit Bonner.
       p.cm.
    Includes index.
    ISBN 0-7603-0732-6 (pbk. : alk. paper)
    1. United States--Military relations--Soviet Union.
    2. Soviet Union--Military relations--United States.
    3. United States--History, Naval--20th century. 4.
    Soviet Union--History, Naval. 5. United States.
    Navy--History--20th century. 6. Cold War. I. Title.

E183.8.S65 B655 2000
359'.00973'09034--dc21   99-052624

On the front cover: Top left: The hybrid cruiser-carrier (CVHG) *Minsk* as she must have looked when she fired flares at the *USS Harold E Holt FF-1074* on April 7, 1984 while in the South China Sea. *Navy League* **Top right:** The *USS Albany CG-10* fires a long-range Talos missile from her forward twin arm launcher and two short-range Tartar missiles from her port and starboard launchers. *TIM – SFCB* **Bottom left:** The Essex class carrier *USS Valley Forge CVA-45* with a load of Grumman-built F9F Panther jets on her forward deck. **Bottom right:** A stern view of a Victor III riding on surface. The riser and pod on the stern is to house a towed sonar array. *U.S.N.I.*

On the back cover: **Top:** The 4,200-ton full load Forest Sherman class destroyer USS C. Turner Joy DD-951, which was armed with three rapid fire 5-inch/54 caliber guns. *Author's Collection* **Bottom:** A Polaris A-1 missile being launched from the deck of the USS Observation Island *EAG-154* on March 1, 1961. *U.S. Navy*

Edited by Michael Haenggi

Designed by Dan Perry

Printed in the United States of America

CONTENTS

At the conclusion of World War II, the United States and the Soviet Union emerged as weary but dominant super powers. Germany, Japan, and Italy lay in physical and economic ruin; and although Great Britain, France, and China shared victory with the Allied nations, they too had suffered. Six years of the most costly war in world history had taken its toll. More than 50,000,000 men, women, and children lost their lives and the financial costs were incalculable. Nations that had at one time been preeminent in world politics were scratching to feed their war-spent populace.

Only the United States and Soviet Union were capable of mounting a continued military presence on an international basis, and as expected, victory resulted in the predictable dissolution of their reluctant wartime partnership. Vast differences in core ideologies and beliefs quickly severed the common thread that bound these countries during World War II. The relationship moved from a cautious alliance characterized by suspicion, secretiveness, and

July 25, 1946, in the Marshall Islands, where the second nuclear detonation—code-named "Betty"—has just erupted from 100 feet beneath the lagoon at Bikini Atoll. This explosion was far more dramatic than the previous atomic bomb test (air burst - code-named "Gilda") on July 1. Observers from many nations, including the Soviet Union, were allowed to witness the new military potential of the United States. *TIM*

bitterness to one of outright hatred and fear. This set the tone for one of the most peculiar and dangerous periods in world history.

The Soviet Union and other nations that embraced Marxist-Leninist doctrine were determined to eradicate capitalism and all those who championed it from the earth. It was quite simple: the United States and her allies had to be destroyed. The Axis enemy had been vanquished, and now there was no reason for these two powers to remain allied—except for peace. Unfortunately, that was not to be. Added to this was the desperate economic position that the Soviet Union found itself in the wake of victory. The cessation of Lend Lease and rejection of Soviet pleas for American loans, coupled with the British and American refusal to allow the wholesale looting of remaining German assets in the western sector of Germany, further exacerbated an already tenuous diplomatic position.

It was inevitable that conflict would emerge between the two new superpowers, and shortly after war's end, most nations aligned themselves with one or the other. By 1950, the type of war, which was a true global war, began to come into focus—a war of ideology, words, pinprick aggression, and ever-escalating military growth. It was unlike any experience the world had ever encountered. Ultimately, it became a war of one-upmanship, which was exercised through diplomatic or military brinkmanship. For the next 46 years, the people of the world were held hostage to what would amount to nuclear blackmail. Never before were selected nations able to eradicate humanity with such dispatch and violence as was possible with nuclear weapons.

It fell to an American journalist to put a face on this novel form of global conflict. Herbert Bayard Swope coined the term "Cold War" in a speech written for Bernard Baruch in 1947, and like Winston Churchill's "iron curtain" reference, these two words seemed to capture the experience in words that were perfectly understandable to all. At various times and in various regions throughout the world, the war heated up and threatened to become a "hot war." The world would hold its collective breath and pray that diplomatic means could resolve the crisis before the superpowers would resort to the use of nuclear weapons.

For the next four and one half decades, the world fully expected a nuclear or massive conventional war to erupt and consume all of humanity. Each side built and maintained huge, expensive arsenals of weapons. The war took on a life of its own, and eventually evolved into a contest to develop, build, test, and stockpile newer and better

An American family "Fall Out" shelter approved by Civil Defense authorities. It could not withstand a direct hit from a nuclear device, yet it could protect civilians from radioactive fallout. One optimistic retailer offered the units for $2,995 (installed) with a 10-year payment arrangement! Today, surviving units are used for family rooms or children's playhouses. *TIM*

weapons for killing all human life. Entire industries were built up employing thousands of workers designed to support the ever-escalating arms race.

Over the span of two generations, the specter of nuclear war haunted mankind. It periodically escalated to the forefront of world politics yet mainly existed as a backdrop to all ordinary human activity. At the height of the Cold War, it was estimated that there were some 10,000 potential military targets in the U.S.S.R. and more than 7,000 in the United States. Added to the military installations on the target list for nuclear attack were cities in the United States and the Soviet Union—the criterion being a civilian population in excess of 100,000 citizens. There were 162 such population centers in the United States and 254 in the U.S.S.R.. The nightmare of air-bursting nuclear weapons over New York City, Chicago, London, Paris, or Moscow was the subject of countless magazine articles, books, television programs, and treatments by all other media.

Generally, the subject was treated with deadly seriousness; however, there were times when films, cartoons, and books satirized nuclear war. In 1964, Stanley Kubrick's *Dr. Strangelove* and the 1965 production of *The Russians Are Coming! The Russians Are Coming!* put the possibility of all-out nuclear war on a humorous and personal level.

The *USS Nimitz CVN-68* with a flight of F/A-18 jet fighters above. The U.S. Navy's aircraft carriers were of grave concern to the Soviet Union. The nuclear variants, which included the immensely capable Nimitz class, posed a threat to Soviet territory and became a symbol of fear. The mobile carrier battle group could strike from anywhere with nuclear or conventional weapons, which has been demonstrated many times over from the early 1950s Korean Conflict to the 1991 Persian Gulf War. The nuclear carrier rivaled the ballistic missile submarine, strategic bomber, and intercontinental ballistic missile as one of the most infamous memories of the Cold War. *U.S. Navy*

Ukraine, where the bulk of the former Soviet Union's military and industrial assets are located. Crime has become a very serious problem, and the most primitive of economic systems—barter—has become commonplace. The people are without a guaranteed supply of food, heat, and other resources. Remaining military units often go without pay for months and are forced to forage for basic needs. Some have reportedly sold off their own armaments simply to exist. Life in the former Soviet Union has always been difficult at best, and despite concerted and desperate efforts to institute reforms, conditions have worsened. The breakup of the Soviet Union and the disintegration of its foundational system have been two of the most significant events in recent world history and will ultimately shape international order far into the twenty-first century.

There is a counterpoint opinion about the seeming end of the Cold War that has gained some notoriety in military and diplomatic circles. While it is true that the Soviet Union no longer exists and the United States is the dominant superpower, that can change during the space of one generation. After all, Imperial Germany was laid waste at the end of World War I, but scarcely 20 years later was again a strong military power. This time, Germany was willingly in the hands of Nazism and its national pride was consumed with revenge and desire for the defeat and subjugation

of those who had ransacked their homeland a generation before.

There are those who put forward the argument that World War II, which was instigated by Nazi Germany, was a natural continuation of the crusade begun in August 1914. The 20-year pause between World War I and World War II was necessary for Germany to rebuild its infrastructure and military, and above all recover its national dignity. Six years of total war finally caused the defeat of Germany and the Axis, and to prevent a future resurgence of German aggression, the country was literally dismembered. It is now again united.

This example of German national resurgence is not an isolated incident in world history, and the possibility exists that the Soviet Union could return to its former prominence, perhaps in a different form. The Russian word *peredyshka* captures and synopsizes the method by which this nation could rebuild itself. It translates as the concept of taking time out from world affairs to put domestic, economic, military, and technological affairs in order for the future. It also is a time for acquiring as much technology from all sources (i.e., the West) as is possible to achieve parity and ultimately superiority. Unfortunately, it can also easily be recognized as a natural pause for regrouping for the next round of global aggression. To some, the Cold War is not over, it is just frozen in time and awaiting a thaw.

bitterness to one of outright hatred and fear. This set the tone for one of the most peculiar and dangerous periods in world history.

The Soviet Union and other nations that embraced Marxist-Leninist doctrine were determined to eradicate capitalism and all those who championed it from the earth. It was quite simple: the United States and her allies had to be destroyed. The Axis enemy had been vanquished, and now there was no reason for these two powers to remain allied—except for peace. Unfortunately, that was not to be. Added to this was the desperate economic position that the Soviet Union found itself in the wake of victory. The cessation of Lend Lease and rejection of Soviet pleas for American loans, coupled with the British and American refusal to allow the wholesale looting of remaining German assets in the western sector of Germany, further exacerbated an already tenuous diplomatic position.

It was inevitable that conflict would emerge between the two new superpowers, and shortly after war's end, most nations aligned themselves with one or the other. By 1950, the type of war, which was a true global war, began to come into focus—a war of ideology, words, pinprick aggression, and ever-escalating military growth. It was unlike any experience the world had ever encountered. Ultimately, it became a war of one-upmanship, which was exercised through diplomatic or military brinkmanship. For the next 46 years, the people of the world were held hostage to what would amount to nuclear blackmail. Never before were selected nations able to eradicate humanity with such dispatch and violence as was possible with nuclear weapons.

It fell to an American journalist to put a face on this novel form of global conflict. Herbert Bayard Swope coined the term "Cold War" in a speech written for Bernard Baruch in 1947, and like Winston Churchill's "iron curtain" reference, these two words seemed to capture the experience in words that were perfectly understandable to all. At various times and in various regions throughout the world, the war heated up and threatened to become a "hot war." The world would hold its collective breath and pray that diplomatic means could resolve the crisis before the superpowers would resort to the use of nuclear weapons.

For the next four and one half decades, the world fully expected a nuclear or massive conventional war to erupt and consume all of humanity. Each side built and maintained huge, expensive arsenals of weapons. The war took on a life of its own, and eventually evolved into a contest to develop, build, test, and stockpile newer and better

An American family "Fall Out" shelter approved by Civil Defense authorities. It could not withstand a direct hit from a nuclear device, yet it could protect civilians from radioactive fallout. One optimistic retailer offered the units for $2,995 (installed) with a 10-year payment arrangement! Today, surviving units are used for family rooms or children's playhouses. *TIM*

weapons for killing all human life. Entire industries were built up employing thousands of workers designed to support the ever-escalating arms race.

Over the span of two generations, the specter of nuclear war haunted mankind. It periodically escalated to the forefront of world politics yet mainly existed as a backdrop to all ordinary human activity. At the height of the Cold War, it was estimated that there were some 10,000 potential military targets in the U.S.S.R. and more than 7,000 in the United States. Added to the military installations on the target list for nuclear attack were cities in the United States and the Soviet Union—the criterion being a civilian population in excess of 100,000 citizens. There were 162 such population centers in the United States and 254 in the U.S.S.R.. The nightmare of air-bursting nuclear weapons over New York City, Chicago, London, Paris, or Moscow was the subject of countless magazine articles, books, television programs, and treatments by all other media.

Generally, the subject was treated with deadly seriousness; however, there were times when films, cartoons, and books satirized nuclear war. In 1964, Stanley Kubrick's *Dr. Strangelove* and the 1965 production of *The Russians Are Coming! The Russians Are Coming!* put the possibility of all-out nuclear war on a humorous and personal level.

At the height of the Cuban Missile Crisis in October 1962, hardware stores did a brisk business in civil defense supplies. Most stores were mobbed and supplies quickly sold out. Many major municipal governments had to broadcast calming messages to the public. *Los Angeles Times*

The Mirisch Corporation Presents

THE RUSSIANS ARE COMING
THE RUSSIANS ARE COMING

MGM/UA

A billboard advertisement for the comedic yet socially revealing 1965 film, *The Russians Are Coming! The Russians Are Coming!* The movie was filmed in Fort Bragg, California, a community that was a real-life witness to Soviet submarines that occasionally surfaced off the northern California coast for a "look-see at America." *Author's Collection*

However comical these productions were, there was no denying the fear that seemed to lurk just beneath the surface when the nuclear arms race was mentioned. Aside from the possibility of an overt act of war, there was continuing anxiety about the more real possibility of an unintentional act of nuclear aggression that would trigger an all-out retaliation and counterattack. The best-selling book *Fail Safe*, which was ultimately made into a major motion picture, was a more sober portrayal of what could happen if there were a nuclear attack. *Fail Safe* brought reality to the hypothesis of accidental unleashing of nuclear weapons. The Cold War was a near half-century of stress and uneasiness for both sides, and despite redundant system and personal safeguards, the potential for a nuclear strike was ever present.

The Cold War lasted from September 1945 until December 1991. It began with the end of World War II, and quietly ceased on December 30, 1991, with the formal dissolution of the Soviet Union, the nation that President Reagan called "The Evil Empire."

Ironically, the victor at the end of the Cold War was not decided by the amount of potential nuclear megatonnage dropped on an opponent, but by the ultimate effect that continued high levels of defense spending had on its national economy.

Both adversaries in the Cold War expended huge amounts of money to build and maintain very expensive military hardware. As the years wore on, the high price tag of preparedness progressively sapped the resources of both sides. Cracks in the alliances became visible at the halfway point in the war. Sustaining high levels of defense spending without a declared war or at least some identifiable battles made less and less sense to the common people on both sides. People in the Soviet Union craved creature comforts and some of the decadence of the West in their daily lives. The citizens of the Western alliance demanded greater funding

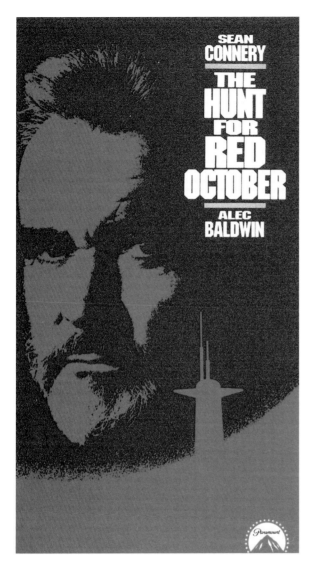

A Soviet Yankee-class nuclear ballistic missile submarine (SSBN) at sea. Although preceded by the ballistic missile–capable Zulu V, Golf I and II, and Hotel classes, the Yankee was the first missile boat that approached the U.S. Navy's George Washington–class SSBN. The Yankee class carried 16 tubes (eight side by side) for SSN-6 "Sawfly" missiles that had a 1,300-mile range. The Sawfly mounted a nuclear warhead and in a subsequent model (#3) had a multiple reentry vehicle system (MIRV). Beginning in 1968, 34 Yankee I–class SSBNs were built. *Navy League*

Paramount Pictures' 1986 *The Hunt for Red October* was not a comedy. It depicted the very real probability of a Typhoon-class SSBN existing for the sole reason of launching multiple nuclear weapons at U.S. targets with impunity and silence. Fortunately, it was fiction. *Author's collection*

of social programs as opposed to escalating military spending.

Change in attitude was inevitable. By the 1980s, most of the Western and Soviet bloc nations had long since reduced their military budgets out of sheer necessity. However the superpowers maintained a concerted military expansionist pace. Fortunately for mankind, the spending rate could not continue, and by the late 1980s, the Soviet Union was crushed by the national debt created by its unrestricted defense spending. So much so that the nation collapsed in spite of a 70-year-long ideology, a substantial infrastructure, and a dedicated military machine. By 1990, the entire Soviet system was under siege and rapidly breaking down on a worldwide basis. Within a year, the Cold War came to an end. The United States and the Western nations had triumphed; however, they too were flirting with economic disaster. Outspending the Soviet Union in national defense had created a huge national debt for citizens of the United States that will still take decades and increased public taxation to resolve.

In the decade that has followed the dissolution of the Soviet Union there has been increasing evidence that its society, culture, military capacity, and economic system are in free fall. The country has been broken up into an eclectic group of smaller states, and most cannot survive on their own. The two largest states are the Russian Federation and

The *USS Nimitz CVN-68* with a flight of F/A-18 jet fighters above. The U.S. Navy's aircraft carriers were of grave concern to the Soviet Union. The nuclear variants, which included the immensely capable Nimitz class, posed a threat to Soviet territory and became a symbol of fear. The mobile carrier battle group could strike from anywhere with nuclear or conventional weapons, which has been demonstrated many times over from the early 1950s Korean Conflict to the 1991 Persian Gulf War. The nuclear carrier rivaled the ballistic missile submarine, strategic bomber, and intercontinental ballistic missile as one of the most infamous memories of the Cold War. *U.S. Navy*

Ukraine, where the bulk of the former Soviet Union's military and industrial assets are located. Crime has become a very serious problem, and the most primitive of economic systems—barter—has become commonplace. The people are without a guaranteed supply of food, heat, and other resources. Remaining military units often go without pay for months and are forced to forage for basic needs. Some have reportedly sold off their own armaments simply to exist. Life in the former Soviet Union has always been difficult at best, and despite concerted and desperate efforts to institute reforms, conditions have worsened. The breakup of the Soviet Union and the disintegration of its foundational system have been two of the most significant events in recent world history and will ultimately shape international order far into the twenty-first century.

There is a counterpoint opinion about the seeming end of the Cold War that has gained some notoriety in military and diplomatic circles. While it is true that the Soviet Union no longer exists and the United States is the dominant superpower, that can change during the space of one generation. After all, Imperial Germany was laid waste at the end of World War I, but scarcely 20 years later was again a strong military power. This time, Germany was willingly in the hands of Nazism and its national pride was consumed with revenge and desire for the defeat and subjugation of those who had ransacked their homeland a generation before.

There are those who put forward the argument that World War II, which was instigated by Nazi Germany, was a natural continuation of the crusade begun in August 1914. The 20-year pause between World War I and World War II was necessary for Germany to rebuild its infrastructure and military, and above all recover its national dignity. Six years of total war finally caused the defeat of Germany and the Axis, and to prevent a future resurgence of German aggression, the country was literally dismembered. It is now again united.

This example of German national resurgence is not an isolated incident in world history, and the possibility exists that the Soviet Union could return to its former prominence, perhaps in a different form. The Russian word *peredyshka* captures and synopsizes the method by which this nation could rebuild itself. It translates as the concept of taking time out from world affairs to put domestic, economic, military, and technological affairs in order for the future. It also is a time for acquiring as much technology from all sources (i.e., the West) as is possible to achieve parity and ultimately superiority. Unfortunately, it can also easily be recognized as a natural pause for regrouping for the next round of global aggression. To some, the Cold War is not over, it is just frozen in time and awaiting a thaw.

CHAPTER 1

THE FOUNDATIONS OF WAR

The Cold War was fought on land, in the air, and at sea on a worldwide basis. In keeping with its overall uniqueness, there was no agreed-upon beginning date. There were no overt military acts nor government declarations of war—it just began, and anyone remotely associated with the military soon recognized it as war. This global conflict was deeply rooted in a series of political, economic, social, and cultural events that occurred from the onset of communism in Russia. For the United States and what were to become its Western allies, the Cold War had its crude beginning during the immediate post–World War I years of 1918–1922.

The Bolshevik Revolution in 1917 toppled the czar and the Revolutionary Government (Bolshevik) negotiated a separate peace treaty with the Germans in March 1918. The Allies did not recognize the new state and openly provided aid to White Russian forces still fighting the Bolsheviks on the northern shore of the Black Sea. Despite Allied intervention, the Red armies closed in on the remnants of the White Russian armies during

the winter of 1920–1921, and forced an evacuation of nearly 100,000 men, women, and children to Tunis. U.S. destroyers *USS Long DD-209*, *USS Fox DD-234*, and *USS Whipple DD-217* were among some three dozen American warships that protected American interests and assisted escaping White Russian refugees. The region was in such violent turmoil that cruisers including the *USS St. Louis* and *USS Pittsburgh AC-4* and new battleship *USS Arizona BB-39* also patrolled the Black Sea as a show of Allied naval might. The Soviet government finally won the Russian civil war in late 1921 but was compelled to ask for aid from the Allies for their famine-stricken country. Through an intermediary, the American Relief Administration, the United States responded with $63,000,000 in relief; however, the United States still refused to acknowledge the new government of the Soviet Union.

American and British naval forces had been sent to the new Russian Communist (Bolshevik) state to quell civil war and protect Western interests. This effort was publicly disdained by leading

The Trident Missile submarine *USS Ohio SSBN-726* on March 12, 1998, near her base in Bangor, Washington. She is commemorating 50 Trident patrols. At any time and anywhere, the Ohio-class submarine can launch one or more of its 24 Trident II (D-5) missiles, which have a range of more than 6,000 miles and multiple thermonuclear warheads. The ballistic missile submarine represented and continues to be a significant deterrence to aggression against the United States and its allies. *U.S. Navy*

In 1982, there was much speculation over a new and monstrous nuclear ballistic missile submarine being built in the Soviet Union. In this line drawing provided to the Office of Naval Intelligence in August of that year, the submarine, code-named Typhoon, was shown launching a missile. In reality, the Russian Navy had designed and was building six of these 25,000-ton submerged displacement boats that carried 20 SSN-20 "Sturgeon" MIRVed ballistic missiles. The Sturgeon had a 4,600-mile range and mounted up to 10 100-kiloton nuclear multiple-reentry warheads. The Typhoons were intended to sit under the polar ice pack and act as a "second strike" weapon system to disrupt and destroy U.S. and Western first-strike recovery efforts. *Navy League*

revolutionaries in Russia, and later prompted Lenin to promise a "funeral dirge over the Soviet Union or Capitalism."

In a strange twist of diplomatic fate it was the Russian Navy that demonstrated its alliance some 60 years earlier with the Union cause during the American Civil War (1861–1865). All other nations were either sympathetic to the Confederate government or simply ignored the pleas of President Abraham Lincoln for support. Russia was the sole world power that openly embraced the Federal cause and for nearly a year (1863) based its Pacific Squadron in San Francisco Bay. Its warships periodically visited ports on the northeast coast of the United States, and there was no denying their value to the Union cause. The other great powers (i.e.,

Tribute to a nuclear holocaust that never happened. An original Polaris A-1 missile from the now-decommissioned ballistic missile submarine *USS Theodore Roosevelt SSBN-600*. This missile sits in a quiet park in the also decommissioned Mare Island Naval Shipyard in Vallejo, California. The Polaris was the U.S. Navy's first submarine underwater-launched long-range ballistic missile. The United States depended on this system as one of its primary deterrents against Soviet attack. Nineteen years after the Polaris' 1960 debut, it was revealed that 75 percent of the warheads on the Polaris A-1s would have failed to detonate. *Author's collection*

Great Britain and France) were caught off balance and realized that attacking the Union could instigate a European war with Russia. The presence of Russian warships actively supporting the Union cause during the American Civil War was a contributing factor in determining the outcome.

Just over a half-century later, Russian revolutionaries witnessed squadrons of U.S. destroyers appear in their harbors as part of the Allied Expeditionary Force. Ostensibly there to protect American lives and business interests, the true purpose was to provide assistance in quelling the civil war. It was widely regarded as unwarranted interference, and set the tone for future relations with the United States and other Western nations. During the period 1919–1922, in places such as Odessa, Novorossisk, and other Black Sea ports, the seeds of the "Cold War" were sown. U.S. Naval forces left the region in late 1922, and it wasn't until the election of Franklin Roosevelt to the presidency of the United States in 1933 that the Soviet Union was formally recognized by the American government.

Relations with the Soviet Union were strained at best prior to and during World War II; however, they were amicable enough to win a war over Nazism and Imperial Japan. Formal agreements between the Allies at the Teheran, Yalta, and Potsdam conferences set the stage for postwar behavior. Once the Axis was defeated, Soviet intentions slid into focus. The Marxist-Leninist doctrine openly preached world domination and now it had a powerful platform on which to begin the journey toward international communism.

At the end of World War II, the Soviet Navy was poorly equipped for combat at sea, but in the decades that followed, it became a navy second only to the United States Navy. Had the Soviet system persevered, it is entirely probable that its navy would have become the dominant force at sea.

In the Cold War at sea, the principal opponents were the United States Navy and its allies, and the Navy of the Soviet Socialist Republics and its allies. The war lasted some 46 years, from 1945–1991. It was a war without heroes, traditional sea battles, and overt patriotic support. It was a war of wills, patience, and wit. It began as a war of cat and mouse, and as the Soviet Navy grew in scope and numbers, it evolved to one of cat versus cat. Both navies existed to prevent an international nuclear holocaust, yet at a moment's notice were prepared and willing to fight any type of sea battle.

Although the Cold War at sea was often popularized as a series of emotionally laden standoff incidents between the primary adversaries, it entailed a far greater range of activity. The Cold War at sea

The hulks of ex-nuclear cruisers *USS Long Beach CGN-9, USS Mississippi CGN-40, USS Virginia CGN-38,* and *USS Texas CGN-39* moored at the inactivation facility at the Puget Sound Naval Shipyard in Bremerton, Washington. 1998 witnessed the end of the American nuclear surface ship navy with the exception of the aircraft carriers. *Author's collection*

Ex-Soviet warships lying aground in Murmansk. Much of the feared Soviet Navy has been scrapped, sold off, or abandoned in the backwaters of one harbor or another. *Greenpeace*

One of the few Soviet MiG-17 fighter aircraft left in the world. There were thousands produced and used by the Soviet Air Force and all of its allies from 1950 to 1980. A few were employed in naval roles but are best remembered for engaging U.S. aircraft in many of the world's trouble spots. This aircraft is at the McClellan Air Force Base in Sacramento, California. *McClellan AFB*

The *USS Pittsburgh ACR-4* in early 1918. This pre–World War I armored 13,680-ton cruiser was one of many U.S. Navy ships that supported the White Russians in their civil war with the Bolsheviks. The White Russian armies were beaten in late 1921 and the Soviet Union became a sovereign nation. *Author's collection*

encompassed the conflicts fought in Korea, Vietnam, and the Persian Gulf. It also included the abortive 1982 Falkland Islands War fought between Great Britain and Argentina. In essence, the Cold War at sea included all combat at sea from 1945–1991. No traditional naval battles were ever fought between the principal adversaries during these years, and the war at sea ended as somberly as it began.

Today, the Western navies are in decline and the Soviet Navy is but a shell of its former glory. Ships that once flew the hammer and sickle can be found in various navies all over the world. For the most part, they have been broken up or are rusting at anchor awaiting their fate. Those that are still operational in the new Russian Federation or Ukraine Navies are often unable to leave port due to fuel shortages and the lack of committed, trained, and obedient officers and crew. The Soviet Navy has died an ignoble death. Sadly, in many ways, the U.S. Navy and its allies have taken the same path. Many of its ships, including the modern nuclear cruisers of the Virginia class, have been scrapped according to the dictates of the accountants. Seemingly, nations can no longer afford large and powerful navies.

This is the legacy of the Cold War at sea. Huge expenditures for combat at sea that never occurred and now the demise of some of the finest warships ever built long before their time. As was predicted by Lenin, the war could be won in any fashion—militarily, culturally, or economically. Ultimately, the Cold War was won by economics.

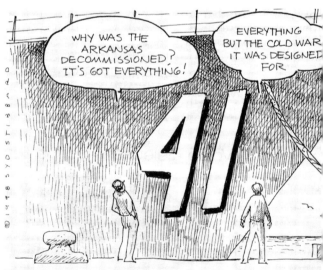

A cartoon that depicts the post–Cold War feeling among naval personnel on both sides of the conflict. Ships were built to fight a "hot" war that never happened, and now they are too expensive to maintain—despite their huge initial cost and obvious remaining military value. *U.S. Navy*

THE POLITICAL CONTEXT

In the two decades following the 1919 Armistice ending World War I, the world experienced some of its most tumultuous political, economic, and cultural change. Communism consumed czarist Russia, Germany rebuilt its economy and military might, Japan tested its modern war machine in China, and the rest of the world agonized through the worst economic depression on record. During this same period, those nations committed to fascism (Italy, Germany, and Japan) secretly (and illegally) rearmed with modern weapons. Western powers contented themselves with peace overtures, appeasement, and slow rearmament.

Despite intelligence reports that the militaristic societies that would become Axis powers were preparing for global domination, the Western powers only gradually faced reality. Initially, Western leaders believed the promises of Nazi Germany, Japan, and Italy, in the hopes that isolated and tolerable aggression would not escalate. International naval limitation treaties (such as the Washington Naval Arms Limitation Treaty of 1922 and its sequels) were adhered to by the West, yet were secretly sneered at by those who sought world domination.

Agreed upon limits on the number, tonnage, and type of warships that could be built were ignored by Japan and Italy. Germany also began a modern naval building program in defiance of protests from other nations. All three modernized their air forces and increased the size of their armies. Peace proved to be a temporary respite between world wars.

The United States, Great Britain, and France rearmed cautiously, and it was not until the last years of peace that they began in earnest to put industry on a war footing. This was partially due to a false sense of security but also due to the lack of popular support for increased defense spending. In the mid-1930s, attitudes began to change and rearmament began in earnest. The possibility for tremendous industrial capacity existed, but it needed time to become fully realized.

When American industrial might was finally brought to bear, the results were extraordinary. At the beginning of the war, the Western powers were ill equipped to fight on one front, let alone on a global basis. However, by the war's end, the United States had produced a staggering 296,000 military aircraft, 86,000 tanks, and 11,900 ships of all types. Much of this was literally given to the Allies.

A propaganda poster displayed during World War II. Popular opinion was reflected by the sentiment of unification for the common purpose of defeating the Axis. In reality, the Allied partnership was fragile at best. Soon after the end of the war, new sides were forged and former allies became enemies. *Author's collection*

15

The oceangoing Soviet submarine L-15 of the "L class" built at the Baltic Yard in Leningrad. These 279-foot-long boats were replicas of a salvaged World War I British submarine. They carried six torpedo tubes in the bow and two aft. All were built over a seven-year period beginning in 1929 and reflected poor technical expertise: of the two built, one was lost on trials and the other by an undetermined accident. Early Soviet submersibles were crude and generally designed for coastal defense. *Author's collection*

More than $11 billion in aid was given to the Soviet Union, including more than 500 vessels of all types. The United States was able to produce what the combined industrial output of Allied factories was incapable of achieving.

During the interwar years, the Soviet Union experienced significant national growing pains, and its acknowledged leader, Joseph Stalin, was more concerned over consolidating and retaining absolute power than improving national defense. To make matters worse, on the eve of the outbreak of war he had just carried out a blood purge to ensure obedience to Communist doctrine and himself. This cost the Soviet Union the finest and

most talented of the officer corps—virtually all of the upper echelon of the naval and army hierarchy was exterminated.

The Soviet Union maintained a large standing army, a mediocre air force, and its navy consisted of obsolete capital ships, coastal submarines, and light forces. Various submarine types were introduced, yet most were crude and technologically deficient. Soviet naval designs were often based on a conglomerate of Western and German models and as a result were barely satisfactory.

In the mid-1930s, Stalin recognized the need for a more sophisticated navy that was capable of fighting on the open sea, but it was not until the

The Soviet 26,000-ton battleship *Marat* (*Petropavlovsk*). This ship was one of three Italian-designed ships built for the Imperial Russian Navy in 1914–1915. They were lightly armored, mounted twelve 12-inch/52-caliber guns, and were considered mediocre by Western standards. The Soviet Navy was hurriedly building modern capital ships when the Germans invaded in June 1941, but all were immobilized. The *Marat* and her two sisters thus represented the capital ship strength of the U.S.S.R. As with many older Czarist-inspired vessels, they were highly unsanitary, and crew habitability was almost nonexistent. The *Marat* was heavily bombed in late 1941, yet was able to help defend Leningrad. This ship, and most other ships of the Soviet Navy was subordinated to the army during World War II. *TIM*

eve of war that words were translated into action. In 1939, a 12,000-ton aircraft carrier, two 35,000-ton battleships, and a number of cruisers, destroyers, and submarines were laid down in various Soviet shipyards. Most were never completed, and of those that saw combat, a large number were easily destroyed by the Germans. By some accounts, the development of Stalin's "big ship" navy, whose ports were all but geographically imprisoned, was more an act of bravado than of strategy. The fact that the Soviet Union had little access to the major oceans and the fact that its merchant marine and navy were easily bottled up plagued naval thought and planning. The large "blue water" navy never came to be and eventually the army conscripted more than 400,000 of its seamen for local defense. Stalin and his senior naval planners had not concerned themselves with how the new navy would be used—just that it would carry the banner of Communism worldwide by sea.

World War II (1939–1945)

World War II was the single most horrific event in the history of mankind. Countries from all continents were willing or unwilling participants, and took sides with the Allies or Axis. The

The "Big Three" reluctantly pose for a photograph at Yalta in February 1945. President Roosevelt (middle) is obviously not well and died two months later. Winston Churchill (right) refused to sit next to Soviet leader Joseph Stalin (left). The Yalta meeting was disastrous for the West. Stalin agreed to declare war on Japan, yet at a high price: Germany was to be partitioned, as was Berlin. Stalin's treachery and Western gullibility haunted the Western allies for nearly 44 years. *Author's collection*

Axis powers included Germany, Italy, and Imperial Japan along with six other, smaller nations. Eventually, the Axis placed some 30,000,000 men under arms, of which 6,000,000 were lost. The Allied powers grew progressively in number to a total of 50 nations, including Great Britain, its Commonwealth nations, France, Norway, China, and ultimately the Soviet Union and the United States. More than 60,000,000 souls were under arms in the Allied cause and by war's end 10,000,000 were killed.

The war began with the unprovoked German attack on Poland in the late summer of 1939 and quickly escalated into an all-out European war. Great Britain followed France and the low countries as the war expanded. Unlike the course of the First World War, France was quickly subdued and many historians agree that Great Britain was within six weeks of being starved into defeat by the Axis U-boat campaign. Had it not been for the United States and its willingness to provide resources, Germany would have triumphed and the occupation of Western Europe been complete. Under one arrangement or another, everything from 50 obsolete "four piper" destroyers to eggs was provided to Great Britain via a seaborne lifeline of merchant ships.

The Soviet Union remained neutral during the first two years of the war, having signed a nonaggression pact with Germany. As it did with all the other treaties and agreements it signed, however, Germany broke this one without provocation. In June 1941, the Soviet Union was actively drawn into the war when thousands of well-trained and committed German troops crashed through their European borders at several points. The objective of their onslaught was the enslavement of the Slavic peoples, and by occupying Moscow—the political, cultural, military, and economic center of the Soviet Union—Hitler was certain of lightning victory. Now it was the Russian people's turn to face the most powerful and victorious army and air force in the world. At first, the battle to slaughter the Soviet Union closely resembled the experience on the western front, where, within weeks, the German war machine ran amok and conquered whatever it attacked. Fortunately for the Russian people, the weather acted as an ally, and continuous ice blizzards combined with intractable mud stopped what most military analysts considered the inevitable—the occupation of Moscow and the certain defeat of the Soviet Union. The German war machine met its first real obstacle at the hands of the Russian weather backed up by the peasant armies of the Soviet Union who were willing to make any sacrifice to win. Some of the fighting in the Soviet Union was the most violent and murderous of the war as the casualty numbers on both sides testified. It was not unusual for thousands to die in one day, yet the armies—often augmented by sailors of the fleet—gave no ground and little quarter. The winter and spring of 1941–1942 and 1942–1943 spelled disaster for the German army in the Soviet Union. When the snow melted, seemingly bottomless mud entrapped entire mechanized divisions and paralyzed an army whose superiority depended on its mobility. Each year seemed worse than the year before. The German army had overextended itself and was slowly forced back out of the Soviet Union and onto home ground.

By April 1945, the roles had been reversed and it was now the Russian peasant armies that overran Germany and occupied Berlin. The Great Patriotic War—as it was known in the Soviet Union—had been won. The cost was almost unimaginable: 25,000,000 men, women, and children of the Soviet Union died as a result. Of this total, 8,000,000 were in the armed forces. Victory had literally been paid for with their blood.

This catastrophic loss was not forgotten by Soviet leadership who faulted the Western Allies for their initial reluctance to open a second front earlier in the war. The United States lost some 414,000 men and women in the armed forces during the war, and according to Soviet claims, the U.S.S.R. suffered an overall death rate 50 times greater.

The Western alliance fought on other fronts as the war expanded to include the United States and Japan in December 1941. The Japanese Navy launched a successful air attack on the U.S. Pacific Fleet moored in Pearl Harbor, Hawaii, and ignited the Pacific phase of World War II. With fighting fronts in Russia, China, North Africa, and now the western Pacific, the war was global and—fortunately for the Allies—included the industrial resources and power of the United States.

The Western Alliance adopted a "Europe First" strategy for defeating the Axis. First, the rapid territorial gains made by the Axis had to be contained, and then rolled back. By late 1942, Joseph Stalin, leader of the Soviet Union, was demanding a "second front" to reduce the pressure on his armies in the east. It came in 1943 with the invasion of Italy, and later the massive attack on the western front in France at Normandy in June 1944.

In a classic pincer movement, the Western forces and the Soviet armies converged on the German heartland, and by mid-1945, the war in Europe was won.

In the Pacific theater of operations, the island-hopping strategy combined with carrier strikes and an unrelenting American submarine campaign slowly pushed the Japanese back to their inner defenses. Within three years, the Japanese homeland was targeted by long-range B-29 bombers operating from formerly Japanese-held atolls in the Pacific, and continuous air attacks began pulverizing Japanese industry.

With the dropping of atomic weapons on Hiroshima and Nagasaki on the Japanese homeland in August 1945, World War II came to an end. At the surrender ceremony many nations were present to witness the capitulation of Imperial Japan—including the Soviet Union, a last-minute

addition to the combatants fighting in the Pacific. The Soviet Union declared war on Japan at the request of the Allies. There was grave concern over the potential for Allied losses in the hundreds of thousands if the Japanese home islands were forcibly invaded. The presence of large numbers of trained Soviet soldiers was deemed essential to defeating Japan on the ground. As it turned out, there was no need for Soviet resources, yet the offer of committing the Soviet military to fight the Japanese had been accepted by the Allies—another incident well remembered by Joseph Stalin.

Post–World War II: Allies Become Adversaries

In September 1945, the Allies were faced with monumental difficulties in Europe and Asia. Europe, and in particular, Germany, had been devastated. Thirty million Europeans were without homes, displaced, sick, and hungry. Many fled their homelands and required medical care, feeding, and transportation back to their villages and cities. Many refugees moved to the West rather than become trapped in a region controlled by the Soviet government. This posed serious logistical problems for the Western allies, and with the exception of the United States, the Allied and former Axis nations had incurred huge public debt and their economies were fragile at best. It was up to the United States to continue a high level of assistance—this time for saving lives. This was not an easy task.

The Soviet Union maintained the largest standing army in Eastern Europe after the war, and in a completely different mind-set, American "GIs" were clamoring to return to civilian life in the United States. Disarmament was on the minds of the Allies—except for the Soviet leadership, which now wanted to loot what was left of German capital assets to pay for the damage to their country. Germany was partitioned into east and west sectors with Berlin administered by four powers (France, Great Britain, the United States, and the U.S.S.R.). The Soviet Union was responsible for providing food for the western sector in exchange for reparations. The plan quickly broke down, however, when the U.S.S.R. was not given a free hand in the west. Food supplies stopped and thousands of refugees starved in what was to be the opening gun of an undeclared cold war.

The new type of conflict escalated as the Soviet Union attempted to install Communist governments in Eastern Europe in lieu of the agreed-upon self-determination. The concept of the "iron curtain" was born; for millions, freedom in the choice of ideology and governmental structure would have to wait for two generations. Winston Churchill

Allied warships crowd Tokyo Bay in September 1945. The surrender of the Japanese Empire occurred aboard the battleship *USS Missouri BB-63* on September 2, 1945. A representative of the Soviet Union was there to sign the surrender document. The U.S.S.R. contributed virtually nothing to the war in the Pacific. The Cold War began almost immediately and the *Missouri* would play a major part at different times in the years to come. *Author's collection*

spoke of an "iron curtain that has descended across a continent" in a speech given on March 16, 1946. The shooting war had ended, yet within months a new type of war was beginning. It would take another two years for the "Cold War" to come into focus and the issues to become clear.

Aside from the growing symptoms of conflict, the underlying theme was evident to anyone who was a student of Marxist-Leninist doctrine. Soviet leaders were firmly convinced that the capitalist system championed by the West and led by the United States was determined to exterminate the Soviet system by any means. This feeling of ideological persecution was reinforced by the popular dislike of the Communist system in most Western nations, especially the United States. Already, terms such as "Red Scare" or "Commie" were entering the lexicon of common Americans, and declared loyalty to "True Americanism" became a watchword in the early postwar years.

Suspicion of Western methods was deeply rooted in Soviet fears of yet another invasion of their homeland. The average Soviet citizen saw World War II as triumph over their hereditary enemy Germany, yet they were not going to relax their guard nor surrender territorial gains for the common good of the world. Aside from protecting its homeland, the Soviet system depended on exporting its doctrine to other nations by any means including propaganda, military aid, and if need be, violent revolution.

To exacerbate matters, in July 1946, the United States invited Soviet observers to witness two nuclear detonations at Bikini Atoll in the Marshall Islands. Operation Crossroads was ostensibly to determine if warships could survive an air burst and an underwater explosion. They survived to a greater extent than was projected. Of collateral diplomatic benefit was the massive power demonstration of U.S. military might for the Soviet and other foreign dignitaries to witness. It was not long before Soviet espionage was able to secure sufficient atomic data for a Soviet nuclear device to be developed, and a whole new dimension to military arms races was added.

Apart from expansion in middle and Eastern Europe, the Soviet Union realized that Greece and Turkey occupied key positions and formed a choke point that could prevent access and escape from its Black Sea ports. A civil war between Soviet-backed Communist rebels and the legitimate Greek government flared up in 1946–1947. In response to this first major attempt on the part of the Soviet system to break out of the U.S.S.R., President Harry Truman issued what has become known as the "Truman Doctrine." In a March 12, 1947, speech to the United States Congress he requested funds to assist the Greek government in its struggle to prevent takeover by Communists. This was later followed up with a military aid package for Turkey.

The speech spelled out much more than a request for military aid. By the words, "support free peoples who are resisting attempted subjugation by armed minorities or outside pressure," it set the tone for U.S.-led anti-Communist activity throughout the Cold War. To reinforce the new American posture, the United States Sixth Fleet was created in 1948 and the battleship *USS Missouri BB-63*, light cruiser *USS Providence CL-22*, and later the new super battle carrier *USS Franklin D. Roosevelt CVB-42* made their presence known in Greek and Turkish ports. The forward presence of the U.S. Navy gave credibility to the Truman Doctrine, and demonstrated to the Soviet Union U.S. resolve to protect its allies.

The battleship *USS Nevada BB-36* shortly after being subjected to the first atomic bomb test of Operation Crossroads being conduced at Bikini Atoll in the Marshall Islands. The orange-painted *Nevada* was used as the "bulls-eye" for the tests. The first test on July 1, 1946, was an air-burst that caused substantial damage to the upper works of many of the 70-odd ships anchored in the lagoon. On July 25, an underwater detonation was far more destructive, yet the *Nevada* refused to sink. She was later expended as a target in July 1948. It was determined that navies still had value in the atomic age. Overall, the United States has detonated 929 nuclear devices from 1945 to 1990 of which 212 were atmospheric. *TIM — SFCB*

U.S. Navy cruisers rest in mothballs at the Philadelphia Navy Yard. Shortly after the end of World War II, scores of warships of all types were put in reserve for future combat needs. Many were sold to foreign countries or broken up for scrap. Most ships were less than four years old, but the advent of jet aircraft and other technology had rendered them obsolete. *TIM-SFCB*

No matter how eloquently expressed, however, a doctrine must have tangible effects. A massive and all-inclusive aid package was necessary to improve stability in Europe.

To cope with the seemingly unsolvable domestic problems of war-ravaged Europe, George C. Marshall, former Chief of Staff to the Army and now Secretary of State in the Truman Administration, proposed an economic aid plan to first feed the peoples of Europe and then direct them to self-sufficiency. It was dubbed the Marshall Plan and in concert with the Truman Doctrine formed the cornerstones of Western diplomatic and economic strategy for European recovery. The Soviets objected strenuously to Marshall's concept, formally declaring that its intent was to reindustrialize Germany as a satellite state for American business interests. It was also characterized as another attempt by capitalist states to obliterate Marxism-Leninism. The war of words was beginning in earnest. Soviet leaders immediately threw political roadblocks in the path of the plan. Their primary vehicle was the Cominform, a Stalinist propaganda tactic that amounted to a formal Communist Information Bureau. Its first act was to convene a conference of Communists from countries all over Europe including France and Italy. Capitalism, colonialism, and all things associated with the decadence of the West were decried, and the group instigated severe action. Communist-inspired strikes and riots broke out all over Europe and were finally subdued by food brought in by the United States. Had the United States not intervened with aid, much of Europe (especially France) could have resorted to Soviet Communism for relief. For the moment, the conflict between Soviet expansionism and Western interests was checkmated.

The undeclared war took another turn with a rather peculiar article that was written for *Foreign Affairs Magazine*. The article was entitled "Sources of Soviet Conduct" or as it was popularly known, the "X article." In reality it was written by a U.S. State Department employee, George F. Kennan, who signed his name as "X" because of his position in the United States government. The piece succinctly recommended the use of counter force corresponding to that used by the Soviets as the political-military solution to anticipated Soviet expansion. The term "containment" was formally introduced, and the resulting concept became the anchor in U.S. and Allied policy toward Soviet ideological aggression. From this date forward, virtually all Western military, political, and economic maneuvering was directed to containing the spread of worldwide Communism as if it were a cancerous disease. With few exceptions (i.e., Cuba and Vietnam), the strategy was relatively successful.

To this point, the Cold War was one of words, minor military actions, and jockeying for position. In February 1948, the war heated up and became reality for the American and Western-allied peoples. A Soviet-backed and -motivated coup was successful in toppling the neutral democratic government of Czechoslovakia, which resulted in the March 10, 1948, murder of its leaders, including pro-Western foreign minister Jan Masaryk. The people of Eastern Europe were still uncertain as to what their political fate should be, but the specter of an entire nation being pulled under the "iron curtain" was highly dramatic. This event, combined with the March 1948–May 1949 blockade of Berlin, forcibly demonstrated that the Cold War had begun. The citizens of West Berlin were fed and provided with heat by the West through round-the-clock flights in and out of Berlin's Templehoff Airport. It was not unusual for aircraft to be landing and taking off at 20-minute intervals regardless of the weather. The Soviets prevented ground transportation, but were unwilling to shoot down unarmed American transport planes. This was not to be the first time that Western ingenuity and resolve would cause the Soviet leaders to stand aside.

The spread of the Communist dogma and its variant teachings was phenomenal. The doctrine of Lenin and Marx was now present on all continents in one form or another. Communist guerrillas were on the move in Malaysia. Great Britain, a nation still determined to maintain worldwide influence, began a counter-insurgency campaign that was initiated by air attacks from the sea in October 1949. The conflict in Malaysia was not resolved

The light cruiser *USS Providence CL-82* was sent with the battleship *Missouri* and destroyer *USS Power DD-839* on April 5, 1946, to the Bosphorus near Istanbul, Turkey. These ships were unmistakably in the region to forcefully demonstrate U.S. resolve to Moscow that Communist insurgency in Turkey and Greece was inappropriate and would be stopped with armed intervention. The *Providence* was a Cleveland-class light cruiser armed with 12 semi-automatic 6-inch/47-caliber guns. In this rare photograph, she is moored in the Mediterranean at Christmas in 1948. *Author's collection*

The *USS Missouri BB-63*. Within seven months of Imperial Japan's surrender, this Iowa-class battleship was showing the flag as a method of stopping the spread of Communism in Greece and Turkey. This example of seaborne power projection was to be repeated many times in the future when U.S. and other Western interests were threatened. The four-ship Iowa-class battleships were armed with nine 16-inch /50-caliber guns with a range of up to 25 miles. They were also the last active battleships in the world. *Author's collection*

The Commencement Bay–class aircraft carrier *USS Rendova CVE-114* lands 84 surplus U.S. aircraft at the port of Istanbul, Turkey, on May 6, 1948. Aside from flag showing by large warships, the United States began a program of military aid as another means to fight the Cold War. The U.S. Navy had a large surplus of relatively new escort aircraft carriers that were pressed into aircraft transport roles. This was also an element of the Cold War at sea, and was just the start of a massive worldwide military aid program for nations that opposed Communism. *TIM — SFCB*

until 1957, when its people were granted independence by the United Kingdom.

The French were also plagued with Communist insurgency in the late 1940s and were ultimately forced to leave Vietnam in 1955. It seemed that all former areas once dominated by Western colonialism were under fire from Communist forces, which in the main were successful. The Western nations had been drained financially by World War II, and there was little defense budget available to counteract popular revolts in distant lands. The United States was obligated to defend South Korea in company with the United Nations when Communist-ruled North Korea invaded it in 1950. This "Police Action," as it was euphemistically termed, was one of the first tests of "containment," and despite the huge loss of men and material, the action was successful in defeating Communist aggression. It was also a proving ground for American- and Soviet-designed jet-propelled aircraft, and at the same time, illustrated the ineffectiveness of conventional anti-aircraft weapons. The war ended in a truce.

Although Soviet-inspired and -sponsored insurrections in various regions of the world became a common staple of the Cold War, it was in Europe that the threat of invasion by the U.S.S.R. and the prospect of another bloody war was most feared. During the immediate post–World War II years, the Soviet military machine was growing in size and technical capability, and no one European nation was capable of opposing it. It was obvious that belligerence was going to be a way of life. It was also evident that the use of tactical nuclear weapons in a European war was possible, and radioactive fallout recognizes no national border. Consequently, in early April 1949, the North Atlantic Treaty Organization (NATO) was established for mutual protection. This very critical alliance initially included Belgium, Canada, Denmark, Iceland, Italy, the Netherlands, Luxembourg, Norway, France, the United Kingdom, and the United States.

In the most significant diplomatic and military alliance since the end of World War II, the

The Soviet light cruiser *Sverdlov* anchored at the British Coronation Naval Review on the evening of June 15, 1953. This was the formal introduction of the Soviet Navy's first post–World War II cruiser class to the world. Obsolete by most Western standards, this all-gun cruiser still represented a potent weapon against merchant shipping. As they did with the gaudy and overdone military parades in Red Square, the Soviets likewise showed off their naval hardware to make the most of its propaganda value. This was just another means of fighting the Cold War. *Author's collection*

Western allies bonded their military might to oppose Soviet aggression. At the outset, the NATO military force was lightweight compared to its potential opponent, but that would change as the alliance strengthened.

Each nation had a specific military responsibility for thwarting Soviet expansion, and within a few years Greece and Turkey (1952) became members, along with the newly accepted Federal German Republic (1954). The existence of a cooperative group of nations and a rearmed Germany was of great concern to Soviet leadership, and in 1955 the Warsaw Pact was created for collective self-defense of its members. Essentially it was a formal joining of Eastern European nations under Soviet military leadership as a counter move to NATO. Each side now had apparent solidarity of ideals and direction in the event of war. For the

Warsaw Pact nations, alliance with the Soviet Union was compulsory, and direction and control was exercised by the Soviet army. NATO operated in a more democratic and equitable fashion and has survived the dissolution of the Warsaw Pact.

The establishment of NATO is often identified as the formal starting gun for the Cold War. It was not that simple. When NATO was formally inaugurated on April 4, 1949, it symbolized a new level in this modern type of war—it was the day that both sides knew they were in a war. It was also the day that both sides recognized that there was a very real probability of another world war—possibly an all-out nuclear war.

The Cold War escalated almost to the point of all-out nuclear warfare in October 1962 with the Cuban Missile Crisis. The Soviet-backed Castro regime in Cuba permitted the establishment of

The heavy cruiser *USS St. Paul CA-73* fires all nine of her 8-inch /55-caliber guns in anger at the North Korean Communist targets. The U.S. Navy was used extensively in the Korean War in many of its primary roles (e.g., shore bombardment, mine warfare, amphibious, and carrier air attacks). It was a cold, bitter, and dangerous war for the U.S. Navy and other United Nations forces that were there to force the North Korean armed forces out of South Korea. The "police action" ended with a truce, and the Cold War continued in the region on more subtle terms. *TIM — SFCB*

nuclear warhead–capable missile launchers some 90 miles from the U.S. mainland. Soviet-built Beagle bombers were also seen being assembled on Cuban airfields by American surveillance aircraft. The United States responded to this form of aggression by initiating a naval blockade, and compelled the Soviet Union to remove the missiles. This was one of the most significant and humiliating reversals ever suffered by the Soviet Union, and for its military hierarchy, it unmistakably demonstrated the need for a powerful "blue water navy."

Both superpowers realized the danger of nuclear war from this event, and shortly after the Cuban Missile Crisis was defused, the first in a series of treaties was signed by the United States and the Soviet Union. In 1963 the Nuclear Test Ban Treaty was signed, and in 1972 and 1974 both nations agreed to limit the proliferation and deployment of strategic arms (SALT I). The superpowers had come to the brink and both had blinked. Of course, Communism was still growing militantly in other areas. The United States now found itself involved in full-fledged civil war in Vietnam. France was forced out by the Communists in 1955. This was less than a decade before the United States found itself on a similar path toward full military commitment to the Republic of South Vietnam. The south was fighting against Communist Viet Cong guerrillas and the regular armed forces of North Vietnam, who were armed with Soviet or Chinese weapons. The Vietnam Conflict lasted until April 1975. The north triumphed over the south just as the last Americans were air-lifted out of Saigon on April 29, 1975. More than 55,000 American lives were lost and billions of dollars were spent in military arms. Also lost was confidence in the American military, which was not to be fully regained until the spectacular Gulf War victory in 1991.

After the United States pulled out of Vietnam, there seemed to be a spirit of cautious cooperation with the U.S.S.R., characterized as détente. President Richard Nixon had opened up China to the United States through his visit there, and the SALT II talks began. There was renewed concern about improved Soviet missile capability, especially the SS-N-20 ICBM (intercontinental ballistic missile), which had a 3,500-mile range and carried up to three nuclear warheads (MIRVs: multiple independently targeted reentry vehicles). The SS-N-20 was a solid-fuel mobile missile system, which, when deployed opposite NATO member nations, caused great—and justified—alarm. This missile system occupied a high priority for discussion at the SALT II conference on the subject of arms limitation. On June 18, 1979, both nations signed the SALT II agreement; however, it was not ratified by the U.S. Senate. Despite this, the United States and Soviet Union abided by its terms. The spirit of détente continued until December of 1979 when the Soviet Union invaded Afghanistan. The United States objected to this military aggression, and for the next nine years, the U.S.S.R. became mired in its own "Vietnam." With the covert assistance of the United States in the last years of the war, Afghan rebels were supplied with the shoulder-held "Stinger" surface-to-air missiles. This system accounted for a number of Soviet helicopters being shot down. This, coupled with a disastrous ground campaign, caused the Soviets to pull out in May 1988. They lost an estimated 15,000 young soldiers, who were mainly conscripts.

The Cold War, which had been on the back burner of many minds for a time, again escalated with Soviet armed involvement in Afghanistan and shortly thereafter, in 1983, the United States deployed the brand-new Pershing II missiles in Europe. These were ground mobile 1,800-mile-range tactical nuclear missiles. This was followed up by President Ronald Reagan's announcement of his plans to develop a system that would intercept and destroy any form of ICBM or submarine-launched ballistic missile (SLBM) launched against the United States or its allies. The Strategic Defense Initiative (SDI) or "star wars" system, as the media labeled it, would consist of a space-based system of interception. The Soviet government was aghast at

High Noon

A cartoon that depicts the level of peril that the West and the Soviet Union found themselves in during October 1962. The Soviets attempted to place medium-range ballistic missiles (MRBM) of the SS-4 (Sandal) type and intermediate-range ballistic missiles of the SS-5 (Skean) variant in Cuba—just 90 miles from the U.S. coastline. The 1,020-mile-range Sandal mounted a three-megaton nuclear warhead and was a relatively reliable and accurate missile. It was capable of hitting St. Louis, New Orleans, and the Panama Canal. The 2,200-mile-range Skean was far more dangerous, as it could devastate most areas in the United States with 5-megaton weapons. Soviet Premier Nikita Khrushchev was obsessive about nuclear weapons and secretly attempted to arm Cuba with a number of missile sites. The United States confronted the Soviet leaders and the missiles were removed. It was the most significant confrontation of the Cold War. Had the U.S.S.R. possessed a "blue water" navy, its resolve might not have collapsed under U.S. determination to escalate this issue to all-out nuclear war. *Los Angeles Times*

A Soviet cruise missile submarine, code-named "Charlie," at high speed. The Charlie class was developed to kill U.S. Navy carrier battle groups and other large Western warships. These 4,700-ton submerged displacement boats were capable of 30+ knots, and carried eight anti-ship SSN-7 missiles. The SSN-7 had a 30-mile range and became operational in 1969. The six boat follow-on class (Charlie II) carried eight SSN-9 missiles with a 60-mile range. Both the SSN-7 and SSN-9 cruise missile types could be fired from below the surface. *Navy League*

The *USS Blueback SS-581*, one of three diesel-electric Barbel-class submarines built with the Albacore-type hull. These were the last conventional submarines built for the U.S. Navy, and often forward deployed in nations that forbade nuclear-powered vessels or weapons. Now the *Blueback* is a tourist attraction in Portland, Oregon. The boat was used in the film *Hunt for Red October*. *Author's collection*

the possibility that such a complex system could negate their entire ballistic missile program, and thus their true power base. The sole endowment of the U.S.S.R. was its military forces, and if its strategic nuclear weapon delivery program were to be neutralized, it would no longer be considered a legitimate superpower.

Mikhail Gorbachev was the new General Secretary of the Soviet Communist Party and the leader of the U.S.S.R. during the Reagan era and later with President George Bush. This leader, more tolerant and farsighted than his predecessors, sought to bring the Soviet Union into the mainstream of the twentieth century. He worked closely with American and Western leadership to foster open relations, or *glasnost*.

He also saw the need to restructure the Soviet economic system and ultimately reduce defense expenditures, which had consumed much of the nation's resources. The Russian translation for this plan of revitalization is *perestroika*. This word became part of the international lexicon and forever will be associated with the leadership of Mikhail Gorbachev. The Soviet military machine continued to flourish partially on its own momentum, but also to maintain the "superpower" illusion. In particular, its navy experienced explosive growth in new vessel types such as the nuclear battle cruisers of the Kirov class, the Slava-class cruisers, and the long-awaited fixed-wing aircraft Supercarrier class: the 64,000-ton Kuznetsov.

Gorbachev's attempts to revitalize the country and allow heretofore forbidden freedoms to Soviet satellite states were commendable, but came too late. The dam finally broke in 1989, and by December of that year, the Berlin Wall was being torn down. The most infamous and internationally known symbol of Communist oppression was smashed by East Germans, assisted by thousands of refugees fleeing the Soviet system. The Soviet Union was imploding—socially, culturally, and economically. Gorbachev's reforms were too little and far too late.

By December 30, 1991, Russian President Gorbachev, in company with Ukrainian and Belarus leaders, declared the Soviet Union extinct. For the Russian people, incredible difficulty and confusion were just beginning. The mega-bureaucratic, monolithic militaristic state that was once the U.S.S.R. was no longer there. The people would have to find something or someone else in which to place their nationalistic faith.

At this time, the rest of the world awoke to find the possibility of nuclear holocaust substantially lessened. For the moment, the world was now a safer place to live—at least in terms of massive nuclear weaponry. Conventional wars continued and will continue unabated, as usual.

Despite the fact that the Soviet Union dissolved itself in the early 1990s, tension remains high between the West and Communist-dominated states and/or those nations that were once dependent on the Soviet Union for weapons and technology. The People's Republic of China has nuclear weapons and a means to deliver them via ICBM or SLBM. Israel, India, and Pakistan also have nuclear weapons. Rogue militaristic nations such as Iraq, Iran, North Korea, Libya, and certain breakaway republics of the former Soviet Union are aggressively seeking means to build nuclear weapons and appropriate delivery systems. The world is still in mortal danger of madmen and their use of weapons of mass destruction.

Naval Aspects of the Cold War

The Cold War was a war of diplomacy, economics, and the most significant arms race in history. It was fought on land, in the air, and on the sea. The men and women of the armed forces on both sides were in a constant state of alert. Both watched each other for any sign of a preemptive strike or attack. Each side had to be prepared at a moment's notice to respond to any sort of provocation, even including a response of massive retaliation. It was a war of calculated and measured response. It included staged public demonstrations of power and technological prowess, but on the other hand, provided humanitarian aid to various nations—all for propaganda value.

Being stationed at sea could often be the most lonely and desperate time for military personnel. Men and women on both sides were separated from their loved ones, often for several months, and in the case of nuclear ballistic missile submarines, separated from humanity itself. It was as if both navies were at battle stations from the time they left port until they returned. In some instances, ships and men never returned to port, and seemingly on a routine basis, submariners and naval aviators were lost due to accidents and mishaps. Soviet and allied warships collided, exploded, and sank in the pursuit of ensuring a forward presence of naval forces. Brinksmanship at sea became an art, and a naval officer in command had to judge how far to provoke his opponent and when to back off. The winner knew how to do both. Shots fired in anger took place in the peripheral wars fought in Korean, Cuban, Vietnamese, and South Atlantic waters. It was all part of the Cold War at sea.

In early 1996, in one of life's ironies, the now Russian, but former Soviet Navy Krivak I frigate, *Pylky FF-702* (foreground), operates in the central Mediterranean with a U.S. Navy Ticonderoga-class cruiser, *USS San Jacinto CG-56*. The *Pylky* had been escorting the Russian fixed-wing aircraft carrier *Admiral Kuznetsov* as part of an international exercise. Just a half-century before, the *USS Missouri* and *USS Providence* were in the same sea, on a mission of preventing the spread of Communism. *U.S. Navy*

The Cold War at sea began with the American and Western allies showing the flag in ports all over the world to reinforce their intention to prevent the spread of Communism. The presence of U.S. and/or other Western warships in a potential hot spot often neutralized Communist efforts and allowed legitimate national self-determination to proceed unhindered by overt Soviet influence. Soviet leaders were quick to notice the value of a surface navy to project power and national interests from the sea. Great Britain, whose empire was on the wane, had mastered this centuries before and now the U.S. Navy emerged as the most powerful in the world. The Royal Navy, on whom the sun had never set, graciously accepted a more subsidiary role in global operations. It was now up to the U.S. Navy to be in the forefront of the effort to contain Communism at sea.

The war at sea also began with U.S. and other Western warships being denied access by the Soviet government or other Communist nations to ports and regions formally open during World War II. U.S. naval patrol aircraft were fired upon and harassed by Soviet fighter planes. The Allied headiness of victory at the end of World War II

The former Soviet Navy Foxtrot diesel-electric submarine *Scorpion* in Sydney, Australia, moored next to the retired *RAN Vampire*, a Daring-class destroyer. Both were part of Australia's Maritime Museum, yet in 1998, the Foxtrot became part of the *RMS Queen Mary* exhibit in Long Beach, California. The Foxtrot was the workhorse of the Soviet submarine force and seemed to be ever-present where Western naval combat photographers were taking pictures. *Author's collection (by Carolyn Bonner)*

attack and missile submarines as well as countering a substantial mine warfare menace. The United States was prospectively tasked with strategic air strikes against Soviet and Warsaw Pact naval installations and large naval units. This included the destruction of Soviet short- and long-range naval aviation potential. To this was added multi-ocean anti-submarine warfare (ASW) efforts, with emphasis on locating and destroying missile submarines. Other NATO forces were to deal with local operations, coastal ASW, and merchant ship interdiction. As the size and capability of NATO sea forces grew and the organization stabilized, the tasks shifted and within a few years, this force became quite effective. In the formative years NATO was not as well equipped as its counterpart in the Soviet Union; however, experience and planning improved naval operations and war-fighting ability.

The "battleless" naval war moved through stages generally dependent on the perceived or actual growth of the Soviet Navy in numbers and capability. Likewise, the Soviet Navy tracked the development of Western technology at sea. Much of what the Soviet Navy achieved during the Cold War was based on espionage and emulating the designs of Western warships and their weapon systems. It was also based on countering Western navy strengths at sea. Soviet naval leadership was in particular concerned about the U.S. Navy submarine threat, and accordingly, built four guided-missile/helicopter Moskva-class cruisers (CHG). These ships were designed to kill submarines.

Of course, as the Soviet Navy grew in stature and capability, it was necessary for the U.S.-led Western navies to take note and counter Soviet strength. The war at sea was ultimately unrelenting, and each side knew that it could heat up at any time.

As the war at sea evolved in the 1960s and 1970s, Soviet attack and missile submarines departed from traditional coastal operations and began patrolling in most oceans and quite near U.S. coasts. The threat of submarine-launched nuclear-tipped ballistic missiles aimed at American and Western cities became a reality. At a moment's notice, ballistic and cruise missile submarines of the Delta IV SSBN class or Charlie II SSGN class could launch their weapons and disappear. It became the mission of the U.S. Navy and its Western allies to prevent such an attack and retaliate when necessary. It was a form of containment at sea. In the latter part of the Cold War, the Soviet Union began to develop and deploy a "blue water" navy that added powerful surface ships and aircraft carrier aviation to its seaborne arsenal. It was at

was quickly eroded as animosity between the Soviet Union and the Western powers escalated. It was then widely recognized that the Cold War at sea would principally be fought in the North Atlantic, consequently attention and resources were directed to that region. This was to be the role of NATO's naval resources.

It was imperative that seaborne lines of communication and supply be kept open and free from Soviet attack. Much of NATO's naval operation was based on maintaining a bridge from the United States to Europe for transporting essential military supplies and troops. This meant combating Soviet

this point that it became clear that the Soviet Union was no longer content to use its navy for the defense of the homeland. Naval bases in friendly nations and "at sea" refueling and resupply allowed the Soviet Navy to expand its sphere of operations and influence far from its shores. The U.S.S.R. had learned that a surface navy could be a valuable adjunct in spreading Soviet Communism internationally. The country's army, air force, and strategic rocket command were capable of a first strike and potentially a credible second-strike nuclear response. A well-found navy allowed a quantum leap in power projection.

By the late 1980s, the Soviet Navy was second only to the U.S. Navy and was building a number of modern ships in all classes, including the Typhoon-class SSBN. This 25,000-ton ballistic missile monster carried 20 SS-N-20 missiles, each with up to ten 100-kiloton nuclear warheads. The purpose of the Typhoon was simple: take station under the polar ice pack and wait for the world to finish its first round of nuclear attacks. Once the United States and its allies had begun recovering, then make the ultimate second strike of 200 nuclear warheads, each five times more powerful than those used in Japan in 1945. The concept of the Typhoon was that of an "on-call doomsday machine." Luckily, this never happened. The late 1980s brought more than an expanded navy; it also brought disaster upon disaster to the Soviet system of government, economy, and its bloated and unwieldy bureaucracy. Dreams of a navy capable of challenging the U.S. Navy in its own backyard and on a level playing field evaporated with the disintegration of the U.S.S.R. Of course, the U.S. Navy quickly followed the path of the Soviet Navy. Both countries soon placed relatively modern ships in reserve or sold them to other nations seeking to improve their naval capability. By the mid-1990s, Egypt, India, Taiwan, Greece, and many other nations had taken advantage of early disposal of highly capable warships. Nuclear warships and, in particular, older submarines (SSNs/SSBNs) began the lengthy, complex, and costly deactivation program.

Had events taken a different turn, speculation provides a vastly different late twentieth and early twenty-first century. If the Soviet Union and its failed economic system had not collapsed under its own weight, it is entirely possible that parity with U.S.-led Western naval strength would eventually

August 27, 1998. The *USS California CGN-36*, last of the U.S. Navy's nuclear surface combatants, is deactivated at the Puget Sound Naval Shipyard. The nuclear cruisers were Cold War creations designed to escort the Nimitz-class nuclear carriers (CVN). High personnel and maintenance costs, and the end of the Cold War, spelled doom for these beautiful and capable ships. The *California* and *USS South Carolina CGN-37* were the last of nine U.S. Navy nuclear cruisers to be deactivated. Nuclear components were removed from the ships and transported to Hanford, Washington, for processing and burial. Nuclear waste disposal in the United States is intense and highly regulated—not so in the Soviet Union. *Author's collection*

have been reached. The rise of the Soviet Navy during the Cold War will always be regarded as phenomenal. A war at sea with the Soviet Navy of the twenty-first century would have been global and catastrophic to both navies. The experience and high technology of the U.S. Navy would likely have prevailed over the sheer number and brute power of Soviet naval weapon systems.

However, in 1945, some 55 years before the turn of the next century, there was no thought of the U.S. Navy engaging the Soviet Navy on equal terms. The U.S. Navy was the most powerful on earth and had ships and weapons to spare. The Soviet Navy was fifth rate at best and represented little threat to anyone. In 1945, there was no conception of a Cold War at sea. That would change.

CHAPTER 3

PRELUDE TO BATTLE: POST–WORLD WAR II NAVIES (1945-1950)

The year that millions of people prayed for, the year World War II came to an end, arrived in 1945. The war was made final aboard the world's most powerful capital ship, the *USS Missouri BB-63* in Tokyo Bay on September 2. In a strange twist of fate for most Americans, the symbolic beginning of the war was on another battleship, the *USS Arizona BB-39*. And appropriately today, both ships quietly rest together in Pearl Harbor, where it all began for the United States on December 7, 1941.

644

Nearly new heavily armed Fletcher-class destroyers are being inactivated at the San Diego Destroyer Base in this November 11, 1945, photograph. The *USS Stembel DD-644* is the outboard ship. Just a quarter-century before, scores of 1,200-ton four-piper destroyers newly built for World War I were moored in the same location awaiting a call to arms. This was "red lead row" for the U.S. Navy destroyer force, and the only visitors were maintenance crews and seagulls. *TIM*

Many naval planners before World War II envisioned a glorious and decisive clash between ponderous lines of opposing battleships. Cruisers and destroyers would act in support by scouting ahead and launching torpedo and gun attacks on the flanks of the enemy battle line. Whichever force had the most ships left afloat would command the sea. This had been the vision of naval strategists since the time when warships changed from wood to steel construction and became steam-powered. The naval battle of Jutland during World War I came close to fulfilling this hoped-for expectation, but the result was indecisive and elusive. Unfortunately, this event kept alive the concept of big ship-to-ship dueling and caused much of the naval thinking and scarce interwar naval funding to be expended on battleships, and worse still, battlecruisers.

Prewar thinking held that the submarine was a novel tool for coastal scouting and defense, and the aircraft carrier for scouting and protection of the battle line. Both existed for the defense of the main battle line and as such received reluctant support until the eve of World War II.

The Japanese aerial attack on Pearl Harbor, launched from six aircraft carriers and the German U-boat campaign in the Atlantic, caused naval strategies to change almost overnight. From the outset of World War II, naval operations varied considerably from what had been expected by most prewar leaders. The massive clash of ponderous lines of opposing battleships never came. There were a number of sea battles between surface ships, but not on the scale that had been expected. War at sea was revolutionized through the use of aircraft and the submarine. The proof of this was found in the large percentage of naval and merchant shipping vessels sunk or damaged by them. U.S. Naval aircraft flying from aircraft carriers or shore bases sank 174 enemy warships and shot down or destroyed 15,000 Japanese aircraft.

The Puget Sound Naval Shipyard in Bremerton, Washington, was a major location for inactive mothball fleet ships. Battleships, heavy and light cruisers, and aircraft carriers were also located in other parts of the country, such as Philadelphia and San Francisco. At least five mothballed Essex-class carriers were captured in this May 1, 1948, photograph. From back to front, they are the *USS Essex CV-9, USS Ticonderoga CV-14, USS Yorktown CV-10, USS Lexington CV-16,* and *USS Bunker Hill CV-17.* Sister ship *USS Bon Homme Richard CV-31* is in the background behind a number of anti-aircraft cruisers (CLAAs). There are three inactive battleships including the *USS Alabama BB-60* just behind the Essex. When the Korean War began, many ships were withdrawn from the reserve fleets and activated for service. *TIM—SFCB*

Likewise, submarines in the Pacific sank an estimated five and one half million tons of the Japanese merchant marine, representing 2,200 vessels and 240 warships. The losses inflicted by gunfire and surface ship–launched torpedoes were considerably less. More than 90 percent of the Japanese merchant marine was annihilated by the American submarine campaign, and alternatively had the United States and Great Britain not placed sustained emphasis on anti-submarine warfare, Germany might have starved England into submission. The day of all gun ship warfare had come and gone. This was true in nearly every theater of the war for both the Allied and Axis navies.

Even as the war drew to a close, technology rendered surface warships further obsolescent with the advent of improved radar, jet aircraft, missiles, and above all, nuclear weapons. The rotary wing aircraft made its appearance during the war, and its naval possibilities were just beginning to be explored. The Allies had developed technology in a number of areas, but so had the Germans. After the war in Europe was over, it became a race to see whether the Soviet Union or its Western allies—who were quickly eroding as allies—could capture the most German scientists and equipment. Twelve years later, when the Soviet Union launched its first satellite, Sputnik, into space, one Soviet official wryly claimed that "their German scientists were superior to American German scientists."

Air Force Major General James "Jimmy" Doolittle, leader of the famous carrier-launched raid on Japan in April 1942. Shortly after the war, despite being visually aware of the possibilities of carrier-based naval aviation, he publicly decried the carrier in favor of long-range bombers. His enthusiasm was warmly received, but short-sighted. *Author's collection*

The battle carrier *USS Midway CVB-41*, one of three built at the end of the Second World War. These 60,000-ton full load carriers had an armored deck and were capable of carrying 137 aircraft. With modification they were also able to carry a large enough bomber to deliver nuclear weapons. This type of vessel greatly concerned the Soviet military. The *Midway* and sister *USS Coral Sea CVB-43* served the U.S. Navy into the early 1990s. *TIM — SFCB*

The twin-engine AJ-2 Savage naval bomber, designed to carry nuclear weapons from the deck of an aircraft carrier. It was the immediate successor to the AJ-1, the first aircraft capable of carrying a large bomb load from the deck of an existing carrier. This type of aircraft was developed at a time (1948) when carrier-based naval aviation might have been phased out in favor of the "big bomber" touted by the U.S. Air Force. The 25-ton Savage had a top speed of 448 miles per hour with an approximate range of 1,000 miles. *TIM — SFCB*

However, the main event in 1945 was the end of worldwide hostilities. For most people, including those in national defense, that was all that mattered. The world of 1945 was free of a global war, and defense spending was being drastically cut worldwide. Aircraft and tank assembly lines stopped and, in many instances, ships that were partially complete were left unfinished. Rather than invest in continued military spending, funds were slashed and redirected to social and educational programs. Millions of citizen soldiers and sailors were coming home and needed to be reintroduced into a peacetime society. It was a massive cultural shock for both the Allies and former Axis countries as the world's cities remained lit up all night and thoughts turned to peacetime pursuits. The shooting war was over in 1945; however, the devastation that had been visited on so many nations would take years for them to completely recover. Peacetime now brought a struggle to feed and house millions of victims. Despite the euphoria of victory, military professionals recognized that the future would not be free of conflict, and preparedness through up-to-date national defense was vital.

The detonation of atomic weapons over Hiroshima and Nagasaki caused many strategists to question the need for ships and navies. One oversight committee in the U.S. Congress stated that the navy was the principal casualty of the atomic bomb. This was near heresy, as the U.S. Navy and its allies had just won a stunning victory in the Pacific and as well as eradicating the German submarine menace. However, advances in weapons technology rendered those victories part of a passing era. The period between 1945 and 1950 was crucial to the survival of all the world's navies. The navies would have to again prove their worth as a viable fighting force in the atomic age.

For navies to survive, they would have to adapt to 600+ mile-per-hour aircraft, nuclear weapons, guided missiles, and continuously improved electronics.

Status of the World's Major Navies 1945–1950
The United States Navy

At the end of World War II, the U.S. Navy was the largest, most powerful seaborne force in history. It consisted of 40 modern fleet carriers, 24 battleships, 36 heavy cruisers, 57 light cruisers, and 450 destroyers. Added to this were 79 smaller carriers, 359 destroyer escorts, and 263 submarines as well as a massive number of support ships and highly mobile amphibious forces. In late 1945, the navy boasted a total of 1,308 combat-capable ships. Most of these vessels were built during the war and were chronologically new, yet on the edge of technological obsolescence. The chief of naval operations recommended a postwar force level of 15 fleet carriers, 11 battleships, 49 cruisers, and 179 destroyers. This was denied by a cost-conscious Truman administration, now quite confident in nuclear bomb–carrying bombers as the first line of defense for the nation. Despite the fact that the 1946 atomic bomb tests at Bikini Atoll (Operation Crossroads) proved that warships could survive in the nuclear age, the navy was still drastically reduced in size. Exactly 2,269 naval vessels were placed in mothballs, dozens were scrapped, many were used in nuclear bomb tests, and some were sold off to nations seeking to improve their naval stature. By 1950, the active U.S. Navy consisted of 15 aircraft carriers of all types, one battleship, 23 cruisers, and 82 destroyers. Manning the fleet was also difficult because the lure of civilian life enticed many away from the naval service. Also, the navy had to adapt in a new age of rapidly changing technology.

Naval Aviation

Added to the skepticism of the Truman administration, the vaunted aircraft carrier was considered even by U.S. Air Force leadership to be headed for the scrap yard. It was the B-29 Superfortress that had delivered atomic bombs to targets on Hiroshima and Nagasaki, causing the Japanese Empire to sue for peace.

The B-29 was the only aircraft capable of carrying the heavy atomic weapon and had an unrefueled range of more than 4,000 miles. There was no carrier aircraft that could perform the same feat, and this prompted many in Congress to question the continued value of the aircraft carrier as a first-line weapon. Even Lt. General Jimmy Doolittle, hero of the 1942 aircraft carrier–launched B-25 raid on Japan, advised the U.S. Congress to consider the aircraft carrier obsolete.

Clearly, it was imperative that the aircraft carrier demonstrate its potential to carry aircraft capable of delivering an atomic weapon to an enemy. This came in the form of the three new battle carriers of the Midway class (*USS Midway CVB-41*, *USS Franklin D Roosevelt CVB-42*, and *USS Coral Sea CVB-43*). At 45,000 tons and with a heavily armored deck, these 968-foot-long ships carried the nuclear bomb–capable 471-mile-per-hour AJ-1 Savage attack bomber. By September 1949, these heavy (27-ton) aircraft entered squadron service and were assigned to the fleet. Further carrier improvements were in the works, too. The navy lobbied strongly for its planned super carrier

The Essex-class attack carrier *USS Philippine Sea CVA-47* in a June 14, 1946, image shortly after being commissioned. Too late for service in World War II, the *Philippine Sea* was used for an Antarctic expedition in 1947 and for the next three years served in the Atlantic and Mediterranean. The Essex class was characterized by tough multi-compartmentalized carriers, which could carry up to 90 aircraft. Shortly after hostilities began in Korea, the *Philippine Sea* was deployed with Task Force 77. This carrier was never upgraded with an angled deck like so many of her sisters, and finished her career in 1969 when she was removed from the Navy List. *Author's collection*

which was finally approved and was to be named the *USS United States CVA-58*. It was specifically designed to carry nuclear-laden bombers, but the project was canceled on April 23, 1949, just days after the keel was laid. This action later caused the whole issue of the sea services being given short shrift to be aired publicly. Naval careers were sacrificed, but the nation again realized the value of a powerful navy.

Of the 27,000-ton Essex class fleet carriers still active at the end of the war, most were mothballed, but four remained on active service. The *USS Leyte CV-32* was assigned to the Atlantic with all three of the Midway class, and the *USS Boxer CV-21*, *USS Valley Forge CV-45*, and *USS Philippine Sea CV-47* were in the Pacific. The fleet carrier force was rounded out with four light carriers (CVLs) and four escort carriers (CVEs).

Fleet workhorse AD Skyraider fighters ready to be launched from the deck of the *USS Yorktown CV (CVA)-10*. The "CVA" designation for U.S. Navy carriers was initiated in 1953 to replace "CV." The well-built heavy-duty Skyraider, or Sandy, as it became known in the Vietnam War, was capable of sustaining much damage and still pushing on to complete any number of diverse missions. This aircraft entered U.S. naval service in December 1946 and was withdrawn in 1974. It was also used by a number of allies. *TIM - SFCB*

During the immediate postwar years, the navy began to develop jet fighters to replace its piston-powered aircraft. The navy did retain the piston-driven Douglas AD (A-1) Skyraider because of its versatility, survivability, and weapons-load capacity. In 1947 the first jet aircraft was introduced to the fleet—the McDonnell FH-1 Phantom. This single-seat fighter was capable of 479 miles per hour. It lasted a mere three years in fleet service as newer designs became available. The FH-1 was followed by the North American FJ-1 Fury, and it, too, was replaced by the McDonnell F2H Banshee. The 532-miles-per-hour Banshee remained in fleet service until 1959, but it was the Grumman F9F Panther that seemed to be the most popular fighter overall. It was capable of 579 miles per hour and was used extensively in the Korean War.

Jet fighters meant heavier and faster aircraft, and the aircraft carriers had to adapt. The navy opted to copy the British ideas of an angled flight deck, and the mirror landing system with the added need for strengthened takeoff and arresting

systems. These alterations were made to most of the carriers on an as-needed basis, and it would take a decade for all of the updates to be completed. The navy, anxious to prove its potential, attempted many innovative schemes. This included the successful firing of a German V-2 ballistic missile from the flight deck of the *USS Midway CVB-41* on September 6, 1947.

In the long run, naval aviation was saved in the postwar years through perseverance and a willingness of naval professionals to publically stand firm on the importance of naval aviation to national defence. Another important factor was their foresight in embracing new technology.

Surface Navy

Many experts opined that the surface navy was virtually obsolete after World War II. The battleship was a favorite target of naval critics and by 1949, only the *USS Missouri BB-63* was still in commission, albeit with a reduced crew and as a training unit.

When she ran aground in January 1950 at Hampton Roads, there were many who called for her decommissioning and the end to the "battleship navy." The fifth in the Iowa class, the *USS Kentucky BB-65*, was incomplete at war's end, and was briefly considered for modification to an anti-aircraft missile battleship. This scheme never made it past the concept stage and America's last battleship was scrapped in 1959. Fortunately, the other 57,000-ton battleships that were armed with nine 16-inch/50-caliber guns were available for recall during various regional conflicts that occurred with regularity.

Cruisers fared little better than their larger counterparts and although their anti-aircraft defense was updated with 3-inch/50-caliber twin-mount guns and improved electronics, they were still regarded as escorts for the fast carriers. The three-ship Des Moines class (*USS Des Moines CA-134*, *USS Salem CA-139*, and *USS Newport News CA-148*) stands out due to its ships' size (21,500 tons full load) and their type of main battery. They had fully automatic rapid-fire 8-inch guns capable of an astounding ten rounds per barrel per minute. Too late for Korean War service, all three nonetheless saw extensive service over the next several decades.

The two-ship Worcester class (*USS Worcester CL-144* and the *USS Roanoke CL-145*) was also vastly different from the traditional cruiser as the ships were armed with twelve rapid-fire dual-purpose 6-inch/47-caliber guns arrayed in six twin turrets. These guns, which were not as reliable as expected, could quickly shift from anti-aircraft mode to anti-ship mode. By the time they were commissioned, high-speed aircraft and the guided missile had eclipsed the need for this type of anti-aircraft cruiser. Their fleet service was short, lasting only nine years, from 1947 to 1958.

The cruiser found its place as a fleet flagship and for shore bombardment duty. In these roles, this type of ship excelled and was quite useful to the navy.

In general, most destroyers at war's end were recent additions of the Fletcher, Gearing, and Sumner classes. They were large (2,000–2,200 tons) and well armed with 5-inch/38-caliber dual-purpose guns as well as anti-ship torpedoes and basic ASW weapons. Scores of these ships were mothballed, and of the 362 smaller destroyer escorts in commission at the end of the war, 356 were inactive by 1948. It was the destroyer-type ship that would largely be used to answer the suspected Soviet submarine threat of the immediate postwar years. Anti-submarine warfare had risen to the task of defeating the U-boats of World War II, but faster and more-elusive craft were expected from the submarine-obsessed Soviet Navy. Of course, the fact that Soviet propagandists informed the world of their intention to build 1,200 submarines by 1965 further exacerbated U.S. fears. There was a rush to design bigger and better ASW platforms such as the Norfolk-class ASW destroyer—the leader in 1949. This approach proved too costly, and as the Soviet threat was discovered to have been overstated, naval planners began to retrofit existing destroyer-type vessels for ASW work.

Eighteen Fletcher-class destroyers and fifteen Gearing types were quickly converted for use as designated fleet escorts (DDEs) on a prototype basis. Improved equipment was added to the traditional depth charges and hedgehog weapons, and were labeled Weapons Alfa (A) and Baker (B), respectively. Weapon A was a trainable rocket boosted by a 250-pound charge that had a range of 1,000 yards and became a standard for most ASW-dedicated ships. Weapon B was a trainable hedgehog mount that used 50-pound charges. Both were designed to counter fast-moving Soviet submarines.

Aside from ASW, the destroyer continued to be used as an escort in fast carrier task forces and for inshore bombardment roles.

The postwar fleet amphibious force was maintained in the form of World War II attack transports, Landing Ship Tanks (LST), and other, smaller, amphibious warfare vessels.

A number of McDonnell FH-1 Phantoms are ranged on the flight deck of the light carrier *USS Saipan CVL-48* in this photograph taken on May 10, 1948. The *Saipan* was being used as a test platform for an entire squadron of the navy's first true jet fighter aircraft. The Phantom was first introduced in 1945 and became fully operational in 1947. VF-17A Squadron operated from the *Saipan* successfully and brought jet aircraft to sea for the U.S. Navy. With a top speed of 479 miles per hour, the Phantom was quickly overtaken by the FH2 Banshee and F9F Panther jets for routine fleet service. Also in 1948, the *Saipan* successfully tested helicopter operations from her flight deck. *TIM — SFCB*

Mine warfare also suffered budget cuts and was reduced to minimum levels prior to 1950 and the Korean War.

Submarines

The U.S. Navy's concern about the rapid development of a hostile Soviet submarine force proved exaggerated but on the plus side, it prompted the United States and Great Britain to reevaluate their own undersea programs. Shortly after the war, both navies began to study the most advanced German submarines that had been captured at the end of the European war. The German Type XXI opened up an entirely new concept in submarine design and laid the groundwork for the nuclear boats of the future.

The U.S. Navy revamped 20 World War II Balao-class boats and 15 of the Tench class. Both had proved themselves in war; however, they attained greater capability after they were converted

The World War II "Liberty ship" *USS Brigadier A J Lyon*, now an aircraft repair ship, has been modified to launch and recover the newly developed helicopter. This July 3, 1946, image was one of the first photographs of an entirely new type of naval aviation yet to come. Within three decades, the helicopter became indispensable to antisubmarine warfare. *TIM – SFCB*

The fifth battleship of the Iowa class, *USS Kentucky BB-65*, being towed away for scrapping in January 1959. She was incomplete at the end of World War II and was considered for various roles such as a platform for radio-controlled cruise missiles; however, scarce funds went into other projects. *TIM – SFCB*

under the Greater Underwater Propulsive Power Program (GUPPY). The boats were turned into jumbo size by slicing them in half and adding a 15-foot section. This space addition allowed for greater battery storage and, coupled with a general streamlining, the boats were capable of 15–17 knots submerged and a diving depth of 600 feet. Also absent were deck guns, and the conventional conning tower was replaced with a "sail" type structure. Success with the GUPPY program led to many more boats being refitted under successive models.

Aside from the mass GUPPY conversion, other boats were selected for such duties as radar picket, and the test use of submarine-launched missiles (i.e., *USS Carbonero SS-337, USS Cusk SS-348,* and *USS Tunny SS-282*). The first missile tested from the deck of a submarine was an Americanized version of the World War II German V-1 or "buzz-bomb." The missile, known as the Loon, was first launched from the *USS Cusk* on February 12, 1947. The test submarine was surfaced just off the California coast when the white painted loon lifted into the air. The success of this test was a vital step forward for national defense.

Two new classes of submarine were built between 1945 and 1950. The six-boat Tang class was designed along the lines of the German XXI model, and all of them entered service in 1951–1952. Still concerned about the Soviet submarine menace, the navy built three "K" class boats that were specifically designed to kill Soviet submarines. These rather small boats (890 tons, 196-foot length, four 21-inch torpedo tube armament) were not as successful as the navy hoped. Fortunately, the much-dreaded Soviet submarine development and building program was still years in the future.

The years from 1945 until the North Korean invasion of South Korea on June 25, 1950, were relatively peaceful for the U.S. Navy. There were various incidents of Soviet fighters shooting down U.S. Navy aircraft (e.g., the April 8, 1950, shooting down of an unarmed Navy PB4Y-2 over the Baltic Sea), but most of the battles of survival were with political leaders and the other services.

The heavy cruiser *USS Salem CA-139* at sea. This fine cruiser was built by the Bethlehem Steel Company Shipyard at Quincy, Massachusetts, and completed after the war. This was the ultimate heavy cruiser of the three-ship Des Moines class. The *Salem* mounted nine 8-inch/55-caliber automatic guns in three triple-barrel turrets and displaced 21,500 tons full load. Often mistaken for battleships, the Des Moines class was well armored and its armament was formidable, yet the day of the all-gun cruiser was over. The era of the jet and guided missile relegated these fine ships into early obsolescence. They were still regarded, however, as symbols of a powerful navy. The *Salem* ended her days where she began and is now a museum ship in Quincy, Massachusetts. *TIM — SFCB*

The navy's value was proved again and again when fleet units were quickly dispatched to the Mediterranean and other regions to stabilize nations that were experiencing political unrest. Throughout the lean budget years, the navy persevered and was finally able to ensure its survival with its performance during the Korean War. One of the first questions asked after North Korean soldiers poured across the border was, "Where are the carriers?" In just over a week, the attack carrier *USS Valley Forge CV-45* and British carrier *Triumph* launched strikes on North Korean targets. In the first year of the see-saw battle to evict the North Korean invaders, the navy grew in strength and respect. Those who championed the cause of the long-range atomic-bomb–armed aircraft as the primary solution to war were proved wrong. Even diehard critics had to agree that the navy had great worth to the nation in the nuclear age as it braced for the rapidly unfolding Cold War.

Other Western Nations

United Kingdom

Great Britain ended World War II in literal bankruptcy. American Lend-Lease and loans kept the country from economic collapse during the war, and a much reduced level of aid continued over the next few years. The country would require decades to fully recover. All of the military services suffered grievously during the war. The Royal Navy experienced a staggering loss of 1,525 warships and 50,000 personnel during the six-year war. Budget-cutting axes decimated its force level of some 900 major ships in commission and 866,000 men and women at the end of the war. By 1950 the number was reduced to 112 active major combat ships of all types, and 140,000 active and National Service personnel. The Royal Navy (RN) also had to face the fact that it was no longer the most powerful navy in the world. Wartime expansion in the United States caused the U.S. Navy to supplant the Royal Navy. This

Light Cruiser *USS Worcester CL-144* at sea undergoing a protective water spray bath designed to remove radioactive fallout in the event of a nuclear attack on the fleet. The two-ship Worcester-class, which included the *USS Roanoke CL-145*, was designed to use the 6-inch/47-caliber gun in an automatic mode for anti-aircraft defense of the fast carrier task forces. The *Worcesters* mounted 12 guns of this caliber in six twin turrets sited similar to that of the World War II Atlanta-class anti-aircraft cruisers (CLAAs). They also had a number of 3-inch/50-caliber medium anti-aircraft guns. There were to have been three ships in this class; however, the end of World War II curtailed construction of the third ship. High-speed jet aircraft of the Cold War rendered these ships inadequate for their intended purpose. They did serve with distinction during their short careers (10 years). After being in reserve for many years, the *Worcester* and *Roanoke* were broken up in 1972. *TIM – SFCB*

change was accepted with grace, mostly due to the fact that both nations had worked so well together during the war. In the Cold War that was developing, the United Kingdom and the United States continued as allies in the common goal of defeating Communism.

During the period from 1945 through 1950, British interests were threatened in a number of areas. In May 1946 while on patrol in the Mediterranean, British cruiser *HMS Orion* and *HMS Superb* steamed through the Corfu Channel and were fired upon by Communist Albanian shore batteries. In October, the Royal Navy again tested the channel for safe passage. It was soon discovered that the waters had been mined by Albanian forces and cooperative Yugoslavians. As the RN squadron entered the channel, destroyers *HMS Saumarez* and *HMS Volage* were seriously damaged by mines. The British withdrew until the following month. Not willing to allow the Albanians the satisfaction of driving British ships out of the Corfu Channel, the British mounted a successful mine-sweeping campaign, which netted 23 mines. For the United Kingdom, the Cold War had begun in earnest.

Eighteen months later, on the other side of the globe, Communist guerrillas began a campaign to infiltrate Malaya and Singapore. British warships responded with air attacks from the carrier *HMS Warrior* and shore bombardment by the frigate *HMS Amethyst*. This particular conflict continued well into the following decade.

One of the most significant precedents leading to the Cold War occurred on the Yangtze River in the middle of the Nationalist-Communist civil war in China.

On February 20, 1949, the British frigate *HMS Amethyst* was fired upon by Communist army shore batteries and badly damaged. Despite the obvious nationality of the frigate, Communist gunners repeatedly hit her with 105-mm shells and forced her aground. A rescue effort by a nearby destroyer, *HMS Consort*, was to no avail, as she, too, was hit. The following day, the heavy cruiser *HMS London* came to the assistance of the stranded frigate, but after firing some 132 8-inch shells and 449 shells from her secondary battery she, too, was repulsed with substantial damage. For the next several months the *Amethyst* was held hostage by intentionally sluggish Communist diplomacy backed up by a heavy concentration of shore batteries. On July 30, 1949, the frigate made a clandestine dash downriver and escaped. With this incident the Chinese Communists made it clear that Western warships were no

The *USS Renshaw DDE-499* (escort) was among several World War II destroyers converted for anti-submarine defense. The U.S. Navy became quite nervous over the capability of some of the German submarines that had been captured by the Soviet Navy. Contemporary escorts and technology were insufficient against the German Type XXI boats, and it was expected that the Soviet Union would soon develop and deploy such technology. As an interim measure, the navy rebuilt some 150 destroyers/destroyer escorts and equipped them with improved sonar, trainable hedgehogs, and Weapon A, shown just above the forward 5-inch/38-caliber gun mount on the Renshaw. Weapon A could fire up to twelve 250-pound fast-sinking explosives to a maximum range of 975 yards in 60 seconds. This was just the beginning of the Cold War at sea between surface ships of the Western navies and the Soviet submarine. *U.S. Navy*

longer welcome in their territorial waters. The Chinese mainland was soon overrun by the Communists, and the door was closed to the West. The ragtag army of the Chinese Nationalist government, led by Chiang Kai-shek, was forced to retire to Formosa (Taiwan) on December 8, 1949.

For the Royal Navy, the years leading up to the Korean War were at once eventful, yet deceptive. The British "robbed Peter to pay Paul," and ultimately the fleet was spread thin all over the world. The final battleship built for the Royal Navy was the 44,500-ton *HMS Vanguard*. Armed with eight 15-inch guns, the Vanguard was too

late for war service. She served in a training role and as the "Royal Barge" for the King and Queen of England. All of the other battleships in the RN were either laid up or scrapped after the war.

The Royal Navy successfully developed three very innovative improvements to carrier warfare, which were quickly adopted by the U.S. Navy. The angled flight deck, steam catapult, and mirror landing system enhanced the ability of the modern carrier in the age of large high-speed (jet) aircraft. Despite this level of design inventiveness, by 1950 there were only five carriers operating in the British fleet. There were some technical advances

Commissioned on September 2, 1946, too late for service in World War II, the Gearing-class destroyer *USS Charles H Roan DD-853* was one of many ships assigned to the newly established Sixth Fleet in the Mediterranean. The presence of the Sixth Fleet forestalled many potential crises and demonstrated U.S. resolve to allies in the region. The 3,160-ton, 391-foot-long *Charles H Roan*, anchored off Cannes, France, on July 4, 1949, served the U.S. Navy until 1973 when she was transferred to Turkey and renamed *Cakmak*. The Gearing class was one of the most celebrated and heavily utilized classes of destroyer in the navy's inventory during the Cold War. *Author's Collection*

in naval aircraft design, but by 1950, the Royal Navy still depended on propeller-driven aircraft. However, jet aircraft came soon thereafter.

The balance of the Royal Navy followed in the path of the larger units and was drastically reduced in size. At the outset of the Korean Conflict, the British had only 15 cruisers, 33 destroyers, 27 frigates, and 32 submarines available for combat worldwide. ASW was becoming a great concern for the United Kingdom as it recognized the potential threat of the Soviet submarine force, and new designs were quickly put on the drawing board. The Daring-class destroyer was first introduced during this period and other significant ocean escort/ASW ships were in the design stage. Even at this time, the Royal Navy was gravitating to its destiny in the Cold War—that of a potent threat to Soviet submarine operations. All in all, the RN would field 123 destroyer-type vessels during the Cold War.

The British fought alongside the United States and other United Nations units committed to resolving the Korean War. Air strikes were launched from RN carriers and destroyers and frigates shelled enemy positions ashore. Its contribution was vital to bringing a conclusion to the war.

France

At the end of World War II, the French Navy consisted of an eclectic group of ships including survivors of its prewar navy, war prizes, and those lent by other Allied nations. It had the use of two aircraft carriers, the escort carrier *Dixmude* and the *Arromanches*, formerly the *HMS Colossus*, an 18,040-ton British light carrier (39 aircraft). The *Arromanches* was acquired from Great Britain in 1946 on a loan basis and was purchased outright in 1951.

The French Navy flew U.S.-made naval aircraft on both carriers until it developed a full naval aviation program.

The French also operated two battleships in the early postwar years. The 49,000-ton giants, *Richelieu* and *Jean Bart*, were initiated before

One of the more controversial vessels built for the U.S. Navy, the *USS Norfolk DL-1*. A fast, high-endurance, and well-armed ASW ship was quickly needed to checkmate the widely anticipated modern Soviet submarine force of ex-German Type 21 boats. The ship here was built in 1959, but the concept of a specialized anti-submarine "hunter-killer" was initiated as early as 1946 and formalized before 1950. The *Norfolk* was armed with four Weapon A launchers, improved sonar, and modest anti-aircraft defense (20-mm, 3-inch/70-caliber guns). Her price tag of $62 million proved too expensive, and she was the only one of the 6,600-ton submarine killers built. Most of the *Norfolk*'s career was spent in experimental testing. *TIM—SFCB*

On February 12, 1947, an Americanized German V-1 (buzzbomb) code-named "loon" was launched from the deck of the World War II Balao-class fleet submarine *USS Cusk SS-348*. This historic event occurred off the central California coastline and was witnessed by few; however, the submarine as a platform for missile launching was proved feasible. This eventually led to the more sophisticated ballistic and cruise missile submarine. *Author's collection*

World War II and completed in 1944 and 1949, respectively. These heavily armed warships (eight 15-inch guns, nine 6-inch guns, and up to 90 smaller AA guns) were operated more out of pride than for their strategic naval value. The French Navy had suffered greatly during World War II, and in the years that followed, this nation sought to regain much of its lost stature in the international community. The *Richelieu* and *Jean Bart* were part of that effort.

The balance of the French fleet was made up of various smaller units and escorts. Four ex-Italian light cruisers of the 5,500-ton Attilio Regolo class were given to France in 1948 and later rebuilt as destroyer leaders of the Chateaurenault class. It was not until the next decade that the French actively began to rebuild a new navy and discard existing units. Its navy was used extensively in the years that followed the end of the Second World War, especially in Southeast Asia.

France became embroiled in the early stages of the Cold War fighting Communist insurgency in its Indo-Chinese holdings. The French Navy flew hundreds of air strikes on Communist positions from former Allied aircraft carriers *Dixmude* (ex-*HMS Biter*) and *Arromanches*. Despite military aid from the United States, which included surplus World War II aircraft, the Communist Viet Minh successfully forced the French government to surrender Vietnam. The war to eradicate French colonialism formally concluded with the 1955 defeat of French forces at Dien Bien Phu by Viet Minh forces after a lengthy siege.

This loss of face in Asia was partially blamed on the United States for not actively supporting France with nuclear weapons against the Viet Minh. The defeat at Dien Bien Phu was a factor that further alienated France from the Western allies and, within a few years, this nation withdrew from NATO and set on a course of its own.

HMS Belfast, a Royal Navy light cruiser assigned to the Far East Station after World War II to represent British interests. The *Belfast* was very much involved in the Korean War, and often she could be found bombarding North Korean troop concentrations and other coastal targets. Typical of the pre–World War II cruisers designed in keeping with International Naval Arms Limitations, the *Belfast* and her sister *HMS Edinburgh* each displaced 10,550 tons, and mounted 12 6-inch (152-mm) guns in her main batteries. Of the scores of cruisers built for the Royal Navy, only the *Belfast* survived and became a museum ship in the Pool of London. *Author's collection*

Also Afloat

Like Great Britain and France, countries such as the Netherlands, Belgium, Italy, Sweden, and British Commonwealth Nations were in difficult financial straits at the end of the Second World War. None could support large navies, so all tended to local defense and a lower level of support for international military operations. None operated battleships; however, the Netherlands did purchase a "Colossus" class aircraft carrier from the Royal Navy in 1948 (*HMS Venerable*) and commissioned it in the Royal Netherlands Navy as the *Karel Doorman R-81*. In a pattern of attempting to find homes for incomplete or nearly new smaller aircraft carriers, the RN also transferred the incomplete Majestic class (*HMS Majestic*) to the Royal Australian Navy in 1949. This 20,000-ton light carrier, now the *RAN Melbourne*, was not fully modernized until October 1955.

Soon after Italy's surrender, its navy still remained a formidable force. The Italian Peace Treaty allotted a certain amount of tonnage to each of the major Allied nations. The result still left a portion of the Italian navy intact, although the remaining ships were not first-line vessels. Italy, a member of NATO, had a navy that consisted of 63 ships, including four older battleships. In the year that followed, Italy initiated a shipbuilding program that thoroughly modernized its navy.

Most of the smaller nations opted to rebuild or expand their navies with ex-U.S. Navy ships and it was not until the 1950s that each nation built warships based on its own design and particular needs. By this time, each naval force had an allotted task in the event of an attack by the U.S.S.R. and its Warsaw Pact nations.

In 1950, the total naval strength of NATO was 1,882 warships of all types. Most were in reserve and only a fraction were actually deployed at sea. The Soviet Navy boasted some 543 ships, of which 360 were submarines, primarily of a coastal variety. Fortunately for the NATO nations, which worked relatively well together, there was no real Soviet naval threat. There were rumors, but little was actually seen of the Soviet Navy.

The Union of Soviet Socialist Republics' Navy
Background

The Russian Navy as a forerunner of the Soviet Navy has had over three centuries of operations. In the twentieth century, the navy suffered its greatest defeat and humiliation. In the war between Russia and Japan, the majority of the czar's fleet was destroyed by the Imperial Japanese Navy during the May 1905 Battle of Tsushumi. This particular operation earned the Japanese Navy a prominent place in the international community, and at the same time disgraced a traditionally powerful European power. The Russian fleet was ill led, consumed with poor morale, and bore a lack of training that was almost criminal. Its ships were unprepared for the disciplined, well-armed Imperial Japanese Navy, and most of its ships were sunk or captured. Added to the aforementioned deficiencies, the Imperial Russian Fleet was unable to sustain itself with fuel and supplies—there was no adequate fleet train, nor any well-arranged provision for maintaining a fleet at sea. The Russians had been compelled to dispatch a fleet from home waters and survival depended on what could be foraged in foreign waters. The need for a separate Pacific Fleet was driven home by this debacle.

The next opportunity for the Russian Navy to perform was in World War I, after it had been partially restored. Its performance for the first three years of this war was mediocre, but it became

HMS Warrior, a Royal Navy Colossus-class light carrier, was completed in 1946, and spent her first two years of service in the Canadian Navy. There were 10 of these 19,600-ton light carriers built in response to a wartime need for inexpensive, quickly assembled "econo-carriers." The Second World War ended before any saw service, and many of this class found homes in friendly navies. They were typical of the small but useful carriers used by navies that could ill afford the large carrier, yet needed seaborne naval aviation. HMS Warrior fought Communist guerrillas in Malaya, and later was sold to Argentina and renamed Independencia. Author's collection

One of the most famous sloops (destroyer type) in the Royal Navy, HMS Amethyst was of the wartime-modified Black Swan class. She displaced 1,490 tons and was armed with six 4-inch dual-purpose guns and a number of smaller close-in weapons. The Amethyst was capable of 20 knots on 4,300 shaft horsepower. This vessel fought Communist guerrillas in Malaya, and was engaged in a running gun battle with Chinese Communist shore batteries on the Yangtze River in 1948. She was hit 53 times by Communist gunfire, yet in true Royal Navy fashion, she escaped and went on to serve for many more years. The Western navies were often the first to feel the bite of Communist aggression. TIM

The Royal Netherlands Navy aircraft carrier *Karel Doorman*. Originally christened in the British Navy as the *HMS Venerable*, she was another in the 10-ship family of British-built Colossus light aircraft carriers. A member of NATO forces, the Dutch Navy had been a navy in exile until the Germans were driven out of Holland at the end of World War II. The Dutch then quickly began to rebuild their naval forces, including the completion of prewar-begun ships, and the acquisition of a new carrier on bargain-basement terms from Great Britain in 1948. The *Karel Doorman* was later refitted with a deck that could support jet aircraft and a steam catapult to launch them. The addition of an aircraft carrier to a NATO country was always welcome and of immense value in the Cold War. Subsequently, the *Karel Doorman* was sold to Argentina and became the *Vienticinto de Mayo*. She was nearly used as a weapon against her original owners in the 1982 Falklands War. There was no wind on the day she needed to launch her A4-C Skyhawks against the British task force, and the old carrier was forced to return to base. Often the weather, not technology, aids or hinders naval combat. *Author's collection*

infamous for its role during the revolution against the czar in 1917. Various ships and their crews either sided with the Bolshevik revolutionaries or remained loyal to the government in power. By 1921, the issue was settled and the loyalists had been exiled, killed, or put into forced labor camps. Unfortunately, many of the navy's better minds were also purged.

As to the inventory of warships at that time, there were few operational units and all were from a former era. Many of the shipyards had been damaged during the revolution, and the state of the Soviet Navy in the early 1920s was pitiful. Rebuilding the navy and the merchant fleet was fraught with problems, including a lack of trained labor in the shipyards and related factories. The "no work, no eat" Communist line was taken seriously, and workers turned to industries that provided some promise of not starving. Eventually, shipyards were supplied with labor, but the workers were often unskilled. Consultants from Italy, Germany, and other countries were hired to train the workers, and the influence of their designs and methods became evident in the finished products.

By 1924, the Soviet Navy had been partially reconstituted, and consisted of two battleships, a lone cruiser, 18 destroyers, and nine submarines. All were rebuilt and obsolete; however, there were now enough vessels to operate small units in the Baltic and Black Seas. At this time the major naval threat to the Soviet Union was thought to be a potential military operation that could be launched against it by an ambitious Baltic nation that would be fully supported by the British and French Navies. This fear was never realized and by 1927, naval planners in the U.S.S.R. began to contemplate building a modern navy.

Over the next few years a series of technologically crude warships were built. A great number of coastal submarines were built, in addition to two cruisers and a small number of Italian-designed destroyers. In the years leading up to World War II, the Soviet Navy continued to expand its undersea capability with the manufacture of 90 submarines split among in the L class, M Class, S Class, and Chuka Class. The surface navy was not

The French escort carrier *Dixmude*. At 496 feet in length and a displacement of 14,500 tons full load, this Charger-class carrier was capable of carrying up to 30 aircraft. Built in the United States and then transferred to Great Britain, it was taken over by the French in April 1945. Two years later on April 2, 1947, air strikes against the Communist Viet Minh in Indochina began. Although the French Navy operated the prewar-built carrier *Bearn*, it was never used in combat. The honor of flying the first combat strikes went to the *Dixmude*, using the former U.S. Navy SBD Dauntless dive-bomber. *TIM —SFCB*

The *Jean Bart*, one of two battleships operated by France in the postwar years. The 49,000-ton *Jean Bart* and sister *Richelieu* were the two survivors of a planned four-ship class. The *Jean Bart* was damaged during the Allied attacks on North Africa, then later rebuilt after the war in Brest, France. These two magnificent ships carried a main battery of eight 15-inch guns disposed in two quadruple barrel turrets located forward. The secondary battery of nine 6-inch guns was sited aft, much like the British battleships *Nelson* and *Rodney*. The *Jean Bart* and her sister were symbols of a formerly defeated nation that wanted to regain its stature in the international community. Both ships served well into the 1960s and represented the interests of France well. *Author's collection*

U.S. Navy F8F Bearcat fighters being unloaded from a U.S. escort carrier, *USS Windham Bay CVE-92*. Many World War II escort carriers were used as aircraft transports to provide military aid from the United States to nations fighting Communism. The Bearcat was relatively new, and this 370-mile-per-hour attack-fighter could carry 11.75-inch rockets or two 1,000-pound bombs. These aircraft were much-appreciated additions to beleaguered French forces slowly being pushed out of Indochina. They discovered, like military commanders of other nations would discover again and again, that air supremacy was not sufficient to win this type of war. Years later, escort carriers would again be pressed into service for the same purpose, but to deliver aircraft to U.S. forces fighting the same determined Communist-led insurgents. *TIM — SFCB*

ignored, however, and at the very last there was a decision to build two 35,000-ton battleships and a number of large destroyers. Joseph Stalin wanted the "most powerful navy in the world," for the sake of having a forceful wedge in international politics. Added to Soviet warship strength was a substantial number of aircraft (1,300+) that were dedicated to naval aviation. These were shore-based aircraft that were ultimately used for reconnaissance, anti-submarine patrol, and anti-shipping raids. The concept of the "stationary aircraft carrier" was thoroughly appreciated by the Stalinist government and continued throughout the postwar years.

World War II – "The Great Patriotic War"

World War II came upon the Soviet Union like a thunderclap. On paper the "people's navy" was well matched to its invader's. Nearly 180 submarines were operational versus half of that number for Nazi Germany. There were 220 warships of all types in various stages of construction, including 90 relatively modern submarines. The Stalinist naval buildup was clearly under way. However, this preponderance of warships was insufficient to guarantee victory at sea. Over the five-year period from 1941–1945, German forces devastated much of the Soviet Navy, including most of its incomplete construction and the surrounding shipyards. This included the two new 35,000-ton battleships. More than half of the surface navy was immobilized or destroyed. Within a few months of the June 1941 invasion, a sustained German air force bombing campaign severely punished two of the three older battleships. Also severely damaged or lost were four of the eight cruisers in the Black or Baltic fleets. The destroyer and undersea forces fared little better. Thirty-six of the 52 destroyers available in 1941 were lost and a minimum of 40 or more of the 180 submarines. The performance of the Soviet Navy in World War II was lackluster, and it suffered most losses from mines and bombing attacks.

During and after World War II, the British Navy supplied warships to Commonwealth nations such as Australia and New Zealand. The Royal New Zealand Navy frigates *Pukaki* and *Tutira* were originally built as the Loch class and at 1,435 tons, were multi-purpose ships armed with one 4-inch dual-purpose deck gun, a small number of anti-aircraft guns, and squid ASW weapons. Within weeks, these ships were sent to the Far East to respond to the North Korean invasion of the South in June 1950. There were ships from other nations as well to enforce United Nations sanctions against the North Korean government. Diplomatic and economic sanctions were backed up with attacks on North Korean military, industrial, and infrastructure targets. *Author's collection*

Anti-aircraft defense aboard Soviet ships was nearly nonexistent and the Germans made good use of their coastal mine warfare campaign. In certain small units, there were individual acts of heroism that proved that the Soviet sailor was not afraid to die. The failure of the fleet as a whole to make a viable contribution, however, was based on ineffective leadership, lack of trained officers, and a "coast defense" mind-set that prevented creativity and unity in large-scale blue water operations.

There were other reasons as well, such as being subordinated to the Red Army and its operations. The army cannibalized ship crews for ground operations without hesitation. Oceangoing warships were used in the defense of Soviet cities, and their heavy guns were employed as field artillery against advancing German armies. The overall consensus was that the navy was a second-rate service in the Soviet armed forces hierarchy.

In response to pleas for assistance during the final years of the war, the United States and Great Britain supplied a number of ships to the Soviet Navy, including the older RN battleship *HMS Royal Sovereign*, which was renamed the *Archangelsk*. The Royal Navy also provided several older submarines, subchasers, and at least eight of the 50 original "four piper" World War I vintage destroyers lent by the United States. The U.S. Navy loaned the older Omaha-class light cruiser *USS Milwaukee CL-5*, which was renamed the *Murmansk*. It also supplied hundreds of other vessels, including icebreakers, modern Liberty class freighters, and smaller warships. Interestingly, the U.S.S.R. refused to return 600 ships and crafts of all types after the war, and in the mid-1950s, more than one-third of the U.S.S.R.'s merchant fleet consisted of ships loaned under the U.S. Lend-Lease Act. The stated reason for refusing to return the ships was simple—the United States did not require other nations to return loaned vessels.

During World War II, the Soviet Navy claimed to have sunk some 1.5 million tons of enemy shipping and at least 37 destroyers and 50 submarines of the German Navy. These losses were never verified, and with an enforced wartime information blackout from the U.S.S.R. the figures

The ex-Italian battleship *Giulio Cesare*, ceded to the Soviet Union under the terms of the Italian Peace Treaty. Renamed the *Novorossisk*, the old battleship served the Red Navy until October 1955 when it was accidentally sunk by a German ground mine. This experience caused an upheaval in the Soviet naval hierarchy. The well-respected and legendary Admiral Kuznetsov was retired in favor of a young and farsighted naval officer, Admiral G. Gorshkov. This 45-year-old officer initiated an enlightened age in the Soviet Navy and over the next 30 years drove it to undisputed prominence in the naval community. The loss of the elderly Italian battleship was the catalyst that ushered in the modern age for the Soviet Navy. *U.S. Navy*

Caught in this rare image is the sole German aircraft carrier, *Graf Zeppelin*, as it appeared when being launched on December 8, 1938. The *Graf Zeppelin* was never completed and shuttled from one location to another during the war in Europe. In 1945, it was seized near Stettin when the Red Army marched in. Despite looking fit and seaworthy, the hulk was sitting on the bottom after being scuttled by a mutinous German caretaker crew. Later refloated, it was overloaded by its salvagers, who were intent on taking everything of any possible use from their defeated enemy—Nazi Germany. For many years it was believed that the ship was lost in a minefield in late August 1947 while under tow to Leningrad. Later it was confirmed that she reached her destination and was subsequently sunk by destroyer-launched torpedoes. In any event, the first carrier in the Soviet Navy was lost before much could have been learned about carrier naval aviation. *TIM*

The Russian-built light cruiser *Krasni Kavkaz* moored with shore boats alongside. Completed in 1932, this cruiser was laid down some 16 years before. The delay was due to the disruption of the Soviet shipbuilding industry by the revolution in 1917 and the war that followed. This coal and oil-burning ship was capable of 25 knots and mounted 7.1-inch guns in her main battery. Based on a pre–World War I design, she was obsolete in 1932 by Western standards. Like much of the Soviet Navy until the advent of Admiral Gorshkov's administration, this ship was in service far beyond its usefulness. Gorshkov disposed of much of the pre–World War II fleet in the late 1950s and early 1960s including the *Krasni Kavkaz. U.S. Navy*

were later deemed vastly overstated. It is likely that most of the enemy shipping destroyed was by aircraft and the total amounted to less than a third of the Soviet claim. Overall, the Soviet Navy was not effective as a surface force and only excelled in supporting amphibious operations. Its submarine campaign was desultory, and at war's end, the navy was in a state of disarray.

Post–World War II: The Birth of a Modern Soviet Navy

One of the principal difficulties facing the Soviet Navy was its geographical limitation to the world's major oceans. The U.S.S.R. was bordered in such a way that access to the sea from its major ports could be made difficult if not impossible by unfriendly nations. Soviet warships had to pass through geographical constrictions that became known as "choke points" in order to enter open water. Access to the open sea was also restricted by many of its ports being frozen during the year. The navy had to be partitioned among four self-contained and essentially independent fleets lo-

cated in the Baltic Sea, Black Sea, Pacific Ocean, and Northern waters. This further complicated the obvious problems of supply, communication, and coordination. During much of the Cold War, through intimidation and diplomatic means, the Kremlin continually sought to overcome these disadvantages, but to no avail.

On the positive side, the Soviet Union was located in one single land mass, and was not dependent on merchant shipping and foreign trade for its survival. Its navy was designed almost from the outset to be a defensive force, and much of its energy was devoted to coastal protection. It was not until later in the Cold War that emphasis shifted to an international naval presence.

It was well known throughout Russia and the world that the Red Army had defeated the Germans on the eastern front during the Great Patriotic War. When the efforts of the navy were mentioned, they were summarily dismissed. For centuries, Russia had wanted to expand its influence beyond its borders. Each opportunity was lost, however, and it was often due in part to the lack of a powerful navy.

It was no different after World War II. Stalin and the senior leadership of the Soviet Union knew that a strong navy was needed, and began a campaign from the ground up to build such a force. One of the first objectives was to ensure that the average citizen understood and appreciated sea power. To this end, maritime and nautical clubs were established in all of the major urban areas. Shows, lectures, and nautical events were sponsored by state-sponsored "Dosflot" organizations.

From an organizational standpoint, the unification of the armed forces in 1945 under a single ministry did little to enhance the prospects of a strong navy, especially since the ministry was obviously dominated by the army. However, in 1950, the centrally controlled defense organization was split into three separate ministries. The navy and its ground-based naval aviation of more than 3,000 mostly obsolete aircraft became its own ministry under the direction of Admiral N. M. Kutznetsov. Kutznetsov was a personal friend of Stalin and shared his desire for a large navy. Thus the Soviet Navy was finally able to expand without major political or economic hindrances.

Status of the Soviet Navy

As noted earlier, shortly after World War II, the Soviet Navy consisted of a hodgepodge of ships that had been loaned by the Western allies; prizes from Germany, Italy, and Japan; and the remnants of its wartime fleets. None of these vessels were comparable to the newer ships of the Western navies. Interestingly, this was not a long-term deficiency because many chronologically modern Western war-built ships were now technologically obsolete. Each adversary now had the opportunity of a fresh start. The United States and its allies began this effort shortly after the war; however, the Soviet Navy was not far behind and would eventually stun the world with its building programs.

Battleships

Nineteen forty-five found the Soviet Union with three obsolete battleships. The *Archangelsk* or *Arkhangelsk* was the ex-*HMS Royal Sovereign* and was due to be returned to the United Kingdom when a suitable replacement could be found among the Italian war prizes. The other two (*Gangut* and *Sevastopol*) had been laid down in 1909, and were both coal fired. None of these ships were capable of operations other than minimal coast defense, and due to their obsolescence, all could easily be sunk by aircraft.

On February 3, 1949, under the terms of the Italian Peace Treaty, the Italian battleship *Giulio*

The ex-U.S. Navy light cruiser *USS Milwaukee CL-5* sits next to a Soviet *MV Molotov* off the Delaware on March 15, 1949. The *Murmansk*, as the old cruiser was identified in the Red Navy, is coming home (to be scrapped). The crew is being transferred to the freighter alongside to avoid contact with the U.S. mainland and possible defection. The ship was simply abandoned, and the Soviets left without a "thank you." The American crew who brought the *Milwaukee* to the Philadelphia Navy Yard claimed it was the filthiest rat and cockroach-infested ship they ever had seen. The ship had to be fumigated before being sold to a shipbreakers. Most warships returned from the U.S.S.R. were in similar condition. *TIM — SFCB*

The *Admiral Makarov*, formerly the German light cruiser *Nurnberg*. This ship, launched in 1934, carried a main battery of nine 5.9-inch guns and twelve 21-inch torpedo tubes as well as a small number of anti-aircraft weapons. The Makarov was employed for many years and eventually scrapped under Admiral Gorshkov's fleet modernization programs. The Red Navy used many of the older ships for front-line duty beyond their technological ability, and then employed them in training roles and finally as accommodation, target, or experimental testing ships. *U.S. Navy*

Cesare was formally ceded to the Soviet Union as a war prize. This 29,032-ton full load ship was initially armed with ten 12.6-inch/43 guns in her main battery and twelve 4.7-inch weapons as secondary battery. Originally commissioned in November 1913, this 36-year-old battleship had graceful lines and was at one time capable of 27 knots. When delivered to the Black Sea Fleet her maximum speed was 23 knots. In comparison to most of the world's capital ships she was slow and thinly armored (maximum 11 inches), which, unfortunately, was a hallmark of Italian design. Among most Italian seamen, these ships were known as the "cardboard class."

She was renamed the *Novorossisk* and her main battery was re-gunned with Russian 12-inch/52-caliber barrels. The *Novorossisk* was also provided with increased armor plating. This addition to the Soviet Navy was used extensively for training and trials, and was the last battleship acquired or built by the U.S.S.R. The old battleship was accidentally lost while at anchor in the Black Sea on October 29, 1955. She quickly foundered after detonating a

World War II German stationary mine. This ended the battleship experience for the Soviet Navy.

Naval Aviation

During the final days of the European war, the U.S.S.R. acquired an incomplete aircraft carrier (ex-German *Graf Zeppelin*). This 33,500-ton full load carrier was 85 percent complete at the beginning of World War II, and was to have carried an air group of 40 aircraft of all types. Its planned role was to accompany and protect commerce raiding ships, yet Hitler's dissatisfaction with his surface navy and ignorance about naval aviation relegated this fine ship to the backwaters. It was moved a number of times and bombed occasionally, but survived to the end of the war. By the time the Russian Army reached the vessel in April 1945, it had been scuttled. It was sitting on an even keel near the mouth of the Oder River on the Baltic Sea. A year later, the now refloated hulk was towed to Swinemuende, where she was loaded with war booty including several sections of incomplete German U-boats. Unfortunately, the

The Soviet light cruiser *Kertch* (ex-*Stalingrad*), a war prize from the Italian Navy. The *Duca D'Agosta*, as completed in Italy 1935, mounted eight 6-inch/53-caliber guns and was equipped for minelaying. The *Kertch* was nimble and quick with a top speed of 36.5 knots, as were many Italian-designed ships. She served the Red Navy for many years and in the late 1950s was leased to the Romanian Navy. The Soviet Navy had literally run all of her machinery beyond any usefulness before turning her over to a satellite state for training duties. *U.S. Navy*

hangar deck was heavily laden and the ship was dangerously top-heavy. In a hurry to loot and take whatever machinery, supplies, or mechanical equipment was available, the Russian crew was less than attentive to the ship's seaworthiness. Russian tugs began pulling Germany's sole bid for carrier aviation to Leningrad on September 27, 1947. It arrived, but rather than be fully examined for future potential it was used as a target hulk. With her went the first possibility of Soviet naval aviation going to sea. The ship may have been a hulk, but the Germans had developed a workable aircraft carrier from which the Soviet Navy could have learned much.

Cruisers

The cruiser force consisted of ex-German, ex-Italian, and ex-American light cruisers and home-built classes dating from World War II and before.

All were considered obsolete when compared to most war-built ships in the Western navies.

The German cruisers were the former *Lutzow*, *Seydlitz*, and *Nurnberg*. The *Lutzow* was transferred to the Soviet Union under the terms of the prewar pact between Stalin and Hitler, and the advancing Russian Army seized the *Seydlitz* in April 1945. Each cruiser displaced 15,200 tons and was 624 feet in length. Their main battery consisted of twelve 7.1-inch guns, complemented by twelve 4-inch guns in the secondary battery. Renamed the *Petropavlovsk* and *Poltava*, respectively, both had been damaged during World War II, but were later rebuilt for service in the Red Navy. Discarding even the most seriously damaged vessels was not a Soviet Navy policy. Everything that could float or potentially be of value to the U.S.S.R. was restored (often to its original obsolete condition).

One of the few Russian-built cruisers, the Kirov-class light cruiser. The Kirovs were designed with definite Italian overtones, and with 110,000 horsepower had an impressive 35-knot top speed. Of the six vessels in this class built, two each were assigned to the Black Sea, Baltic Sea, and Pacific Ocean. *U.S. Navy*

The Red Navy also ended up with war prizes from Japan, with whom it was at war for a mere 26 days. The ex-Japanese destroyer *Harutsuki* was one of these prizes, and like other ships taken from defeated Axis countries, was tested and used exhaustively. The *Harutsuki*, displacing 3,500 tons full load, was a first-line Imperial Japanese Akizuki-class large destroyer built in 1944. Normally heavily armed with a mixture of ASW, anti-ship anti-aircraft weapons, she was transferred to the Soviet Union in 1947 without armament. The Russians named her the *Pospeshny* and she served in non-combat roles. The *Pospeshny* was just another in the eclectic force that marked the Soviet Navy just after World War II. *U.S. Navy*

The *Nurnberg* was taken over by the Red Navy in 1946 and renamed the *Makarov*. This 7,000-ton light cruiser mounted nine 5.9-inch guns in her main battery and a mix of lighter weapons for anti-aircraft defense. The *Makarov* utilized 12,000-shafthorsepower diesel engines for cruising, and steam turbines for full power. This economical combination of propulsion systems was efficient and attractive to the new owners, and this particular ship served the Soviet Navy for many years.

The *Murmansk*, which was the former *USS Milwaukee CL-5*, was a post–World War I Omaha-class light cruiser. These ships had four funnels and broadside 6-inch guns. They mounted a main battery of ten 6-inch/53-caliber guns and displaced just over 7,000 tons. These ships were obsolete at birth and during World War II were assigned to duty in less important areas. The *Milwaukee* had been assigned to the South Atlantic as part of the famed "banana fleet" and with little advance notice, it was secretly and quickly assigned to a Russia-bound convoy. The American crew worked with the new owners for six days and then, in a brief ceremony, the ship was handed over in the harbor at Murmansk. The American crew was not allowed to set foot in the city and only the

ship's photographer was permitted (under heavy escort) to take a picture of the ceremony from a nearby hill. The photograph was diplomatic evidence that the cruiser had been transferred, in case the Russians claimed otherwise later. The Soviet crew members were polite yet firm in their request for guidance and training. The Red Navy officers were unusually meticulous in accounting for all equipment, ammunition, and stores promised. They expressed no gratitude, and the American crew was simply asked to leave its ship and board a transport sailing for New York. This suspicious, high-handed attitude was ever present when U.S. or Western forces negotiated with the Soviet military. It foretold the postwar relationship with great clarity.

After Italy surrendered, there were demands for much of the still viable Italian fleet to be given to the Soviet Union en masse. In lieu of a wholesale transfer, older ships such as the *Milwaukee* and the British *HMS Royal Sovereign*, combined with scores of smaller ships, were transferred. These would later be exchanged on a strictly enforced basis for selected units of the Italian Navy.

Even before victory in World War II, the Western Allies sensed that a large, powerful Soviet

The Soviet Navy *Silnyi* or *Silni* of the "S" or "improved Gordi" class destroyer built during World War II. These fast (36 knots) and heavily armed vessels mounted four 5.1-inch guns and carried stowage for up to 80 mines. They were handsome ships and served well into the 1960s, primarily in the Baltic. None were upgraded to carry surface-to-air missiles and retained their all-gun armament throughout their careers. *U.S. Navy*

Navy had the potential for causing substantial grief in the postwar world.

The *Milwaukee* was returned to the United States in March 1949 in exchange for the Italian light cruiser *Emanuele Filberto Duca D'Aosta*. The former Italian cruiser was renamed the *Stalingrad* and entered service with the Red Navy in the Black Sea Fleet. Built in 1934, this 7,789-ton cruiser mounted eight 6-inch/53-caliber guns (main battery) and six 3.9-inch weapons in her secondary battery. As with most Italian prewar designs, this ship was nimble footed at 36.5 knots with her Parsons geared turbines developing up to 110,000 shaft horsepower. Also in keeping with Italian naval design in the interwar years, this ship was lightly armored with a maximum of 4 inches in critical areas. The Red Navy made good use of this cruiser for many years in the Black Sea and she was later equipped for laying mines, a favorite Soviet naval tactic.

The Soviet Navy also employed four classes of cruiser that were built in local shipyards. The oldest was the 8,030-ton *Krasni Kavkaz*, originally laid down in 1914 and armed with four 7.1-inch guns (main battery), and twelve 4-inch guns in the secondary battery. Similar was the *Krasni Krim* at 6,934 tons, but this light cruiser sported a fifteen

Uritski-class 1,150-ton destroyer (Soviet) built during World War I, and retained for coastal patrol and minelaying well into the late 1950s. This destroyer was capable of 25 knots and carried up to four 3.9-inch guns and older model torpedoes. The class was obsolete when completed in 1914, and again disproved the fear of a massive Soviet Navy of comparable ability to Western navies in the 1950s. The Soviet Navy was reluctant to send any ship to the scrap heap. *U.S. Navy*

The 2,225-ton Leningrad class of Soviet destroyer was launched in the late 1930s, and was quite fast at 39.3 knots (trial speed). Much assistance was received from French naval designers with this type and most ships survived the war to be assigned to the Baltic or Far East. They mounted four 5.1-inch guns in their main battery yet were not equipped for minelaying. *U.S. Navy*

5.1-inch/55-caliber main battery. Both were originally capable of approximately 30 knots, burned coal, and served the Red Navy in less strenuous roles well into the 1950s.

The five-ship Soviet-built Chapaev class displaced 15,000 tons full load and carried twelve 6-inch guns in four triple turrets. These were backed up with eight 4-inch dual-purpose weapons and 28 37-mm anti-aircraft guns in twin mounts. These ships also carried facilities for up to 200 mines and could steam at speeds in excess of 35 knots. This was based on prewar design, yet most served well into the early 1970s.

The last of the postwar class of cruiser was the popular 11,500-ton full load Kirov and "improved Kirov." There were two ships in the original class (*Kirov* and *Molotov*) and the primary difference was in the arrangement of their superstructures and upper works. The four-ship "improved Kirov" variant had a more streamlined silhouette than their predecessors. Both mounted nine 7.1-inch guns in three triple turrets in the main battery with a secondary battery of eight 4-inch dual-purpose weapons. All were capable of carrying 60–90 mines, and could steam at just under 35 knots full

speed. Only three of these ships survived into the 1970s and were then relegated to training roles. The Kirov and Chapaev classes were design precursors to the most famous (and feared) of all Soviet gun cruisers, the Sverdlov class. This class was on the drawing board in the late 1940s. However, none were launched until 1951.

Destroyers and Other Escort Vessels

The Soviet destroyer force consisted of numerous separate classes during the early postwar period. They, like much of the rest of the Red Navy, came from a number of sources outside of Russia. It is also difficult to determine the exact number of ships that survived the war. The Soviets routinely changed pennant numbers and ship names as well as fabricating the number lost or currently operational.

During the period 1945–1950, the Red Navy had a mismatched destroyer force of 13 types. These included eight elderly (1918 vintage) former U.S. Navy "Wickes" class four piper destroyers from the Royal Navy; several ex-German, -Italian, and -Japanese destroyers of varying capability; and at least eight identifiable Russian-built

The Soviet Union concentrated on building submarines that could most effectively defend the country against invaders, yet a large number of long-range (10,000 miles at 9 knots), high-endurance boats were built in the 1,500-ton oceangoing "K" class. These submarines were built in the early years of World War II, and carried 20 torpedoes and ten 21-inch tubes plus two 4-inch deck guns and two 45-mm anti-aircraft guns. They were also equipped for minelaying and carried a crew of 62. Most of this class served the Red Navy well into the nuclear-power age of submarine warfare. *U.S. Navy*

ships. All of the foreign acquisitions were carefully studied and exhaustively tested.

Accordingly, none were suitable for operational service as their power plants were worn out from other exercises. The mainstay of the Red Navy were the eleven ship "R or later Gordi" 2,500-ton class; eleven ship "S or Improved Gordi" 2,150-ton class; eight vessel "G or Gordi" 2,150-ton class; and six ship "Leningrad" class of 2,582-ton destroyers. All carried four 5.1-inch/53-caliber guns in their main battery and a minimum of six 21-inch torpedo tubes; they could steam at 36 knots+ and were fitted for laying mines. All were variants of one another and were remarkably similar in look and performance. They were stylish yet somewhat brutish-looking with their high forward superstructure. From the lessons learned from other navies and its own growing ability to produce quality warships, the Soviet Navy began to design a postwar destroyer class that was comparable to those in the West. The first of what would become known as the "Skory or Skori" class was built in 1949, and over the next several years 70 vessels were commissioned. These 3,500-ton, heavily armed ships with speeds up to 38 knots brought international respect to the Soviet Navy—something its leaders craved.

Other destroyers and frigates in the Soviet medium naval forces inventory were older and a few dated from before the 1917 Revolution. Most of the frigates and patrol vessels came from foreign sources or had an obvious foreign design influence.

The relatively modern mine warfare and fleet train force owed much to foreign influence and included 34 well-armed and well-found U.S.-built Admirable-class minesweepers (650 tons, 3-inch/50-caliber gun and 20/40-mm anti-aircraft weapons. They were diesel powered and capable of 16 knots).

Submarines

The submarine force constituted the bulk of the Soviet Union's naval potential in the initial post–World War II years, and this phenomenon continued throughout the Cold War. The influence of late-war German submarine design was unmistakable in the Soviet boats built in the years following the end of the war. The Red Army looted and brought back everything remotely related to the undersea warfare. This included the purchase of certain U-boat crews to serve as instructors in the Soviet Navy.

The primary goal of the Soviet submarine force was to protect the country from attack and invasion. By 1950, a strategy had been developed and endorsed by the Kremlin. The plan was founded on a 15-year submarine building program, which would provide 1,200 boats of varying capability to adequately maintain three defensive rings around the homeland. One hundred small submarines would patrol the inner ring closest to the coastline; the intermediate ring would be patrolled by upwards of 900 medium-range submarines and the outer ring by 200 long-range attack boats. The objective of the intermediate-

"SHCH-II" or "Shtcha" class medium endurance–class Red Navy submarine built in large numbers (100+) over a 12-year period from 1935 through 1947. These boats were the backbone of the defensive perimeter around the motherland. They displaced 620 tons on the surface and carried six 21-inch torpedo tubes. Named for fish, many of the early models were discarded as unsuitable during the war, yet more than 60 survived into the early 1960s as patrol units in the Baltic and Black Seas. *U.S. Navy*

and long-range submarines was to sink enemy shipping in the open ocean before it had the opportunity to provide supplies to attacking and invading forces. This plan was to be in place and operational by 1965; however, it was fraught with problems and never came to fruition. Nuclear power, U.S. and Western navy submarine-launched ballistic missiles, and the need to defend Russia from attack from carrier-launched aircraft intervened long before this plan was implemented. However, in the first years after the end of World War II, the Soviet submarine force faced more basic difficulties.

The submarine force was not standardized, and even by 1950 it consisted of a minimum of 16 different boat types and different variations of more popular models. As with the surface navy, many of the boats were ex-German and Italian war prizes or stolen booty. Some of the boats were disassembled when captured in 1945 and later completed in Soviet shipyards. Added to these were boats built in Russia before and during the war.

The new classes were either German boats or those built based on later models (Types XXI, VIII, and XXIII). In the midpoint of World War II, Germany realized that its submarine fleet could provide relief from the allied onslaught by eluding ASW tactics. This meant vastly improved submerged performance. It was not until the final months that the prefabricated Type XXI was available for oceangoing service and the smaller version (Type XXIII) for coastal work. The designs were streamlined with welded hulls, and capable of double the underwater speed of contemporary boats. They were air-conditioned and had silent auxiliary electric motors for combating enemy listening devices. They were designed for performance under water and could remain submerged for most of their patrols through the use of an air breathing *schnorchel* (snorkel) and high-capacity batteries. In essence, the Type XXI was the first true submarine. All of the Allied navies wanted to examine and test this design, but the Soviet Navy was obsessed with acquiring these revolutionary

"MV" type coastal patrol submarine built in the last year of World War II. They were a variation of a smaller "M" class of coastal submarine built earlier in the war. Sixty-three of "MV" boats were built in sections, many after being transported by rail to distant yards. They displaced 350 tons on the surface and carried two 21-inch torpedo tubes. Surprisingly, they were capable of a 4,000-mile radius on the surface, and 100 miles at five knots submerged. Over 60 of these small but lethal boats survived well into the 1960s. *U.S. Navy*

boats. There was even talk of radar-evading paint on the *schnorchel* and electronic counter-measures.

In the years that followed the war, the Red Navy used captured boats for operational work and began the design of what would be its most significant immediate postwar submarine class. It was a 1,350-ton boat capable of 15 knots submerged, and it carried six 21-inch torpedo tubes. Code-named the "Whisky" class, more than 100 of these medium-range submarines and its many variants were produced. The first was launched in 1951, as was its big sister, the 19-boat "Zulu" class. The Zulu and its modified successors were long-range 2,200-ton boats capable of 15 knots underwater. They also provided the prototype for the first Soviet ballistic missile program at sea in 1956. The introduction of these boats to the international naval community confirmed fears that the Soviet Navy was interested in more than coastal defense.

In the very early years of the Cold War, the mainstay of the submarine fleet consisted of 19 prewar-designed "K" class 2,067-ton large seagoing boats, 33 "S" class 780-ton medium-range boats, and more than 60 "Sctcha" class 620-ton medium-range submarines. The "K" class was the largest seagoing boat and carried ten 21-inch tubes. It was capable of 10 knots submerged and could operate at long distances for extended patrols. The two medium-range classes carried six 21-inch torpedo tubes and had a maximum speed of 8 knots submerged. All were fitted for laying mines.

The Soviet Navy also operated coastal patrol submarines, of which the "M" class was the most prominent. These were small (161–205-ton) boats with two 21-inch torpedo tubes. The boats were capable of seven knots underwater. They were quite portable and could be transported by rail to wherever they were needed.

Prelude to Korea

In first few years (1945–1950) of the Cold War, all of the worlds navies with the exception of the Soviet Union downsized to dangerously low levels. However, Western navies did not abandon research and development. The development of jet-powered naval aviation, improved submersibles and ASW, as well as guided missiles and nuclear bomb defense, went forward. The Western navies also placed many of their newer vessels in ready reserve or mothball preservation. Reactivation of needed units in an emergency could be accomplished quickly.

It was just a matter of time before a Stalin-inspired and Soviet-sponsored outbreak of war occurred. The fear of Communism and the Soviet Union was growing among military, political, and diplomatic professionals, but it was not until actual fighting broke out that the common citizen recognized that an undeclared world war had begun. It began in Korea during the early summer of 1950.

CHAPTER 4

THE WAR BEGINS: NAVAL OPERATIONS (1950-1970)

The Korean War

Over the five-year period from 1945 to 1950, it became increasingly apparent that an undeclared war of global proportions had begun. No single incident confirmed the existence of this new type of war; however, a series of events culminating in the unprovoked invasion of the Republic of Korea on June 25, 1950, brought the "Cold War" into focus. This attack marked the end of minor skirmishes and shallow apologies, and the beginning of the forcible spread of Communist dogma at the point of a gun. This was the next most serious test of Western resolve since the 1948–1949 failed Soviet blockade of Berlin. It was also to be another and more violent expression of Western "containment" of the Communist

A Panther jet attack fighter is being readied for launch from the *USS Philippine Sea CVA-47* on August 24, 1950, just weeks after the invasion of South Korea by its northern neighbor. The on-scene carriers immediately began to pound North Korean targets within days of the late June invasion in a war that eventually cost the lives of 54,246 U.S. service personnel. *TIM – SFCB*

menace by meeting Soviet encroachment with "unalterable counterforce." The time for words had passed, and the Soviet Union—and in particular, Joseph Stalin—sought to test the United States and its allies. Would they defend a nation not part of Europe? Would they commit men and materiel to a shooting war? Would they risk world war so close on the heels of the greatest war in human history?

Korea was partitioned much like Germany at the end of World War II. The United States received the surrender of the Japanese garrison south of the 38th Parallel, and the Russian Army accepted the surrender of the Japanese occupation army north of the same line. Shortly after the war, the United Nations announced its intention to supervise free elections in Korea, and as expected the Soviet government objected. The country was thus split into two separate entities. The south became the Republic of Korea (ROK), a democratic republic, and the north became the Democratic People's Republic of Korea, a Communist-backed dictatorship.

The Soviet Union decided to make an issue of the Korean partition, and at the same time determine the extent that the United States would back up its words with decisive military action. At the Kremlin's instigation and with China's approval, six North Korean army divisions consisting of 110,000 men backed up by more than 1,000 pieces of artillery crossed the 38th Parallel into the south on June 25, 1950. These reasonably skilled and determined invaders quickly pushed through poorly trained and inadequately deployed ROK forces. They occupied the capital city of Seoul by June 28, 1950, just three days into their campaign to unify the north and south under Communist rule.

The United Nations responded within hours to the crisis and ordered the North Korean armed forces to vacate the south. Fortuitously, the Soviet delegates to the United Nations were boycotting it due to a disagreement over Nationalist Chinese membership in the United Nations. The U.N. Security Council resolution was adopted without Soviet participation and made the upcoming war to evict North Korean armed forces from the south an initiative of the United Nations rather than just the United States.

There was little that the United Nations or the United States could do immediately following the invasion. There also was some concern over the possibility that the invasion of South Korea was just the opening gun of a larger effort that could include attacks on Formosa and NATO nations in Europe. For the present, however, hostilities were limited to the Korean Peninsula.

The U.S. Navy was in Korean coastal waters within days, but budget cutting in Washington had reduced the far-eastern naval forces to a bare minimum. The Seventh Fleet consisted of one Essex-class aircraft carrier (*USS Valley Forge CVA-45*), two cruisers, a dozen destroyers and a small number of auxiliaries. The British had one light carrier of the Colossus class available, *HMS Triumph*, cruisers *HMS Belfast* and *HMS Jamaica* and a few destroyers. Overall, there were few assets available in the region, and even counting the total Allied naval strength, there was barely enough to mount any kind of a suitable response. Within a week of the invasion, surface forces were called upon to engage the North Korean Navy. Allied surface forces including the light cruiser *USS Juneau CLAA-119*, light cruiser *HMS Jamaica*, and destroyer *HMS Black Swan* encountered four Soviet-provided, North Korean Navy–operated G-5, 14-ton motor torpedo boats (MTB). They were escorting a troop- and supply-laden convoy of 10 trawlers off the coast of South Korea. In the only true surface action of the war, the North Korean force attacked the Allied unit with smaller-caliber guns. The larger ships made short work of the G-5s and the following day (July 3rd, 1950) destroyed a number of the North Korean supply vessels. There was a lesson in this action for the Soviet Navy. The employment of torpedo or gunboats as a method of coast defense had limited application, and fighting a blue water navy means having one of your own. This surface action was the first and last of the Korean War. The rest of the war at sea consisted of round-the-clock carrier air strikes, shore bombardment, amphibious operations, and mine warfare.

The *USS Valley Forge CVA-45* and *HMS Triumph* began launching air strikes on July 3rd, 1950, over North Korean targets, and Panther jet fighters from the *Valley Forge* knocked down two Soviet propeller-driven Yak-9 fighters over Pyongyang. It was obvious from the beginning that

The escort carrier *USS Badoeing Strait CVE-116* steams with most of her air group on deck with wings folded. These 23,875-ton full load "jeep" carriers carried up to 34 aircraft and the *Badoeing Strait* was used extensively off Korea. Often, the F4U Corsair was flown from her decks to support Marine and Army ground troops as well as for other strike roles. The weather and operating conditions were often appalling and dangerous for pilots landing and taking off from her 557-foot-long by 105-foot-wide flight deck. This tested naval and marine pilots to their maximum ability, and at the same time demonstrated the resolve of the United Nations to push the invaders back above the 38th Parallel. *TIM – SFCB*

The anti-aircraft cruiser *USS Juneau CLAA-119*. These ships were designed to provide a curtain of heavy anti-aircraft gunfire over fast carrier task forces. They were beautiful purpose-built ships, but were top heavy and did not perform as expected due to the lack of sufficient gun directors for their twelve 5-inch/38-caliber dual-purpose guns. The first few days of the Korean War quickly thrust the *Juneau* into what was the naval officer's dream—a surface battle. Joined by British ships, the *Juneau* destroyed North Korean torpedo boats and the group of trawlers they were escorting over a two-day period from July 2 through July 3, 1950. The *Juneau* served with distinction during the Korean War, and was decommissioned in July 1956, having been in service for a mere decade. Jet aircraft exceeded the speed her gun directors could track, and it was time for a new type of anti-aircraft defense—the surface-to-air missile. *TIM – SFCB*

Near the 38th Parallel, off the Korean coastline, the Iowa-class battleship *USS New Jersey BB-62* opens fire with all nine of her 16-inch/50-caliber guns. In this image captured on November 24, 1951, the battleship again demonstrated its value in shore bombardment. Each gun can throw a one-ton projectile up to 25 miles. Ultimately, all four of the Iowa class provided gunfire support to United Nations forces during the Korean War. In April 1968, the 24-year-old battleship was again summoned from reserve status to pound Communist targets during the Vietnam War. *TIM – SFCB*

LST 799 sits high and dry on a pier in the harbor of Inchon on January 9, 1951. This graphically demonstrated one of the major obstacles to an amphibious landing in this harbor. The tidal range can be as high as 31 feet, and can strand ships up to the size of a light cruiser, making them easy targets for shore batteries. Four months earlier, a combined allied naval and ground assault force made a successful and miraculous landing at Inchon and routed North Korean defenders. A key objection to the planned landing was the danger of unexpected tidal ranges—General MacArthur ignored the warnings and the landing was a success. *TIM –SFCB*

the Soviet Union provided the equipment and the North Koreans the manpower.

In the United States, a phenomenon was taking place that was not anticipated by the Soviet Union. Joseph Stalin and his advisers fully expected the United States and the United Nations to allow South Korea to be consumed by the North Korean military onslaught. As a matter of policy, the United States had publicly excluded South Korea from its strategic defense of the Pacific, preferring to state its support of Nationalist China and Japan. Shortly after the invasion, the United States sensed that a Communist takeover of Korea threatened Japan. Its position was quickly restated to include the defense of South Korea. This change of policy became the catalyst that inspired a major reevaluation of America's national defense. To add action to words, the Truman administration initiated a call-up of the military reserve and activation of dozens

of ships that had been in mothballs. All types and classes of warships were needed, especially aircraft carriers, cruisers, destroyers, and minesweepers.

By late July 1950, the Essex-class carrier *USS Boxer CVA-21* arrived in Japan as an aircraft transport bringing scores of P-51 Mustang fighter aircraft, spare parts, and ground crew for the air force. The Boxer had no air group available for combat.

In her stead, the *USS Badoeing Strait CVE-116*, an escort carrier with piston-driven aircraft, began flying air strikes on enemy targets in late July 1950 and eventually completed three tours of duty off Korea during the war. The small carriers were not jet capable, so they used aircraft such as the F4U Corsairs for close-in ground support such as was needed around the Pusan Perimeter and the Inchon landing in September 1950. The CVEs also maintained ASW patrol around fleet

The destroyer *USS Ernest G Small DD-838* was hit by a floating mine on October 7, 1951, off Hungnam, Korea. Her bow as far aft as the superstructure was severely damaged and nine men lost their lives. While she was slowly steaming out of the area, on October 11, heavy seas began to work the bow and endanger the survival of the ship. In this rare image, the *Small* is backing away from its bow, which is literally tearing loose from the ship. The bow later sank, and the destroyer made its way to a shipyard in Kure, Japan, steaming in reverse for over 400 miles. A temporary patch was made to enable the destroyer to safely return to the United States.

The *USS Ernest G Small* with 85 feet of its bow missing steams into Long Beach Harbor. The *Small* was repaired over a 12-month period using the bow of the partially completed *Seymour D. Owens DD-767*. She, like so many U.S. Navy and United Nations ships, had run or would run afoul of mines off Korea. The Soviet Navy was well versed in mine warfare, and readily shared their knowledge with the North Koreans. Until the United Nations instituted a serious anti-mine warfare program, a large number of casualties resulted. The *Ernest G Small* was back at sea by early December 1952. *TIM — SFCB*

concentrations and provided long-distance over-the-horizon airborne early warning.

By August 1, 1950, the *USS Philippine Sea CVA-47* had arrived and with the *Valley Forge* began pounding enemy targets. Aside from hitting military targets, the carriers began the systematic destruction of road bridges, rail bridges, and train marshaling yards.

Interdicting the flow of supplies would eventually wither the enemy. United Nations forces also imposed a full naval blockade around Korea, and when not on patrol, cruisers and destroyers would pound targets on the coastline, paying particular attention to trains along the coast. As the war progressed, the destruction of North Korean or Red Chinese supply trains that habituated the coast became somewhat of a routine. Late in the war, the "Train Busters Club" was formed and the honor of destroying the greatest number of trains (three) fell to the *USS Endicott DMS-35*, a high-speed minesweeper converted from a Bristol-class destroyer. During the early

days of the war, the navy was strapped for ammunition, and many gunnery officers were hampered from meeting call fire or target of opportunity requirements. Ammunition for 5-, 6-, and 8-inch guns had to be transported to the war zone before any concentrated gunfire missions could be initiated. Once this occurred, surface ships shot up any and all ships or boats attempting to supply the enemy and inland targets spotted doing likewise. Of course, the North Koreans were at the same time mining waters where Allied ships were known to be, and shore batteries were targeting areas where United Nations ships might unknowingly steam through.

The North Koreans employed mines quite effectively, and despite the efforts of U.S. Navy mine warfare forces, several destroyers (e .g., *USS Brush DD-745* and *USS Walke DD-723*) were damaged and four minesweepers were lost. It is estimated that more than 4,000 contact and magnetic mines were provided by the Soviet Union. North Korea made excellent use of this weapon.

One of the most hazardous duties in the Korean War at sea was in a minesweeper. The Admirable-class minesweepers *USS Pirate AM-275* (shown) and *USS Pledge AM-277* were sunk almost simultaneously off Wonsan Harbor, North Korea, on October 12, 1950. Twelve men were lost in this extraordinarily unfortunate incident. Another U.S. Navy minesweeper, the *USS Magpie AMS-25*, was lost a few days earlier on September 29, 1950. The North Korean Navy employed hundreds of mines in their campaign to destroy and demoralize United Nations naval forces. The mine can be an inexpensive equalizer in naval warfare. *TIM — SFCB*

The *USS Helena CA-75*, an 8-inch gun heavy cruiser in the U.S. Seventh Fleet, prepares to assist the Chinese Nationalist evacuation of the Tachen Islands off the coast of Red China. The Communist-controlled Chinese military was continually provoking or attacking Nationalist Chinese outposts by air attack or artillery shelling. The U.S. Seventh Fleet, which operated in the region, was always ready to support the Nationalists with ships such as the *Helena. TIM —SFCB*

Within weeks of the invasion, it was apparent that a bold stroke was needed to prevent a complete disaster. General Douglas MacArthur (United States), Commander in Chief of the Far East, decided to conduct an amphibious landing at Inchon, 150 miles to the rear of the North Korean Army. Fundamentally, the attack was intended to sever the enemy's overextended supply lines and disrupt crucial communication, command, and control operations. The navy fully supported this maneuver, but others pointed out the inherent dangers at Inchon—in particular a tidal range of up to 30 feet. If the landing were miscalculated or delayed, the entire assault force would be at the mercy of the North Koreans and potentially wiped out.

Seasoned naval and marine officers in combination with MacArthur's staff set the landing time for 0633 on the morning of September 15, 1950, only 82 days after the North Korean invasion. On September 15, after a two-day softening up by naval attack units, some 230 ships of all types converged on Inchon (Port of Seoul), and began the assault, with the 1st Marine Division on the point of the spear.

The U.S. Army 7th Division joined the Marine advance and within days recaptured Seoul and destroyed the North Korean Army. By October 19, 1950, U.S. forces now controlled the North Korean capital, Pyongyang. The tables were turned in one of the most daring and providential strategies in the history of military warfare. It was the U.S. Navy, Marines, and Army, supported by the Air Force, that accomplished what many saw as a miracle. From that point forward, the navy's value was never again seriously challenged. Politicians, military professionals, and the public recognized that no one branch of military service could adequately defend the nation. A balanced form of national defense was the answer to protecting the United States and the free world.

United Nations forces, including a rejuvenated ROK army, were quick to roll up the enemy, and after the minesweepers had cleansed the North Korean port of Wonsan of nearly 3,000 contact and magnetic mines, the 1st Marine Division landed unopposed on October 26, 1950.

Allied forces were experiencing increased harassment by Soviet-built attack and bomber aircraft over Korea and the Sea of Japan. In November 1950, the air war took on a different aspect. The Russian-built MiG-15 jet fighter was introduced and began to attack United Nations forces from bases in Manchuria. This new fighter was capable of over 600 miles per hour and mounted 23-mm or 12.7-mm guns. Ultimately,

The radar picket ship *USS Watchman AGR-16,* leaving her base at the Treasure Island Naval Station in San Francisco, California, for duty in the mid-Pacific. Beginning in April 1958, she and 15 other specially converted Liberty ships from the World War II era idly steamed in a predetermined area out in the Pacific and radioed information on any unidentified aircraft closing on North America. She and her sisters spent a yearly average of 200 days at sea, and were rotated systematically from their patrol areas. They provided over-the-horizon radar detection for the Continental Air Defense Command with the primary assignment of warning of an incoming Soviet bomber attack. The program ended in September 1965 after improved detection methods had been developed. *Author's collection*

150 MiG-15s joined the fight, and were usually flown by Soviet Air Force pilots in Chinese uniforms. The MiGs were painted with Chinese Air Force markings. Pitted against the MiG-15 was the U.S. Air Force F-86 Saber jet and the navy's F9F Panther. The U.S. fighters proved an even match for the Russian jets, downing more than 200 Soviet-piloted MiGs during the stalemated air war. The era of piston-driven aircraft dominating the battle space was over, and that of the high-speed, high-altitude aircraft begun.

The rapid advance of Allied forces was reversed by the Chinese, who literally smuggled an army of 300,000 professional soldiers across the Korean border in late November 1950. Eight fully equipped Chinese Army divisions mounted an offensive that forced the United Nations to abandon much of their gains in North Korea. By December 24, 1950, 105,000 ROK and U.S. troops as well as 91,000 civilians had to be evacuated by the navy from the port of Hungnam. The navy was also able to prevent the enemy from capturing 350,000 tons of equipment and supplies by transporting it to safety.

As 1951 began, the war assumed a new face when more than one half-million Chinese soldiers

began to push the United Nations, which now included 16 countries, out of Seoul and southward some 50 miles from the 38th Parallel. By March 1951, the United Nations was again in control of Seoul, and the North Koreans had been driven back across the 38th Parallel. For the next two years, the naval war in Korea was one of carrier air strikes, shore bombardments, and fighting Soviet-built aircraft from carriers such as the *USS Essex CV-9, USS Bon Homme Richard CV-31,* and *USS Princeton CV-37.* By the end of the war, eleven Essex-class carriers were assigned to serve in the Korean Theater. Among the many air strikes in 1951 over Korea, three stand out as being spectacular in their audacity and delivery. The first was the May 1, 1951, attack by the aircraft from the carrier *USS Princeton CV-37.* Eight AD-4 Skyraiders were launched to carry out what was the first torpedo attack since the last days of World War II. The Skyraiders released Mark 13 aerial torpedoes aimed at the Hwachon Dam. The torpedoes hit the target mark and the result was a disruption of North Korean supply lines when the Han and Pukham River valleys were flooded. A similar attack was made during World War II by British Lancaster bombers (No. 617 Squadron) dropping specially designed skip bombs that breached the Mohne and Eder Rivers on the night of May 16–17, 1943.

The second carrier strike was again made by AD Skyraiders flying from the *USS Essex CV-9,* against the North Korean Communist headquarters in Kapsan. The October 29, 1951, attack was so well coordinated and timed that it occurred precisely 13 minutes after the party faithful sat down to dinner. More than 500 of the Communist Party elite were killed in this raid, which did no damage to other parts of the city. The North Korean government immediately offered a substantial bounty for those "murderers from the sky."

The third attack again starred the ever-popular and durable Skyraider that was involved in the first of six experiments using radio-controlled drone-guided bombs. On August 29, 1952, the *USS Boxer CV-21* launched an F6F-5K (former Hellcat fighter) radio-controlled by two AD Skyraiders. The target for the explosive-laden drone was a railroad bridge in North Korea. This attack was essentially a repeat of the German use of radio-controlled drone bombs such as the one that hit the *USS Savannah CL-42* on September 11, 1943, off the coast of Salerno. The drone attack controlled by the Skyraiders also set the stage for the future development of air-launched cruise missiles.

A Texas Tower radar station situated out at sea with the task of detecting a Soviet bomber attack on the continental United States or the North American continent. The Tower was a 6,000-ton steel platform that supported three radar-shielding domes. The structure was embedded in concrete-filled caissons that extended down 48 feet into the continental shelf. Fifty to 70 personnel were assigned to these self-sustaining stations, and this type of duty (150 miles off the coast) was tedious and dangerous during a storm. As with other stopgap measures to defend the United States from Soviet air attack, technological advances in radar and satellite imagery rendered them obsolete. Although operated by U.S. Air Force personnel, their placement at sea made them a part of the Cold War at sea nonetheless. *U.S.N.I.*

The Spanish destroyer *Almirante Ferrandiz,* formerly the Fletcher-class *USS David W Taylor DD-551,* during the change of command ceremony at the Treasure Island Naval Station on May 15, 1957. The United States Navy loaned and sold a number of warships to nations friendly to Western interests, and in this transfer, the Spanish Navy was loaned the *Taylor* and the *USS Capps DD-550* for a period of five years. This was the first of five Fletcher-class destroyers loaned to Spain, and helped ensure a continued pro-Western stance. Spain joined NATO in December 1981. *Author's collection*

Periodic shore bombardment was carried out by all four of the Iowa-class battleships, whose 16-inch guns were always welcomed by ground troops. Heavy cruisers such as the *USS Helena CA-75* and a number of Gearing- and Sumner-class destroyers rounded out the surface forces that fought in the war.

After months of difficult negotiations, an armistice was agreed upon and signed by the Communists and the United Nations on July 27, 1953. An uneasy peace settled over the region. Six hundred thousand Koreans lost their lives as well as an estimated 1 million Chinese. The United Nations lost 55,440 personnel, and of this, 94 percent were from the United States. The political and military result of the Korean War was that the United States emerged as a superpower and was

destined to lead the free world in its battle to stave off Communist domination. For the U.S. Navy, it was a difficult and different kind of war than the one it had been so successful in just years before. Most importantly, the navy was again appreciated and found a definitive role in national defense.

Post Korean War and the Early 1960s

At the end of the Korean Conflict, the world was clearly divided into two different camps: Western oriented and Communist dominated. There was an ongoing arms race between these two camps, and soon there were propaganda, civil defense, and cultural races. It also became a struggle to conquer space and realize mass destruction weapons development through technology. The West claimed clear leadership in all contests. The

Soviet Union made a giant leap in catching up with the United States when it detonated a hydrogen bomb in August 1953. Two years later the U.S.S.R. detonated a thermonuclear device (H-bomb), which was dropped from a long-range bomber. Having a nuclear weapon was one thing, but having the method to deliver it meant real danger to West. When Russia attained this ability, it caused grave concern in the Western world because both sides had relative weapons equivalency. This technological stride by the Soviet Union was impressive, but it was the successful launch of a man-made satellite called Sputnik into space on October 4, 1957, that stunned the world. This was followed up by the launch of another satellite carrying a dog named Layka on November 4, 1957. Both Soviet satellites weighed substantially more (184 pounds and 1,120 pounds respectively) than the U.S. version (3.5 pounds), and were transported into space by the SS-6 Sapwood ICBM. This missile had a range of 6,200 miles and, aside from boosting satellites into space, could also transport a three-megaton nuclear weapon into U.S. territory. Despite the race for space and unrelenting missile development tied to the continuous threat of nuclear war, it was the brush fires in a number of regions that brought both forces into conflict.

In the years that followed the Korean War Truce, the Cold War at sea took many nontraditional forms. The U.S. Seventh Fleet became a permanent fixture in the Western Pacific and the Sixth Fleet assumed the same role in the Mediterranean. The presence of the large jet-capable carriers in all parts of the world acted as a powerful deterrent to Communist activities—at least in the coastal areas. The aircraft carrier became a prime method of enforcing U.S. will and diplomacy in almost every region bordered by the sea. This was true throughout the Cold War and beyond. Deterring Communism and countering the growing Soviet military machine was not the sole prerogative of U.S. and NATO naval aviation. With the advent of nuclear power at sea, submarines could truly fight the kind of war first envisioned by their designers. Limitless undersea operation turned the submarine into a strategic weapon when it was married to the ballistic missile. The U.S. Navy had been experimenting with various cruise missile variants in the Regulus program during the late 1950s, but it was not until the commissioning of the Polaris ICBM-armed George Washington class of SSBN on December 30, 1959, that the program became credible. Other nations including France, Great Britain,

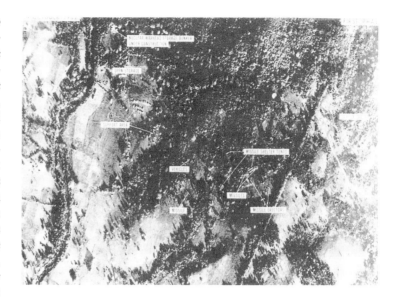

Aerial photographs of Russian missile installations under construction in Cuba. This image and others confirmed that the Soviet Union was building a network of strategic missile bases in Cuba that could launch nuclear-tipped weapons at much of the southern United States. This knowledge led to the Cuban Missile Crisis in the fall of 1962. *TIM*

A Soviet Foxtrot-class diesel-electric attack submarine running on the surface. It has obviously been at sea for a long period. Foxtrot F-911 was "held down" by U.S. Naval patrol planes (P2V Neptune) and Gearing-class destroyer *USS Charles P Cecil DDR-835* for 35 hours during the Cuban Missile Crisis in October 1962. Besides enforcing a shipping quarantine around Cuba, U.S. destroyers forced Soviet submarines to leave the area, including another Foxtrot. This boat was brought to the surface by grenades dropped by the *USS Cony DDE-508*. The Foxtrot class had a very long range (19,000 miles), carried nuclear-tipped torpedoes, and was a highly capable vessel. The Cold War nearly heated up into a global conflict in the fall of 1962. *Author's collection*

The Gearing-class destroyer *USS Vesole DDR-878* was one of many destroyers that enforced the U.S.-imposed "quarantine" on Soviet weapons being delivered to Cuba. The *Vesole* became famous when she was photographed escorting the Soviet freighter *Volgoles* out of the Caribbean area. The *Volgoles* was transporting a full deckload of ballistic missiles as she sailed into the open Atlantic. President John F. Kennedy's ability to intimidate Premier Khrushchev was made possible by the U.S. Navy. The value of a powerful navy became apparent to the Kremlin from this incident. *TIM*

and of course the Soviet Union followed suit with their own programs and U.S. dominance did not last long. As a result, the Cold War at sea assumed a new character—perhaps the most feared of all.

In the aftermath of the Korean War, surface ships of NATO and the U.S. Navy were often occupied in patrolling the most likely hot spots of the Cold War. Multinational forces of destroyers carefully monitored ship traffic near the Korean, Vietnam, and Formosa (Taiwan) coastlines. Interdicting Communist supplies and guerrillas being smuggled into friendly nations was a full-time job. During the day, junk and small boat traffic was at a minimum. As soon as the sun set, radar scopes lit up like Christmas trees as hundreds of small craft plied back and forth, ignoring the forcible search and seizure activities of naval patrols. Most craft were innocent, but a large number carried men and weapons, usually hidden beneath false decks and in stinking holds. The tenacity of these guerrillas was admirable, and a portent of the future

when war broke out in Vietnam. Occasionally, the naval patrols netted contraband, but a large portion of it slipped through.

During this period, there was intermittent artillery shelling of shore islands such as Quemoy and Matsu that were garrisoned by a 100,000-man Nationalist Chinese army. Within easy range, the Red Chinese mounted a concentrated barrage that lasted from August through December 1958. The Seventh Fleet was ordered to protect supply transports to the islands. The threat of air strikes from nearby carriers caused the shelling to diminish.

The U.S. Navy completed mass evacuations of civilians fleeing from Communist control. During August 1954, U.S. Navy landing craft transported more than 300,000 civilian and military personnel from North Vietnam to the south. The question as to how Indochina (now Vietnam) was to be realigned was answered with a demarcation between the north and south at the 17th Parallel as part of the Geneva Accords of 1954–1955. In general terms, the United States indicated that it would provide military support to the anti-Communist regime in South Vietnam. In early February 1955, the Seventh Fleet was again called upon to relocate some 29,000 Nationalist Chinese soldiers and civilians from the Tachen Islands to their new home in Taiwan. For those people that desired to avoid Communism, the U.S. Navy was most obliging.

Military assistance was provided to a number of nations friendly to the West. The U.S. Navy and the United Kingdom's Navy had a huge surplus of relatively new World War II-built warships, many of which were either sold or loaned to selected navies around the world. South American and NATO members were able to modernize their navies and at the same time make a commitment to oppose the spread of Communism. In 1951–1952, the U.S. Navy sold six Brooklyn-St. Louis–class light cruisers to Argentina, Brazil, and Chile. To ensure some degree of regional power balance, two were sold to each nation. One, the Argentine Navy *General Belgrano* (former *USS Phoenix CL-46*), was sunk by a British nuclear submarine (*HMS Conqueror*) in the 1982 Falklands Islands War. Since the final days of World War II, this was the first time that a major warship was sunk by torpedo. These were but a few of the diplomatic and political actions taken. There were military incidents as well. Soviet submarines ventured long distances from their homeland and, in combination with electronic-laden fishing trawlers, began a sustained surveillance of Western naval operations. Later, the ships would also interfere with U.S. Navy and other Western vessels by violating commonly understood international rules of the road. In February 1959, an investigating team from the radar picket destroyer escort *USS Roy O Hale DER-336* boarded the Soviet trawler *Novorossisk* seeking to confirm reports that the ship had been cutting transatlantic cables. No proof could be found. The use of destroyer escorts for radar picket such as the *Hale* was quite commonplace during the 1950s. The aerospace defense of the continental United States was dependent on an early-warning system that could detect incoming Soviet bombers. Radar was not developed to the state where it had a comprehensive over-the-horizon capability, so ships (either escort destroyers or converted Liberty ships) were stationed at intervals out at sea to provide warning to the Continental Air Defense Command. It was lonely and difficult work that required the crews to be kept at sea for many months. Submarines were also pressed into the early-warning radar picket role, and the ultimate radar-equipped submersible was the 447-foot-long *USS Triton SSRN-586*. Commissioned in 1958, the 6,770-ton *Triton* was the largest submarine in the world at that time. Ostensibly to provide early warning to task forces, she went out of service in 1969. In the early years of the Cold War at sea, it seemed as if naval aircraft were in a more precarious position than ships or submarines.

U.S. Navy patrol aircraft (P2V Neptune) were periodically shot down by MiG fighters as they flew through international air space in close proximity to Communist-held territory. The Chinese also shot at or attacked U.S. naval aircraft near their territorial borders, but were not as successful as their Russian counterparts. It was significant that well-armed U.S. aircraft usually downed Communist attackers, but the unarmed patrol planes were at their mercy. Occasionally, an apology was offered by the Soviet Union but more often Russian delegates in the United Nations denounced the United States and its "imperialist stooges" as warmongers. The war of words found a ready forum on the floor of the United Nations Security Council. The word "crisis" became a popular description of any Communist maneuver that resulted in a confrontation with the West. Another phrase that worked itself into the world's lexicon was "peaceful co-existence," which was coined to describe two wolves circling over a frightened rabbit. Words were finally translated into action in Cuba in the fall of 1962.

Cuban Missile Crisis

Cuba is an island nation 90 miles from United States. It had significant emotional, political, and

The anti-submarine aircraft carrier *USS Essex CVS-9* at sea during the October 1962 Cuban Missile Crisis. Her S2F Tracker and WF-2 Tracer aircraft supplemented by Sea King helicopters made her a formidable opponent to any Soviet submarine in the region. The *Essex*, lead ship of the famous 27,000-ton fast-attack aircraft carriers of World War II, played a major role in driving Soviet submarines out of the Caribbean. This ship demonstrated U.S. Naval resolve and ability to hunt down, and if need be, kill an intruding submarine. *U.S. Navy*

economic ties to the United States dating back to 1898 and the Spanish-American War. Primarily an agricultural country (sugar) with heavy investment by U.S. business interests, throughout the late 1940s and into the 1950s, the country had become subject to a corrupt form of totalitarian rule. Unfortunately, control of the government fell into the hands of Fulgencio Batista, who systematically looted the country and ruthlessly dealt with any opponents. By 1958, much of the country was exasperated with Batista, his henchmen, and policies. His government, seemingly committed to acquiring wealth at the expense of the Cuban citizenry,

The end of the Cuban Missile Crisis in late 1962 did not end the hostility between Communist Cuba and the United States. Western economic embargoes had virtually devastated the island nation's fragile economy, yet this did not prevent the Cuban Air Force from attacking innocent fishermen operating within international waters—or welcoming hijacked U.S. commercial airliners. The radar picker destroyer escort *USS Kretchmer DER-329* shown in this February 21, 1963, image has just rescued two men whose shrimp boat was attacked and sunk by rockets fired from two Cuban MiG fighters. *TIM — SFCB*

had also lost support from the United States. It was allied with various crime syndicates in the United States and overall was one of the most corrupt and brutal governments in the Western Hemisphere. Not surprisingly, a popular revolution swept Batista out of power and into exile on January 1, 1959. Guerrilla revolutionary Fidel Castro became the leader of Cuba a week later and shortly thereafter declared that he was a devoted student of Marxist-Leninist doctrine. Two years later, the Castro regime was further alienated from the United States due to a quixotic and amateur military venture in the Bay of Pigs. From April 17–20, 1961, 1,400 Cuban exiles (freedom fighters) invaded Cuba with the intent of rousing the populace against Castro. The invasion and short battle were an abysmal failure, and U.S. Navy forces just over the horizon were instructed to remain neutral. This fiasco further embarrassed the United States as it became well known that the attack was sponsored by the U.S. Central Intelligence Agency and related covert military personnel.

Soviet leadership was ecstatic over the solidity of Castro's hold on Cuba and his political views, which meshed well with those of the Kremlin. It was welcome news to the U.S.S.R., whose leadership was becoming anxious over the obvious nuclear weapons imbalance with the United States. The United States had developed superiority in submarine-launched (George Washington–class SSBN) and land-based ballistic missiles, and its Strategic Air Command was far more capable than the bomber and rocket forces of the Soviet Union. The ballistic missiles sited in Soviet territory had a limited range and were not able to hit all areas of

the continental United States. The possibility of having a friendly state where Russian bombers and missiles could be based was too tempting to resist for Premier Nikita Khrushchev. Much of the United States would be at risk, and both nations would be on an even playing field.

The United States was now faced with a potential Soviet puppet state within dangerous proximity to its shores. Aside from Castro's overt commitment to Communism and the fervent support of his people, there was another more compelling reason for concern. The Russians were shipping arms and sending hundreds of military advisers to Castro. By late 1962, Cuba had received a substantial amount of military aid, including 60 MiG-15s, 30 MiG-17s, and 20 MiG-19s. It was also rumored that the Cuban Air Force had the MiG-21 attack fighter. This aircraft was capable of 1,285 miles per hour and mounted two 30-mm machine guns. It was also able to stand up against most Western fighter aircraft and could shoot down a U.S. Air Force U-2 reconnaissance aircraft. The Soviet Union also provided the Cuban Navy with seven Komar guided-missile patrol boats. The Komar class was the first missile-armed (two SS-N-2) boat of this type in the world. Also received were a number of Kronstadt submarine chasers, P-4 and P-6 motor torpedo boats. The planned expansion of the Cuban Navy with six Skory-class gun destroyers ended as the result of the international crisis in October 1962.

The United States became most alarmed when its aerial surveillance revealed the presence of Soviet missiles on Cuban soil that could carry a nuclear weapon into the continental United

States with little or no advance warning. A U-2 overflight of Cuba also detected IL-28 Beagle bombers being assembled at various Cuban military airfields. The missiles installations being readied in Cuba were of two different sorts: the medium-range ballistic missile SS-4 Sandal, with a range of 1,200 miles and a one-megaton weapon, and the intermediate-range ballistic missile SS-5 Skean with a range of more than 2,200 miles and a five-megaton weapon. Intelligence reports indicated the presence of 42 Sandal missiles and 32 Skeans on Cuban territory as the crisis unfolded. It was later confirmed that no Skeans had been received in Cuba; however, 36 nuclear warheads for the Sandals, six nuclear bombs for the Beagles, and 80 nuclear warheads for cruise missiles were delivered. Had these weapons become operational, many cities within the continental United States would have had less than a three-minute warning before impact. The events that took place in October 1962 brought the superpowers to the brink of nuclear combat and global war. Premier Khrushchev was known for his volatility, but in this context the stakes were far too high for hasty words or action. The time for compromise and reflection was at hand.

On October 22nd, President Kennedy appeared on television and advised the nation that the U.S. Navy was to begin a blockade on the following day of Soviet shipping carrying offensive weapons to Cuba. The "quarantine" was to be enforced by Task Force 136 consisting of the ASW carrier USS Essex CVS-9 supported by a number of destroyers and cruisers. Within three days, 52 surface ships were enforcing the blockade, and by November there were 115 destroyers and two cruisers on station. The emergency was so real that many ships in repair and overhaul status were literally patched together and sent to sea. Providing air cover would be the carriers USS Enterprise CVAN-65 and USS Independence CVA-62, accompanied by escorting surface forces. The idea of a quarantine was not wholly endorsed by Kennedy's military advisers. Some preferred a full-scale invasion and military defeat of Castro and his armed forces. Kennedy opted for a diplomatic solution.

The United Nations Security Council was next asked to censure the Soviet Union for threatening world peace with a probable nuclear holocaust. The U.S. Navy, in concert with warships sent by other South American navies, began to interdict and examine ships heading toward Cuba. More than two dozen cargo ships were known to be steaming for Cuba, and within a day of the quarantine being established, most reversed course

out of the Caribbean. In order to show the seriousness of Kennedy's intentions, two Soviet ships were stopped. One of the vessels was examined by boarding crews from destroyers. Its cargo was found to be harmless. By October 26th, Premier Khrushchev caved in to pressure and fear of massive nuclear war. He notified President Kennedy in writing of his intention to remove offensive missiles from Cuban soil providing that the United States refrained from invading Cuba and lifted the naval blockade. Later he demanded that the United States also remove its offensive missiles from Turkey as a further condition of his compliance with removing the missiles from Cuba. This was already planned, and on October 28th, Khrushchev notified the United States that offensive missiles in Cuba were being removed as well as the medium-range Beagle bombers. By late November 1962, the crisis was over. U-2 flights and other forms of surveillance confirmed the removal of weapons stipulated in the Kennedy-Khrushchev agreement. Destroyers watched and inspected Soviet cargo ships as they left Cuba and verified missile components and allied systems were being transported back to the Soviet Union.

In addition to providing an effective blockade, the navy was also able to locate, track, and harass Soviet submarines of the diesel-electric Foxtrot class that were patrolling in the region. This was the first real test of U.S. Navy anti-submarine warfare (ASW) ability. The USS Essex CVS-9 had been converted for ASW work, and with her improved sonar and purpose-built aircraft (Grumman S2F Trackers, Sikorsky HSS-2 Sea Kings, and Grumman WF-2 Tracers) she contributed much to detecting and hounding uninvited Soviet submarines out of the area.

The value of a large, powerful (and modern) navy was firmly understood by Soviet leadership. Had the U.S.S.R. had such a navy, it would have been more able to protect its political and military advances and effectively challenge the U.S. Navy.

The removal of offensive weapons of mass destruction from Cuban soil did not mean an end to rancor between the United States and its neighbor. Various forms of harassment by the Cuban government continued during the Cold War. For example, on February 6, 1964, Castro ordered the closing of the fresh water supply to the Guantanamo Bay Naval Base. The base then became self-sufficient and later refused Castro's offer to turn on the water faucet.

The end of the Cuban Missile Crisis was a milestone in the Cold War, and served as a reality check for both superpowers. A year later, a positive step

The destroyer *USS Maddox DD-731* spent much of its career life in the Seventh Fleet. During the Korean War it was a member of the "Train Busters" club, responsible for shooting up enemy coastal railways. On August 2, 1964, the *Maddox* was conducting an electronic surveillance of North Vietnamese defenses in the Tonkin Gulf when she was attacked by three Soviet-made P-4 torpedo boats. With the assistance of on-call carrier aircraft, the attackers were driven away. This and later incidents in the same waters gave credence to the political declaration of war against North Vietnam by the Johnson administration. The *Maddox* was a Sumner class (short-hull 2,200 ton) destroyer and never received a FRAM update. She never really left the Far East, and in July 1972 was transferred to Taiwan's Navy as the *Po Yang. TIM —SFCB*

A pair of F-4 Phantom jets based on the *USS Ranger CVA-61*. The Phantom was a very popular and rugged aircraft for naval and marine pilots. It had a top speed of Mach 2+, and a combat ceiling of 71,000 feet. This two-seat version entered service in 1962 and became one of the key combat planes in the Vietnam War. The air war over Vietnam was tedious and dangerous. Targets in the north were some of the most heavily defended since Berlin, Germany, during World War II. There were 6,000 anti-aircraft guns and over 200 SAM sites around Hanoi, Haiphong, and other significant industrial areas in North Vietnam. During the 11 years of the Vietnam War, approximately 200 U.S. aircraft were downed by enemy surface-to-air missiles (SAM) and 2,100 by conventional short-range anti-aircraft gunfire (AAA). *Author's collection*

was taken to slow down the nuclear arms race. In September 1963, a treaty banning all atmospheric nuclear testing was ratified by the U.S. Senate. On October 10, 1963, the treaty signed by the United States, Great Britain, and the Soviet Union went into effect. At sea the war continued unabated.

The West and the U.S.S.R. were developing some extremely powerful and innovative means of using the sea to maintain an arms balance. The George Washington-class ballistic missile submarines was joined by the more powerful five-boat Ethan Allen SSBN-608 class in late 1960 and the 8,250-ton Lafayette SSBN-616 class built from 1962–1967. By the late 1960s, the United States had 41 active ballistic missile submarines armed with 656 Polaris ICBMs. Great Britain had four Resolution-class SSBNs that mounted 16 Polaris missiles, and France was building four boats in the

Le Redoubtable-class SSBN with 16 Polaris-type ICBMs. The Soviet Union was also building a number of ballistic and cruise missile submarines such as the Echo and Hotel classes, which carried a limited number of missiles.

U.S. Naval aviation had taken a quantum leap forward after the Korean War and now had a nuclear super carrier, the *USS Enterprise CVAN-65* and eight other super carriers to complement the modernized Essex class. With the exception of Great Britain and France, no other nation had a significant carrier-borne naval aviation program. The Soviet Union, still in a defensive mentality, maintained a naval air force that it claimed numbered in the thousands.

To further emphasize the degree of power projection from the sea, the U.S. Navy carried out Operation Sea Orbit from July 31, 1964–October

The aircraft transport *USNS Core AKV-41*, formerly the *USS Core CVE-13*. The *Core* was a Bogue-class 14,000-ton full load 496-foot-long escort carrier commissioned on May 5, 1942. She served throughout World War II and was converted to an aircraft transport in 1959. With its spacious flight and hangar decks this civilian-manned aircraft ferry could transport dozens of fixed and rotary-wing aircraft from U.S. ports to Vietnam. High-capacity derricks were located fore and aft, as shown, and could unload their cargo quickly. Sister ship *USNS Card AKV-40* was sunk in the Saigon River by a Viet Cong mine on February 5, 1964. As the war effort heightened, even vessels on the way to the breakers were rejuvenated for one further service to the U.S. military. *TIM*

1, 1964. The nuclear carrier *USS Enterprise CVAN-65* was escorted by the nuclear missile cruiser *USS Long Beach CGN-9* and the nuclear missile frigate *USS Bainbridge DLGN-25* on a cruise around the world. The significance of this cruise was that it was accomplished without refueling and proved the endurance or "forward presence" potential of a carrier battle group in the nuclear age. These ships could remain near Soviet- or Communist-held territory almost indefinitely and be able to launch nuclear-armed missiles and aircraft at a moment's notice.

The Vietnam War: 1964–1970

The next major evolution in the Cold War at sea occurred on the other side of the world in the Tonkin Gulf in August 1964. However, leading up to the events that would initiate the Vietnam War, there was a growing number of annoying incidents at sea between the West and Communist states.

The U.S. Navy suspected the U.S.S.R. of using fishing trawlers to cut or damage transatlantic cables, and the U.S.S.R. complained bitterly about electronic jamming of its communication systems. As part of the U.S.S.R.'s campaign to disrupt Western naval exercises, Soviet naval air force Badger bombers and other aircraft periodically harassed American carrier task forces. Various smaller

Russian vessels were often seen in proximity to carrier operations and periodically interfered with ship-to-ship refueling. Frequently, U.S. and other Western warships had to maneuver to avoid Soviet ships that were deliberately attempting to cause a collision. The Soviet press reported that U.S. naval aircraft had flown dangerously close to Russian ships more than 1,000 times, and U.S. warships had put Soviet ships at unnecessary risk at least 20 times.

Over Laos, two U.S. Navy F-8 Crusader fighters from the carrier *USS Kitty Hawk CVA-63* were shot down in June 1964 just over a month after the aircraft cargo ship *USNS Card* was sunk while tied up in Saigon, South Vietnam. A mine attached to the hull by the Viet Cong (Communist guerrillas) was blamed. The United States had been providing military aid and advisers to the South Vietnamese in their effort to prevent Communist-led North Vietnam from annexing them into one country.

On August 2, 1964, the destroyer *USS Maddox DD-731* was slowly cruising in the Gulf of Tonkin on a "desoto" mission designed to identify North Vietnamese radar transmissions. The 300-mile-long by 250-mile-wide Gulf of Tonkin was regarded by the Red Chinese and the North Vietnamese as their lake, and Western warships were unwelcome. After three days of the *Maddox*

A river patrol boat used in the Mekong Delta for minesweeping during the Vietnam War. It carries radar and is heavily armed with machine guns and small arms. These and hundreds of other "Riverine Force" boats fought a fierce and deadly "brown water" war against enemy mines, shore fire, and arms smugglers. As the war wound down for the United States, the entire U.S. Navy brown water force was turned over to the South Vietnamese Navy. After South Vietnam was conquered by the North Vietnamese Army, many of these boats were captured. Within a very few years, these well-built and very capable boats were inoperable due to poor maintenance and repair by their new owners. *TIM*

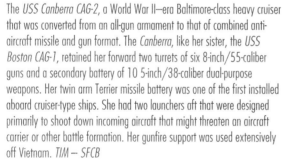

The *USS Canberra CAG-2*, a World War II—era Baltimore-class heavy cruiser that was converted from an all-gun armament to that of combined anti-aircraft missile and gun format. The *Canberra*, like her sister, the *USS Boston CAG-1*, retained her forward two turrets of six 8-inch/55-caliber guns and a secondary battery of 10 5-inch/38-caliber dual-purpose weapons. Her twin arm Terrier missile battery was one of the first installed aboard cruiser-type ships. She had two launchers aft that were designed primarily to shoot down incoming aircraft that might threaten an aircraft carrier or other battle formation. Her gunfire support was used extensively off Vietnam. *TIM — SFCB*

idly steaming up and down the coastline at 30 miles out, the North Vietnamese dispatched three Soviet-designed P-4 motor torpedo boats to first shadow and then attack the lone destroyer. As the P-4s came within 10,000 yards of the *Maddox* and began to launch their ancient but potent steam-powered torpedoes, the destroyer opened fire with her main battery of 5-inch/38-caliber guns. The *Maddox* had increased her speed to flank (32 knots), and as two of the boats continued to within 2,000 yards, she opened fire with her 3-inch/50-caliber anti-aircraft guns and began to dodge the torpedoes that had caught up to her. The *Maddox* was hit by a sole bullet, but in contrast did terrific damage to her determined attackers. As the *Maddox* began to leave the battered and sinking P-4s in her wake, three Crusaders from the carrier *USS Ticonderoga CVA-14* arrived and began to strafe the enemy boats. The result of this confrontation was little damage and

no casualties in the *Maddox*. The Pentagon and, in particular, the Johnson administration were anxious to further confirm that an actual unprovoked attack had occurred against U.S. naval forces.

On the night of August 5, 1964, the *Maddox* again steamed into the Gulf of Tonkin in company with the more modern destroyer *USS C. Turner Joy DD-951*. That evening and until midnight, both ships claimed that they were attacked by North Vietnamese craft. The *Maddox* fired 64 rounds from her main battery and the *Turner Joy* fired a like number. Some 84 contacts were reported and 22 torpedoes were seen to pass by the ships. Aircraft from nearby carriers examined the area the following morning and found no after-battle evidence in the form of wreckage or bodies. Sixty-four carrier aircraft sorties were launched against inland targets by aircraft from the *Ticonderoga* and the *USS Constellation CVA-64* in retaliation for the unprovoked attacks on the U.S. destroyers. Two dozen North Vietnamese Navy patrol boats and a large petroleum facility were claimed destroyed.

Years later, after discussions with North Vietnamese naval officers who were present in nearby

The *USS Oriskany CVA-34*, the most modern of the Essex-class aircraft carriers, is about to fuel the destroyer *USS Bradford DD-545*. The *Oriskany* was often deployed off Vietnam (Yankee Station) during the war, and launched thousands of sorties against enemy targets. She also launched attacks against North Korean targets years before and her pilots shot down at least two MiG-15 attackers during that war. The Naval Tactical Data System (NTDS) was installed aboard the *Oriskany* in early 1961, which was the electronic precursor to the AEGIS system of the 1990s' Burke-class destroyers and Ticonderoga-class missile cruisers. A fire aboard the *Oriskany* in October 1966 resulted in the death of 44 men, yet the carrier was back on station within months. Decommissioned in 1976, the old carrier was towed to Beaumont, Texas, in May 1999 for probable scrapping. *TIM — SFCB*

bases, it was discovered that the U.S. sonar contacts were the result of an overeager operator and freakish weather conditions that caused ghost images on radar. The Johnson administration was under pressure from conservative elements in the Congress to adopt a more "hawkish" attitude in Southeast Asia. The attacks in the Tonkin Gulf permitted a legitimate armed response by the United States, and silenced President Johnson's political opponents.

The U.S. Congress abdicated some of its war-making powers to President Johnson after the Tonkin Gulf incidents were reported. The "Tonkin Gulf Resolution" was quickly approved by the House and Senate. This enabled a full-scale buildup of military forces and direct involvement of U.S. forces in the Vietnamese civil war.

The war in Vietnam did not begin with the Tonkin Gulf Resolution. This action was one of many almost predestined steps in U.S. military involvement in Southeast Asia. It began with promises of military aid and technical advisers shortly after World War II. Direct assistance was stepped up after the Geneva Accords in 1955, and quietly escalated by quantum leaps up through late 1964. By the time the *Maddox* was engaged by North Vietnamese torpedo boats, there were more than 15,000 advisers in South Vietnam and $500 million in aid had been provided in 1963 alone. At the end of 1964, 23,000 American military personnel were based in Vietnam. Communist leadership in Hanoi decided to escalate the struggle and began to pour personnel and materials into South Vietnam as well. The Soviet Union was all too happy to provide military aid of its own.

Nineteen sixty-five was a key milestone year in what was quickly becoming known as the Vietnam Conflict (war). The U.S. Navy was now committed to its now traditional role of providing carrier air strike support both tactically and later strategically. "Yankee" and "Dixie" stations were established at sea. Both were mythical locations at sea where attack aircraft carriers such as the *USS Hancock CVA-19*, *USS Ranger CVA-61*, and *USS Coral Sea CVA-43* operated and launched strikes against targets in the north or wherever directed. Nearly all of the U.S. Navy's carriers were rotated in and out of these stations during the war. By the end of 1965 carriers had launched a phenomenal 55,000 sorties. Among the most popular aircraft, during the early phase of the naval air war, were the AD Skyraider, F-4 Phantom, A4C Skyhawk, and F-8 Crusader. The Skyhawk was probably the most famous of all naval aircraft that fought in the Vietnam War. It was produced in large quantities and used by other navies as well. Its speed was over 600 miles per hour and it had a 1,740-mile range. It was designed to carry a nuclear weapon, and its role in Vietnam varied from ground support to bombing. The multi-use of purpose-built aircraft was common in this war. When the need arose, aircraft had to be sent—any aircraft that could do the job.

The naval air war escalated through a series of strikes against critical North Vietnamese targets such as power installations, bridges, and transportation and supply centers as well as known military bases or marshaling areas. Often the attacks were made in concert with the U.S. Air Force, such as the March 2nd "Rolling Thunder" attacks on targets in North Vietnam. The loss of air crews began to mount as the number of strikes increased. The August 10–12, 1965, period witnessed the greatest loss of naval aircraft to date. Surface-to-air missiles and conventional anti-aircraft gun batteries accounted for six U.S. aircraft shot down over this three-day period. The North Vietnamese initiated a systematic defense of key military and industrial installations. As students of Soviet air defense doctrine, they used every means at hand, including having individuals fire their rifles at incoming U.S. aircraft. They were provided Soviet-made 23-mm rapid-fire anti-aircraft guns and scores of the SA-2 Guideline surface-to-air missile (SAM). This was the most used SAM system in the world during this period. The SA-2 carried a 286-pound warhead and had a range of 31 miles. As the war progressed in Southeast Asia, methods were developed to improve the chances of an aircraft avoiding this missile. Low-level attack on heavily defended sites remained difficult in view of the curtain of fire often put up by North Vietnamese defenders.

There were a growing number of encounters between naval aircraft and Soviet-built MiG-17s during the early phase of the war. The F-4 Phantom, F-8 Crusader, and even the A1 Skyraider were frequent victors over their North Vietnamese opponents.

The naval air war was one of a number of operations of the U.S. Navy in Vietnam. Interdiction of enemy supplies was attempted through the use of a search and seizure program at sea, dubbed *Operation Market Time*. Patrol ships (e.g., destroyers, destroyer escorts, and Point-class U.S. Coast Guard cutters) began a planned inspection of junks, small craft, and other ships transiting along the Vietnamese coastline. Also used in the coastal surveillance force was the "Swift type, PCF," (Inshore Patrol Craft) a shallow-draft, all-metal patrol boat. The Swift boat was based on the successful

The *USS John S McCain DL-3*, a 4,770-ton full load Mitscher-class frigate commissioned in 1952. The *McCain* was armed with two 5-inch/54-caliber guns and four 3-inch/70-caliber guns in twin mount enclosures. To combat the feared early Soviet submarine menace, this class was armed with Weapon A. Four of the Mitscher class were built as ocean escorts, yet even after extensive updating with ASROC, these ships were considered unreliable and a bad idea. The U.S. Navy experimented with different ship types that were intended to meet and defeat modern Soviet submersibles. In 1962, the *McCain* accompanied the carrier *Wasp* when she and the balance of an ASW task force entered the Baltic Sea—the backyard of the Soviet Union. *Author's collection*

The Forrestal-class super carrier, *USS Ranger CVA-61*, at sea with her air group on the flight deck. The *Ranger* displaced 78,000 tons full load and her armored flight deck was 1,039-feet-long by 238 feet at its extreme beam. She was capable of 34 knots on 280,000 shaft horsepower. On June 4, 1963, the super carrier was harassed by Soviet Badger bombers while on patrol in the Sea of Japan. The carrier's combat air patrol convinced the Russian pilots to break off. She also saw much service off Vietnam, and in 1993 was decommissioned in 1993, and placed in reserve at the Puget Sound Naval Shipyard in Bremerton, Washington. *TIM*

crew boats used in the Gulf of Mexico in support of the offshore oil-drilling program. The Navy also employed landing craft, small minesweepers, and Coast Guard patrol boats (WPB) to cover the 1,000-mile coastline of Vietnam. This meant stopping a craft and sending a boarding party to examine cargo manifests and thoroughly search for weapons and related supplies. Thousands of sightings and searches were made, with some result, but not on the scale anticipated. The Viet Cong simply took steps to avoid the naval patrols.

The more heavily armed American ships were also available for call-fire missions along the coast, and successfully able to assist ground troops on a number of occasions. Having a destroyer with 5-inch/38-caliber guns was a godsend to troops pinned down by the Viet Cong or North Vietnamese Army (NVA) regular troops. Light and heavy cruisers (e.g., *USS Oklahoma City CLG-5* and *USS Canberra CAG-2*) were sometimes available to lend support with their 6- or 8-inch guns. It seemed ironic that the U.S. Navy had converted older cruisers to carry surface-to-air missiles as rapidly as funding would allow, and now its World War II–type armament was most in demand.

Victory and Liberty ships from World War II and Korean War use were reactivated to form a continuous sea train of cargo being transported into Vietnam. By late 1965, there were 175 ships transporting approximately 725,000 tons of cargo to Southeast Asia monthly. Of course, not all shipping lines were willing to carry cargo to the war zone. On occasion, seamen from Greek and Mexican freighters refused to work on ships sailing for Vietnam, with the backing of their governments. From the outset, the Vietnam War was unpopular. Escort carriers of the Bogue and Commencement Bay class were activated and converted into aircraft transports (AKV). Equipped with high-capacity derricks, these ships could carry dozens of rotary and fixed-wing aircraft to the war zones. They were manned by civilian crews and carried no weapons.

The "blue water navy" was not the only navy to participate in this war. The "brown water navy" that sailed the rivers of Vietnam played an important role which was reminiscent of that in the U.S. Civil War, when river warfare was common.

Named the "Riverine Force," various older inshore-capable boats and later purpose-built patrol craft began the very dangerous process of intercepting Viet Cong supplies and often found themselves in firefights with shore batteries and heavy machine guns. The "blue water" may have belonged to the U.S. Navy, but when it turned brown, there was a constant struggle for control.

A Soviet Tupolev Tu-16 Badger on an anti-ship patrol with an AS-2 Kipper cruise missile under its fuselage. The navalized version of the Badger (C) was used for reconnaissance and potential anti-ship combat. First introduced in 1954, the twin-jet bomber (similar to a U.S. Air Force B-47), was armed with six 23-mm automatic guns and could carry bombs, AS-1 "Kennel" cruise missiles, and later the AS-2 "Kipper" standoff anti-ship missile (inset). The Kennel had a 55-mile range and the Kipper a 115-mile range. Both were typically armed with high explosives. The Tu-16 was a familiar sight to Western navies, and together with the four-engine turbo prop Bear, and the ever present trawlers, dogged most fleet activities. *Navy League*

As the Soviet Navy grew in stature, power, and numbers, it began to assign its more high-priced vessels to "accompany and interrupt" Western naval activities. An anti-ship missile-armed, 5400-ton full load "Kynda" class missile cruiser is shown taking station off the port quarter of the *USS Little Rock CLG-4* and the *USS John F Kennedy CVA-67* in the Mediterranean on October 30, 1969. The Kynda class was first seen by Western observers in 1962 who were astonished to see a blue water ship whose main armament was eight SSN-3 "Shaddock" anti-ship missiles. The Shaddock had a range of 400 miles and could carry conventional or nuclear warheads. In this photo, the *Kennedy* is the target of choice for the Kynda. *Navy League*

Perhaps the most famous of all Soviet surface-to-surface tactical weapons was the SSN-2 "Styx" missile. It is shown being rolled on a loading cart to a fast-attack craft such as a Komar missile boat. Many Soviet bloc and client state navies made use of this 2.75-ton weapon, which could reach a speed of 650 miles per hour using a two-stage solid propellant motor. It has been used in a number of wars, and although somewhat simple in design and guidance system (active radar homing), it is effective. Since becoming available to the Soviet Navy in 1958, the SSN-2 went through a number of updates. One of the most attractive qualities of this missile is that it could be installed aboard small, inexpensive boats and readily compete with heavy steel ships. *Navy League*

The overall name for the Allied effort to suppress enemy supply lines and troop movements in the inland waterways of South Vietnam was "Operation Game Warden." It began slowly in December 1965 with older landing craft that were converted for river use by means of armored protection and heavy armament. The river gunboat was reborn to fight on the waters of the Mekong Delta and the swampy areas around Saigon (a total of 7,000 square miles). As the war continued, the first craft were replaced with Swift boats, Coast Guard cutters, and the famous River Patrol Boats (PBR). These were 32-foot-long fiberglass-hulled boats that relied on water jets rather than the rudder and propeller system for propulsion. This enabled the PBR to maneuver in tight areas and virtually ride on top of the water. They carried a crew of four and were armed with three 50-caliber machine guns and a 40-mm grenade launcher.

The river craft were serviced ashore or by one of four modified Land Ship Tanks (LST) that also acted as a hosts for HU–I B Huey helicopters that provided air cover and surveillance. By the time Operation Game Warden was completely on line, there were scores of boats on patrol. However, it was never sufficiently effective to prevent resupply of the enemy.

The U.S. military was doing its best to assist the South Vietnamese against insurgency from the north, but civilian policies that drastically interfered with military operations prevented success. The policy of "graduated response" or "strategic gradualism" was at the core of civilian direction of the military in Southeast Asia. The concept of applying pressure to the level that causes your enemy to "cry uncle" is well known on the school playground, but the result can be far different when attempted by nations. Had pressure been mounted in the form of unrelenting violence and destruction, which the U.S. military was quite capable of, then perhaps the effect might have been different in Vietnam. Hobbling the military by declaring pauses in bombing, such as first occurred May 12–18, 1965, ultimately proved disastrous. A sustained campaign to a desired conclusion was required for success in war, as was demonstrated time and time again during World War II. Civilian control of the military is necessary for a democracy to survive; however, when that control exceeds common sense and intrudes on tactical operations, then military failure is usually the outcome. President Johnson and his civilian advisers had set upon a course that doomed the war in Vietnam to a stalemate if not an out-and-out defeat of American interests. Such was the beginning in 1965 whereby at the end of the year, there were 181,000 U.S. service personnel in the war.

The war assumed a wider aspect during the final years of the 1960s. More troops, ships, and aircraft were committed. The USS New Jersey BB-62 was recommissioned for service in Southeast Asia. Her 16-inch guns pounded targets within 20 miles of the coastline just as they had before during the Korean War.

More surface-to-air missile sites were erected by the North Vietnamese, and the port of Haiphong and the City of Hanoi were saturated with redundant air defenses. On October 31, 1968, President Johnson ordered a complete halt of all forms of bombardment whether from land, air, or sea on North Vietnamese territory. This was the tenth bombing halt since 1965 as part of the U.S. plan of "strategic gradualism." Each delay enabled the North Vietnamese to rebuild and improve their air defenses, making them progressively more formidable to attacking U.S. aircraft.

American soldiers, sailors, and airmen and their Western allies (a very small contingent) fought the war with heart and soul, but there was no true front line or definitive victory(s) that would compel the North Vietnamese to capitulate. The U.S. and South Vietnamese forces were continuously exposed, and their enemy could disappear in the night or be right alongside them. It was unnerving and frustrating. To compound matters, during the final months of Lyndon Johnson's term as U.S. president, the interference of his top-level civilian advisers and their absolute control over minor aspects of the war brought the allied campaign to a grinding halt.

Up through the end of the decade, the Vietnam War could have been most characterized as a massive U.S. military buildup, which was hobbled by political obstruction. By January 1968, there were 486,000 military personnel "in country" (assigned to Southeast Asia), and this number was expected to rise. By the time Richard Nixon took office as President in January 1969, the war had become extremely unpopular with many Americans, and around the world there was little public support. The war was also beginning to take its toll in U.S. service personnel killed, those missing in action or wounded and the much publicized and severely mistreated POWs (prisoners of war). The cost to the taxpayers had risen to an astonishing $30 billion per year, and still there was no end, nor any potential resolution in sight. Just days after Nixon took the oath of office, formal truce talks began in Paris between the United States and North Vietnam, and the force level of U.S. personnel in Vietnam officially peaked at 546,000 on January 31, 1969. Bowing out gracefully seemed to be the new administration's unspoken agenda for extracting itself from the war. "Peace with Honor" became a well-used slogan as well as "Vietnamization."

The U.S. military in Vietnam began a process of turning over weapons, equipment, and responsibilities to South Vietnamese forces. The ultimate objective was to enable the South Vietnamese to stand on their own as a trained and fully equipped military force. With sufficient numbers and modern battle-proven weapons and tactics, the South Vietnamese should have been able to rout the Viet Cong and prevent absorption by North Vietnam. Or so the theory went. The U.S. Navy began to turn over ships and aircraft in the coastal forces to the South Vietnamese Navy as well as patrol areas heretofore the responsibility of U.S. forces. By late 1969, the U.S. Navy had turned over 229 ships and vessels of all types to the South Vietnamese Navy.

The first reduction of troops occurred in June 1969, with 25,000 leaving Southeast Asia. This continued at an accelerated rate throughout the

A Komar fast-attack craft. This class and others, such as the OSA variants, were designed as an inner defense against Western and U.S. aggression against the Soviet homeland. They were armed with anti-ship missiles and close-in 30-mm machine guns. *Author's collection*

rest of 1969. In August, the North Vietnamese released the first three of hundreds of POWs that they had imprisoned in and around Hanoi. They reported conditions that were abhorrent and an affront to any civilized society. Extracting large contingents of U.S. personnel from Vietnam was satisfying to most Americans who saw this as the beginning of the end of U.S. involvement in a civil war. Unfortunately, it was also a period of confusion for the U.S. military, which had an inability to find its place in the overall strategic plans of the United States. Its conventional posture of unhampered war-fighting had been seriously injured, and during the time it sought to recover, much of its confidence was lost. It was not fully restored until the stunning victory in the 1991 Gulf War.

Other Global Naval Activity During the 1960s

Although the war in Southeast Asia and the Cuban Missile Crisis had captured the lion's share of the public interest during the 1960s, the Cold War at sea was being fought in many other locations in different ways. Activities in the North Atlantic, Mediterranean, and even off the coast of Korea were reported, but did not achieve a high-profile level. However, all instances where Western and Communist-controlled states came into contact at sea were part of the Cold War and contributed to the big picture.

The Western Atlantic, Gulf of Mexico, Gulf of California, and eastern Pacific along the West Coast of the United States have generally been recognized as the exclusive territory of the United States Navy and its allies. Soviet warships of any type, including submarines (that were known to patrol these areas), were quite rare and only welcome after certain diplomatic niceties had been exchanged. On the other hand, the Kremlin considered the Black Sea and Baltic Sea as their

The U.S. spy or electronic surveillance (ELINT) ship *USS Pueblo KL-44*, later *AGER 2* at the Puget Sound Naval Shipyard in Bremerton, Washington, on her commissioning day, May 13, 1967. The *Pueblo* was one of three converted coastal-type U.S. Army cargo ships designed to carry some of the most sophisticated listening equipment then available. The *Pueblo* and sister ships *USS Banner AGER-1* and *USS Palm Beach AGER-3* also carried sonar sensors to record submarine signatures. Data was to be gathered by idly patrolling close off Communist-controlled ports and coastlines. None of the vessels were armed with any significant defensive weapons and there was no effective means to destroy equipment and intelligence data should they be attacked. The *Pueblo* was attacked and boarded by the North Korean Navy and much of her highly classified material was captured. The small-ship ELINT program was cancelled after the loss of the *Pueblo. U.S.N.I.*

The ubiquitous Soviet trawler that could be found in the vicinity of most Western naval forces and off the coastlines of the major allied powers. This is a "Pamir" class intelligence gatherer, and was one of two built in Sweden in 1959–1960. Likely it was the *Peleng*, which displaced 2,240 tons full load with a range of 21,000 miles at 12 knots. Originally designed as powerful diesel oceangoing tugs, they were converted to their new role in 1965. Unlike most Western vessels employed in surveillance activities, the Pamir class mounted three quad launchers for SAN-5 "Grail" point defense surface-to-air missiles. This missile system was used for close-in defense and carried a 5.5-pound blast fragmentation warhead out to 3,000 yards (estimated). Most Soviet ships, including innocent-looking trawlers, were heavily armed. *TIM*

"lakes." Any incursion by either of the superpowers into one of these zones that were under the unofficial hegemony of the other superpower was considered a dangerous flaunting of power.

In May 1962, the U.S. Navy deployed a powerful anti-submarine unit built around the ASW carrier *USS Wasp CVS-18* into the Baltic Sea. Six destroyers and the destroyer leader *USS John S McCain DL-3* accompanied the *Wasp*. The purpose of entering the Baltic Sea was ostensibly to visit Kiel in West Germany, but it was obvious that the United States was demonstrating its naval power in the Soviet Union's backyard. Also significant was the type of force selected. A battle force with an attack carrier at its center could have provoked a serious international incident, but an ASW carrier

with escorts was less threatening. It served to illustrate the mobility of a blue water navy, and the United States' and NATO's ability to develop special units to hunt down and kill Soviet submarines. The U.S.S.R. was still in the process of building its navy and could do little in opposition. Four years later, the Soviet government protested the presence and suspicious activities of the *USS Forrest Royal DD-872* and *USS Harry E Yarnell DLG-17* while they were operating in the Black Sea. When ships of the Soviet Navy encountered U.S. or NATO counterparts, both sides cruised close to one another and carefully observed and photographed one another's vessels with particular attention to armament, electronics, and performance. While the crews were advised to refrain from any gestures or

The first U.S. aircraft carrier to employ the British-invented "angled landing deck" was the *USS Antietam CV-36*. Built too late for service in World War II, the *Antietam* did fight in the Korean War and earned two battle stars for her efforts. In May 1952 this Essex-class 27,000-ton fleet carrier was placed out of service to be converted for angled deck flight operation experiments. In early January 1953 she emerged from the New York Navy Yard to begin testing. The angled deck proved to be quite successful and was adopted for use in all future attack carriers. The *Antietam* continued as an anti-submarine warfare carrier (CVS) and was later decommissioned in May 1973. *Author's collection*

remarks that might inflame a situation into an incident, U.S. sailors often barbecued beef on the fantails of their ships and allowed the fragrant smoke to drift down on their cabbage-eating audience. Conversely, American sailors watched with some envy as Soviet sailors openly consumed beer and liquor. Each had their pressure points.

After the Cuban Missile Crisis, the U.S.S.R. began responding to U.S. and Western naval activities through planned harassment by aircraft, intelligence-gathering trawlers, and later, submarine and surface warships. In June 1963, six Tu-16 Badger medium-range bombers approached the *USS Ranger CVA-61* while she was steaming some 300 miles east of Japan and in international waters. The Badger was capable of 535 knots and in combination with its larger brother, the Tu-95 four-engine Bear, were assigned to all of the Soviet Navy's four major fleets. These aircraft provided reconnaissance and naval strike capability, so when six Badgers began an unannounced appearance, they were intercepted by the Ranger's combat air patrol and escorted away from the carrier. Unfortunately, five years later a similar incident involving a Badger

resulted in tragedy for the bomber's crew. On May 25, 1968, the Badger made several low-level passes on the *USS Essex CVS-9* while the antisubmarine warfare carrier was operating in the North Sea. On the fourth pass, the bomber's wing tip struck the water, causing the aircraft to lose control and crash. The six-man crew was killed instantly. These incidents were a sample of the nuisance campaign that intensified as the Soviet Union became more confident in its standing within the international military community. Soviet commercial interests at sea also began to venture beyond home waters. Fishing trawlers (or what appeared to be fishing trawlers) always seemed to be lurking in the immediate areas where U.S. Navy exercises were being held. In October 1965, 36 Russian fishing boats just happened to be near a U.S. nuclear test site in the Aleutians. A few months later, a large number of Soviet fishing vessels arrived in the Gulf of California on a brief "fishing expedition."

In the early 1960s the Soviet Navy began to flex its muscles in the Mediterranean and by June 1964 maintained a permanent anchorage site (Kithira) where its ships could be fueled or re-provisioned without having to return to a Communist-controlled or friendly port. This was significant as it allowed for a forward presence and removed one of the great disadvantages posed by Russian geography. Soon, warships flying the hammer and sickle began to visit ports in the eastern Mediterranean and into the South Atlantic. In the years that followed, the total number of Soviet ships that could be deployed to the Mediterranean increased dramatically, as did the speed with which they were on station.

Nineteen sixty-six witnessed another leap for the Russian Navy when a squadron of its submarines successfully circumnavigated the world. In October of that year, the Swedish Navy twice attacked what was believed to be a Soviet submarine within its territorial waters.

In October 1967, after the abbreviated Arab-Israeli War, an incident significant to the entire international naval community occurred. The Israeli destroyer *Eilat*, formerly a 2,555-ton full-load British "Z" class, was engaged by Egyptian anti-ship missiles and sunk. The attack, on October 25, 1967, was made on the destroyer as she was patrolling 15 miles off Port Said, Egypt. Four Soviet-supplied Styx missiles were fired from the confines of the harbor and struck the *Eilat* in succession. The fourth missile actually hit what was left of the ship as she turned over and sank. The first missile was not detected by the *Eilat* until it was within six miles of the vessel, and there was

The nuclear carrier *USS Enterprise CVAN-65* was the epitome of the attack carrier concept. Later the CVA or attack carriers became multifunctional when the CV designation was approved in the early 1970s. When the *Enterprise* was commissioned on November 25, 1961, she was the most powerful warship ever built. Her length was 1,119 feet with a maximum beam of 256 feet. The "Big E" was propelled by eight A2W reactors and geared turbines that provided a top speed of 36 knots. Her fuel was uranium with an estimated 140,000-mile range at 36 knots or 400,000 miles at 20 knots. Subsequent developments in nuclear technology enabled even greater ranges. She soon became combat active in the Cuban Missile Crisis and later throughout the Vietnam War. When first commissioned she had no defensive armament and relied upon her air group and cruiser-destroyer escorts for protection. In 1968 she was armed with one point defense missile system and later, close-in weapons system (CIWS) - Vulcan Phalanx 20-mm Gatling guns. *TIM*

no time to take evasive maneuvers. Had she been able to respond, her guns, including anti-aircraft weapons, would have been useless against the highspeed Styx. Over one-third of the destroyer's crew was lost during the attack. It was the first time in history that an anti-ship missile had been used to sink a heavy warship—and it was of Soviet manufacture. The Styx was originally introduced to the Soviet Navy in 1958–1959 as a tactical surface-to-surface weapon. It had a range of 26 miles, carried a warhead of up to 882 pounds, and although its guidance system (active radar seeker) was crude, it was effective. More than 1,200 missiles have been manufactured and exported to many client states. The Soviet Navy OSA- and KOMAR-class missile boats were armed with the Styx, and after the loss of the *Eilat*, all surface ships were at the greatest risk since the introduction of armored fighting ships during the American Civil War. A small, inexpensively built boat armed with one or more of these missiles could locate, target, and destroy cruiser-type ships out of their gun range (15–18 miles). This single incident had a critical impact on naval warfare, and most navies began preparations to defend against this new threat.

On the other side of the world, the United States was diplomatically and militarily embarrassed on January 22, 1968, when one of its intelligence-gathering ships, the *USS Pueblo AGER-2*, was captured in international waters by the North Korean Navy, and forced to sail to Wonsan Harbor at gunpoint. One of the crew was killed during the unprovoked attack, and it was not until the following December that the crew was set free. The loss of this ship provided a bonanza of technology for the Soviet Union and technicians carefully examined all of the sophisticated equipment found on board. The *Pueblo* was one of three prototype conversions designed to ply the world's oceans gathering electronic information on the Soviet Union and its allied nations. Up to 30 AGER's were planned, provided the *Pueblo* and her sisters were successful. The *Pueblo* became a tourist attraction in Wonsan, and the U.S. Navy abandoned the program, at least in that form. The United States elected to resolve the *Pueblo* issue diplomatically rather than widening the war in Asia. Diplomatic efforts were successful after the North Koreans had extracted as much propaganda value as possible.

Within months of releasing the crew of the *Pueblo*, the North Koreans compounded matters

The nuclear missile cruiser *USS Long Beach CGN-9*. The *Long Beach* displaced 17,350 tons full load and was 721 feet in length. Her intended role was that of an ocean escort for the carrier *Enterprise*. The cruiser was armed with two twin Terrier launchers forward to deal with incoming enemy aircraft at medium ranges and a twin Talos launcher aft for targets at long ranges. She carried up to 166 surface-to-air missiles in her magazines and in 1961, she was a formidable warship. The *Long Beach* carried ASROC for ASW defense, and was later modified to carry Standard missiles and Harpoon anti-ship weapons. When first built, her electronic automated systems were state of the art; however, they were hard wired. With rapid advances in computerization, she became obsolete, and due to space limitations and costs, was not considered for upgrade to AEGIS. She ended her days in the nuclear recycling program at the Puget Sound Naval Shipyard in 1994. *Author's collection*

An ASW pilotless drone, DASH hovers over a destroyer and hopefully will land on the specially built mini-heliport, which was built on many destroyers and frigates in the 1960s. The concept of a drone carrying Mark 46 ASW torpedoes out to a distant submarine contact was highly attractive as was the ability to equip dozens of escort vessels with the system. Unfortunately, the program was unsuccessful in the U.S. Navy and was soon abandoned, but not before scores of World War II destroyers were converted under the Fleet Rehabilitation and Modernization program (FRAM). *Author's collection*

by shooting down an unarmed U.S. Navy EC-121 airborne electronic-surveillance aircraft. The four-engine aircraft was a one of a large number of Lockheed Constellations that had been converted to troop transport or electronic eavesdropping. On April 14, 1969, it was on a routine patrol mission some 90 miles out into international waters in the Sea of Japan when North Korean fighters shot it down. None of the 31 crew was found alive, although a concentrated search did result in the recovery of some wreckage and two bodies three days later. The U.S. Navy responded with a massive buildup of naval force off the North Korean coast. Aircraft carriers *USS Enterprise CVAN-65*, *USS Ranger CVA-61*, *USS Ticonderoga CVA-14*, and *USS Hornet CVS-12* were joined by 17 escort vessels in the Sea of Japan as they conducted operations for a week beginning on April 20.

The 1960s ended with the United States slowly withdrawing from the Vietnam Conflict and at the same time strengthening its alliance with NATO. The Soviet Union was no longer confining its activities to local waters, and was beginning to pose a major threat to allied supply lines at sea. The Mediterranean Sea was being shared by the U.S. Sixth Fleet and a number of Soviet surface ships—a phenomenon not anticipated. There was uneasiness in the West over the expanded Russian surface fleet, and growing concern over the Soviet nuclear submarine force and its combat-tested cruise missile capability.

On the other hand, Soviet leadership was anxious about the seaborne ring of U.S. submarines whose missiles were targeted on Russian cities. Accordingly, they commissioned two hybrid, guided-missiles—ASW helicopter cruisers, the *Moskva* (1967) and *Leningrad* (1968), both tasked to kill U.S./ NATO ballistic missile and attack submarines. The Kremlin was determined to protect Mother Russia from U.S. submarine-launched ballistic missiles (SLBM).

The second major threat posed was the U.S. carrier battle groups that could launch aircraft armed with nuclear weapons against Soviet targets. For that contingency, the Russian navy developed cruise missile armed submarines (Echo class) and

An octuple ASROC launcher aboard the decommissioned destroyer *USS Hoel DDG-13*. This anti-submarine rocket entered service in 1961 and was launched from a trainable eight-tube launcher. It could not be guided in flight. Its warhead consisted of a Mark 46 homing torpedo or a Mark 44 nuclear depth bomb. In escorts built in the 1970s and beyond, ASROC could be launched from the Mark 10/Mark 26 standard surface-to-air missile launchers. *Author's collection*

similarly armed Kynda-class cruisers. Complementing this force was the Tu-95 Bear strike bomber armed with anti-ship missiles.

At the end of this decade, there was no sign that the Soviet Union had abandoned its traditional role of defending its own soil and that of its allies. It was now more capable of responding in kind to threats posed by NATO and the United States.

The Cold War at sea for NATO and the U.S. Navy during the two decades since the beginning of the Korean War had been one of imaginatively facing the challenges of Communism worldwide. It appeared that ship-to-ship engagements were no longer a part of traditional combat at sea. Now it could be a firefight in a muddy Southeast Asia marsh from the decks of a fiberglass jet boat or it might be carrier-launched air strikes on ground targets in support of allied troops. Warships bombarded shore targets and took shore battery fire in return. Carrier battle groups had to contend with Soviet spy trawlers that often interfered with their operations, and Soviet-made or -piloted aircraft periodically shot down helpless patrol aircraft. Legitimate long-range Soviet fishing trawlers displacing up to 1,400 tons, supported by 500-foot-long fish transports were operating in areas traditionally fished by U.S. interests. By the late 1960s entire fleets, including refrigerator ships, tankers, and oceangoing tugs were hard at work harvesting twice the U.S. annual catch within miles of U.S.

The much modernized Dealey-class ocean escort, the *USS Bridget DE-1024*, at sea in June 1965. The Dealey class was built as the U.S. Navy's first effort to combat the anticipated Soviet submarine problem. The *Bridget* retained her forward twin 3-inch/50-caliber mount, Weapon A, and ASW torpedoes. Her aft 3-inch mount was removed in favor of a DASH landing platform and hangar. Despite these updates, the Dealey class was never really considered a competent ASW unit, and by 1974, all except the lead ship *Dealey DE-1006* and the *Hartley DE-1029* were sent to the shipbreakers. The *Dealey* was transferred to the Uruguayan Navy and the *Hartley* to the Colombia Navy. *TIM*

territory. There was little that could be done, and often the U.S. Coast Guard just stood by helplessly watching the gluttony of a nation sworn to destroy the United States. This new type of war tested the nerves of its contestants as well as its resources and navies.

Cold War duty at sea during this period was far different from the naval battles fought and won just a quarter-century earlier; however, it too was dangerous, and a "winner take all" proposition.

Status of the World's Major Navies 1950–1970
The United States Navy

The Korean War demonstrated the need for a powerful navy with emphasis on naval aviation. Without the rapid response support of U.S.

and British aircraft carriers in the region, it is certain that the North Koreans would have consumed all of South Korea long before any other U.S. or allied military rescue operation could have been mounted.

In the years that followed, the navy found its role split into a number of missions. Defense against the Soviet submarine force was vital, as was having a credible nuclear response available on a 24-hour basis. For these contingencies, specially trained hunter-killer groups were formed around modified Essex-class aircraft carriers, and nuclear-powered ballistic missile submarines were rapidly designed, built, and deployed around the world. A littoral warfare capability was initiated and proved quite successful during the Vietnam War, as did the development of a brown water or Riverine force to fight in the Mekong Delta. The introduction of nuclear power to the super carriers and their escorts allowed for a continuous forward presence in the more volatile regions of the world. This provided an unmistakable and authoritative demonstration of U.S. power. The Pentagon and the people of the United States again realized that the world is primarily covered with water, and without a navy that can go anywhere anytime, national defense and free trade would be in jeopardy.

For the U.S. Navy, and for that matter, all of the world's navies, the 1950s was a period of readjustment from World War II naval techniques to the age of jet power and nuclear weaponry and energy. It was a time for research and design of new methods to fight the war at sea. The 1960s were the years for using the new concepts, refining techniques, and making improvements based on experience. It was also the last decade without the mass benefit of automation and computerization. The period from 1950–1970 was one of the most significant periods in naval history, as so many technological and weapon system advances were made. The momentum continued into the next decades with the introduction of the microchip. The marriage of nuclear power to unlimited vistas in the exploding electronic revolution would again revitalize and change the navies of the world.

Naval Aviation

On July 1, 1950, the United States had a mixed bag of 14 active carriers with 1 in ready reserve. This force consisted of three Midway class (CVB), four Essex class (CV), three light carriers (CVL), and four escort carriers (CVE). Over the five-year period from the end of World War II, the U.S. Navy's carrier capability had shrunk to 12 percent of its wartime strength. The value of carriers was demonstrated during the Korean War, with more than 30 percent of the total missions being flown from the decks of U.S. aircraft carriers. In addition to the strike and support missions of the type flown in Korea, the navy felt that it would soon have to face a huge number of Soviet submarines. Rather than destroying Russian submarines individually during convoy or hunter-killer operations, nuclear strikes against hardened Soviet submarine bases were forecast as the best way to curb this menace. There were a number of improvements and modifications necessary to maximize the potential of naval aviation at sea, and initially a major program was begun to rebuild several of the successful 27,000-ton Essex-class carriers.

As early as 1945, the navy began planning to enhance the Essex class to handle high-speed and heavier aircraft. The gross weight of an early World War II Grumman F4F "Wildcat" fighter was 8,100 pounds, whereas the Korean War F9F "Panther" jet was 19,000 pounds. Naval aircraft would become even heavier by the Vietnam War (the F8U Crusader weighed in at 34,700 pounds). Clearly the Essex-class of World War II was incapable of operating the heavier jet aircraft until certain major modifications were made. Beginning in 1947, the Ship Characteristic Board initiated a base plan (SCB-27) to begin rebuilding several of the Essex class ships. Two of the class, the *USS Bunker Hill CV-17* and *USS Franklin CV-13*, were excluded from consideration due to the severe damage they received in World War II, and three others were not selected for other reasons. Eventually 19 of the 24 carriers in this class were modified under one or more of the five sequential programs that began with SCB-27. The primary characteristics consisted of the installation of more powerful catapults (steam), angled flight decks, deck landing mirror systems, stronger deck arrestor wires, and increased bunkerage for jet fuel. Selected ships received other improvements such as large pilot ready rooms, increased bomb and munitions storage, and air-conditioning.

Of all the Essex-class carriers that were rebuilt, the *USS Oriskany CVA-34* received the highest level of modernization. Items such as a light metal cladding of the flight deck, a fully enclosed and sealed hurricane bow as well as an arrestor wire system much stronger than that on other Essex class conversions were added.

Of the carriers that received a major refitting, seven became attack versions, eight were used as specially built ASW Hunter Killer units, and three became helicopter attack carriers. Although it was one of the carriers considered for major modification, the *Antietam* was used for experimental purposes only and withdrawn from service in 1963.

The Essex class served in a number of critical roles until the advent of the heavier Phantom II jet fighter, which weighed 55,500 pounds. This aircraft and those that followed required a Midway class or one of the super carriers beginning with the *USS Forrestal CVA-59*. With the introduction of the super carriers into the fleet, the Essex class began to recede into the less glamorous ASW, training, and amphibious missions. Many served with distinction during the Vietnam War, providing air strikes and support to ground forces, yet by 1976, the last of the class had been withdrawn from service and many had been scrapped.

The *USS Henry B Wilson DDG-7*, one of the highly successful and popular Charles F. Adams class guided-missile destroyers built from 1959 to 1963. They carried two 5-inch/54-caliber guns for surface targets and shore bombardment, ASROC, ASW torpedoes, and a single aft-sited twin arm Terrier surface-to-air missile launcher. These were rugged and sturdy escorts that could defend a task force against most threat types. They were used extensively off Vietnam in naval gunfire support assignments. The *Henry B Wilson* is shown steaming into San Francisco Harbor in the late 1960s. *Author's collection*

The navy also made use of light carriers and escort carriers during the 1950s. Most of the Independence class (13,000 tons full load, 623-foot length, 45 aircraft, and 32 knots top speed), were employed as stopgap ASW carriers and later for pilot training and reservist cruises. Three of the eight World War II survivors were made available to the Spanish Navy (*Dedalo* ex-*USS Cabot CVL-28*) and to the French Navy (*Bois Belleau* ex-*USS Belleau Wood CVL-24* and *Lafayette* ex-*USS Langley CVL-27*) and carried out a variety of missions for many years.

The U.S. Navy also modified two postwar light carriers as communication platforms, (*USS Saipan CVL-48/AGMR-2* and *USS Wright CVL-49/CC-2*); however, there was no place in modern naval aviation for the light carrier. The same held true for the escort carriers. A small number were

used operationally during the Korean War, yet those that were not converted to aircraft transports were later sold for scrap.

The Midway-class battle carriers designed during World War II were the most able to bridge the gap between World War II and the Cold War. These were the largest aircraft carriers in the world at 60,000 tons full, with a 968-foot-long flight deck. The Midway class was heavily armored with an 8-inch side belt and a 3+-inch-thick flight deck. The three ships in this class (*USS Midway CVA-41*, *USS Franklin Roosevelt CVA-42*, and *USS Coral Sea CVA-43*) were capable of 33 knots based on a 212,000-shaft horsepower propulsion plant and a hull shape identical to the Iowa-class battleship. The Midways were able to carry the heavier aircraft and, with modification, launch and recover the A3D Skywarrior,

The *USS Valley Forge LPH-8* preparing to launch her helicopter assault landing force of marines in an exercise off Bangkok, Thailand, on May 15, 1962. Prior to the construction of helicopter assault ships (Iwo Jima, Tarawa, and Wasp classes), three former Essex-class attack carriers were converted as a temporary measure to develop this new technique of assault troop insertion. It was a great success, and this type of assault has become a lynchpin in Marine Corp–Navy cooperative operations. The *Valley Forge* and her two sisters (*USS Boxer LPH-4, USS Princeton LPH-5*) served throughout the 1960s and were decommissioned by the end of 1970. *TIM - SFCB*

which was the successor to the propeller-driven AJ Savage bomber. In order to compete with the U.S. Air Force's "nuclear super bomber" and retain a role in the strategic defense of the United States, the navy had to prove that carrier-based naval aviation could deliver an atomic punch to the Soviet Union. The aircraft carrier most adaptable to this role was the Midway class, and all three carriers were subjected to major overhauls during the 1950s and 1960s. Each of the three had individualized characteristics, and the *USS Midway* was the carrier that most closely approached the super carrier "Forrestal" class. Her refit lasted from 1966 through 1970 and reportedly cost $202 million. The high cost and unusually short duration of the refit were sufficient reasons for not making further improvement to her two sisters.

All three of the Midway class rotated in and out of the Vietnam War with carriers in the Essex class and the new super carrier class. Throughout their service lives they have always been attack carriers and not relegated to lesser missions. Ultimately, the super carriers of the Forrestal class were to replace these ships at the end of the century.

The U.S. Navy Super Carrier

At the end of World War II, it was the dream of naval aviation to be one of main legs supporting national defense. The aircraft carrier had taken the war to Japan and played a major part in that country's destruction. However, it was well known that the atomic bomb, delivered by an air force B-29 super fortress, had caused the enemy to capitulate.

In order to compete, the navy needed a carrier far larger and more powerful than even the Midway class. In 1948, the super carrier (*USS United States CVB-58*) was authorized in the fiscal year 1949 federal budget. The *United States* was planned to be 1,089 feet in length, 80,000 tons full load with a propulsion plant generating 280,000 shaft horsepower. Its primary role was to carry a nuclear strike force of 54 Savage AJ or larger bombers. Their targets would be strategic, including suspected hardened Soviet submarine bases. The concept was imaginative, but the timing was wrong. Five days into construction, CVB-58 was canceled and its funding and materials transferred to the very pleased air force for the much-coveted B-36 strategic nuclear bomber.

A key factor in the Polaris program was the availability of spare parts, provisions, missiles, and repair services in close proximity to the patrol areas of U.S. ballistic missile submarines. The USS Proteus AS-19 was one of the most notable, having been converted to service Polaris boats during 1959–1960. The submarine tender's overall length was increased from 529 feet to 574 feet by the addition of a 44-foot-long "plug." Specialists at the Charleston Navy Yard placed the ship in dry-dock, cut it in half, and floated the aft portion some 50 feet back. The "plug," consisting of 12 separate prefabricated sections, was installed in stages and the ship welded back together. The new section carried the Polaris missile magazine and handling facilities. The electric generating power of the modernized tender was increased to 15,000 kilowatts, which was sufficient to power most shipyards. The overall workmanship resulted in one of the finest pieces of modern naval architecture. The Proteus was often moored in Holy Loch, Scotland, and serviced submarines such as the USS Patrick Henry SSBN-599, seen here coming alongside in this March 9, 1961, photograph. It was vital to keep the SSBNs at sea, and having their support ship close to patrol zones reduced transition time. TIM —SFCB

The naval hierarchy suspected that the large carrier was being compared to the prewar battleship as being expensive and having a questionable strategic value. The Korean War changed thinking in the Pentagon, the White House, and Congress. There was still a definite place for the aircraft carrier in national defense, albeit not as the primary strategic weapon. However, the contemporary carriers in the Essex and Midway classes would soon be outstripped by the new heavier and faster jet aircraft that would be vital in any conventional or nuclear wars in the future.

The lead ship of what would become the super carriers was the USS Forrestal CVA-59. This 78,000-ton, 1,039-foot-long vessel carried 80–95 modern aircraft, up to and including the 72,000-pound A3 Skywarrior nuclear attack bomber. The Forrestal set the mold for all super carriers that followed, including the ultra-modern Nimitz-class nuclear attack carriers. It also introduced weapons cost "sticker shock" to the U.S. Congress with a price tag of $189 million. It was the first aircraft carrier that incorporated all of the latest design features based on World War II experience and the needs of jet aircraft. The flight deck was armored and angled to facilitate rapid launch and recovery operations. All of its lifts from hangar to flight deck were external, and its island structure was small with an integrated smoke funnel. Four powerful catapults were installed and the Forrestal was capable of 33 knots on 260,000 shaft horsepower. The bow was not open to the elements and sported a sealed hurricane enclosure. All in all, this was a marvel in carrier aviation and was a quantum leap from anything any other nation had to offer, including its sisters in the Midway class.

The Forrestal was commissioned on October 1, 1955, and was soon followed by the USS Saratoga CVA-60, USS Ranger CVA-61, and the USS Independence CVA-62. Each would have some differences from the other as experience would cause modifications, but essentially the first four of the super carriers were considered members of the Forrestal class. By January 1959, just over three years from the Forrestal entering fleet service, the fourth of the class, the Independence, was also at sea.

All four of this class were deployed off Vietnam at various times, and the Independence and Saratoga were on station carriers supporting the blockade of Cuba in 1962.

The follow-on class to the Forrestal was the Kitty Hawk/America. This class included three ships, the USS Kitty Hawk CVA-63, USS Constellation CVA-64, and USS America CVA-66. They

One of the key factors that support a far-reaching blue water navy is its ability to maintain a continuous forward presence. The U.S. Navy perfected at-sea replenishment of combat ships during World War II, and reached the high point of this technique with the Sacramento-class fast combat support ships. The *USS Sacramento AOE-1* was built by the Puget Sound Naval Shipyard in 1963, and despite its inordinately high cost, set the standard for future fast replenishment ships. The *Sacramento* served throughout the Vietnam War and enabled the carriers and their escorts to remain on Yankee and Dixie stations for extended periods, thus allowing improved air support for ground operations. *TIM*

were slightly longer at 1,062 feet and heavier at 60,100 tons, but there were other important differences between the two classes. The Kitty Hawk/America class had two aircraft elevators forward of the longer island structure and a separate radar mast was located just aft. This class was also armed with defensive missiles (Terrier) and no 5-inch anti-aircraft guns. All were completed over a period of four years, from 1961–1965, and all carried out missions in Vietnam.

The next and final fossil fuel–powered super carrier was the *USS John F Kennedy CVA-67*, commissioned in September 1968. This ship was at the apex of conventionally powered super carriers having been the beneficiary of the experiences of her seven sisters. Although the ship was originally planned to be nuclear powered, the price tag of nearly $500 million was too difficult for the Congress to swallow, knowing that without nuclear power, the cost would be less than one-half as much. She, too, was in a class by herself with a displacement of 87,000 tons full load, and distinctive with a canted smoke funnel to re-

duce caustic fumes that corroded aircraft and electronic antennas. The *Kennedy* was not armed with defensive missiles until 1969 when the short-range Sea Sparrow system was installed. Aside from financial considerations, the new carrier was not destined to defend itself from all aerial threats—this was becoming the responsibility of its guided missile escorts.

The frontal piece of American naval aviation during the 1960s was the nuclear-powered *USS Enterprise CVAN-65*. Begun in 1958, the 89,600-ton, 1,119-foot-long super carrier was the largest warship in the world. Driven by eight nuclear reactors, the "Big E" developed 280,00 shaft horsepower and could steam for three to four years without being refueled. Nuclear power truly allowed a continued forward presence. She was able to carry far more jet fuel, and for the modern (and thirsty) aircraft coming into fleet service (F-4 Phantom and F-14 Tomcat), this was vital for sustained operations.

The *Enterprise* was initially deployed in the Atlantic and served in the 1962 Cuban Blockade;

The grandfather of nuclear power at sea was the *USS Nautilus SS-571*, which entered service on January 1, 1954. It was the first nuclear-powered submarine in the world and carried a crew of 109. The *Nautilus* led the way for the submarine to be exactly what it was originally designed for—unlimited submerged operations. *TIM*

The U.S. Navy's first ballistic missile submarine, *USS George Washington SSBN-598*, at sea after her June 9, 1959, launching. She was created by slicing a Skipjack-class submarine into two halves and inserting a 130-foot-long center section to house 16 Polaris A-1 missile tubes (eight side by side aft of the sail). The importance of having SSBNs on station was so critical to national defense that two crews (Blue & Gold) rotated every 56 days. As with the rest of the Polaris program, the construction of the first boat was quickly accomplished, and the program was a huge success. Over the next decade, the George Washington class was expanded to four boats and then two successively larger and more capable classes (Ethan Allen and Lafayette) were built. The next ballistic missile submarine class was the Ohio (1979), which was designed to carry a much more powerful weapon: the Trident missile. *Author's collection*

however, it was soon apparent that her proper theater of operations was in the Pacific, where her range would best serve the country. Just prior to deployment in the Vietnam War, she and her two nuclear escorts, the *USS Long Beach CGN-9* and *USS Bainbridge DLGN-25*, made a demonstration cruise around the world without refueling. Operation Sea Orbit sent a meaningful message to the Soviets about contemporary U.S. Naval power.

The period from 1950 to 1970 was crucial to the development of U.S. naval aviation. It began with the possibility of being put second to the air force and consigned to the backwaters of national defense. It ended with the most powerful ships the world had ever seen, which were able to be in almost any trouble spot within hours. The carrier's place in the future was assured by farsighted naval officers such as Admiral Hyman Rickover, who championed the use of nuclear power in the U.S. Navy.

Surface Navy

As stated earlier, the U.S. surface fleet had all but disappeared into mothballs by June 1950 when the North Koreans crossed over into South Korea. Many were reactivated for the emergency, and the battleships, cruisers, destroyers, minesweepers, and amphibious forces measured up quite well throughout the Korean War. Men and materials had to be moved from the United States to the battle fronts, thousands of mines had to be swept, enemy positions bombarded, and the carriers protected from air and submarine attack. From early 1951 through the spring of 1952, surface ships of all types fired just under half a million rounds of ammunition at Communist targets in Korea. Ground troops always knew that ships lying offshore could blast an enemy out of their way or rescue troops facing heavy opposition. Some of the destroyers fired so many 5-inch projectiles in so short a time period that they literally began to shake themselves apart. As with the aircraft carrier, there was a resurgence of appreciation for the navy's surface forces. Of course, it was imperative that the surface force modernize along with naval aviation and the submarine forces. Ironically, the Soviet Navy was responsible for U.S. planners still adhering to the concept of ship-to-ship combat. In the early 1950s, the Russians began commissioning a large number of Sverdlov 6-inch all-gun cruisers in company with its new all-gun destroyers of the Skory class. This was a throwback to a past era, but the U.S. Navy could ignore the possibility of one or more of these ships confronting U.S.

After the success of the *Nautilus*, the U.S. Navy changed from the use of the German-type XXI submarine hull shape and adopted the "albacore" or "tear drop" shape for its attack submarines. The initial class was the "Skipjack," and the *USS Scorpion SSN-589* (shown being launched on December 18, 1959) was one of six boats. She was armed with six 21-inch torpedo tubes and had a submerged speed of over 30 knots. The *Scorpion* was powered with a single reactor and steam turbines. Unfortunately, the *Scorpion* was lost with all hands on May 17, 1968, in the Atlantic. Extensive sea bottom surveillance was done by the *USS Mizar AGOR-11* and the wreckage was finally located 10,000 feet down. A faulty trash ejector latch was blamed for the loss. *U.S.N.I.*

forces. Fortunately, U.S. Navy resources were devoted primarily to guided missile and nuclear power technology and the ship-to-ship duel remained just what it was—improbable.

For the remaining four Iowa-class battleships, the answer was simple. They were sporadically brought out of reserve to provide precision and devastating coastal gunfire support that was not possible from bombers or other smaller ships. All four of the Iowa class participated in the Korean War. However, the only battleship reactivated for the Vietnam War was the *USS New Jersey BB-62* in late September 1968. After a minor overhaul and the addition of state-of-the-art electronics she was shelling enemy positions in September 1968. There was some thought given to rebuilding existing battleships into missile or half aircraft carrier platforms, but cost compared to the value of such ships was questionable. Consequently, the battleship remained what it was—the ultimate gunfighter, only employed when absolutely necessary due to the high cost of maintenance and personnel requirements.

The cruisers were also used for gunfire support and often as fleet flagships. By the mid-1950s, it became evident that they had become wholly inadequate as anti-aircraft defense platforms. The solution was to retrofit certain heavy and light cruisers with guided missiles. To this end, the navy began developing what was known as the "three T's" for the Talos, Terrier, and Tartar missiles. The Talos 6b1 had a range of 100 miles, the Terrier 40 miles, and the Tartar 17.5 miles. This was the first major family of U.S. Navy sea-launched surface-to-air missiles. All had teething problems, but with this capability, modified cruisers such as the *USS Boston CAG-1* and *USS Canberra CAG-2* could defend themselves and other ships. By late 1957 six light cruisers of the World War II Cleveland class were refitted with Talos or Terrier missiles (Galveston-class CLG). By the early 1960s three Baltimore-class heavy cruisers were completely rebuilt from the hull upward as missile cruisers (Albany class CG).

During the Vietnam War, the *USS Chicago CG-11* shot down a North Vietnamese MiG attacker with a Talos missile at a range of 48 miles. The *Chicago* was also a central air controller for fighter air cover and was responsible for directing U.S. fighters in downing twelve MiGs during one mission.

On July 20, 1960, the first Polaris A-1 missile fired from a submarine emerges from the surface from the *USS George Washington SSBN-598.* The Polaris program moved at a near frenzied pace, and greater pressure was applied in 1957 when the Soviets launched Sputnik and their first successful intercontinental ballistic missile. The survival of the nation was at stake, and in order to bring the Polaris system on line, the navy had to settle for a 1,000-mile-range missile rather than the 1,500 mile specified. It all came together on July 20, 1960, and the *George Washington* was soon operational. *U.S. Navy*

The late 1950s also marked a watershed for the American cruiser when the *USS Long Beach CGN-9,* a nuclear cruiser almost solely armed with guided missiles, entered fleet service. Aside from being nuclear powered, the *Long Beach* was the first cruiser built from the keel up since World War II. She was armed with Terrier and Talos missiles initially, and later two 5-inch/38-caliber single mounts were added after the navy succumbed to criticism of the great cruiser being unable to fend off torpedo boats.

The *Long Beach* proved to be too expensive for an entire class to be built, so the navy contented itself with two fossil-fuel guided-missile cruiser designs; the nine-ship Leahy class (1961–1962), and the nine-ship Belknap class (1963–1965). Both classes were similar in displacement, length and cost—which was far less than a nuclear-powered version.

The U.S. Congress approved funding for four more nuclear-powered missile cruisers during the

1960s, primarily to serve as escorts for the *USS Enterprise CVAN-65.* The *USS Bainbridge DLGN-25* was commissioned in April 1961, the *USS Truxton DLGN-35* in December 1964, and the two-ship California class begun in 1967.

The cruiser had evolved from a shore bombardment platform to a fast anti-aircraft escort for fleet operations. All of these new cruisers were capable of 32 knots and had an ASW capability with ASROC (ballistic missile with nuclear depth charge or homing torpedo) and the 12.75-inch torpedo. Unfortunately, none had permanent facilities for helicopters, which made them far less capable in ASW operations than ships so equipped. ASW was a completely different matter, and given great attention by the Navy. The Soviet-threatened 1,200-unit submarine force was taken quite seriously, and shortly after World War II, the U.S. Navy began to develop means to meet this contingency

Anti-Submarine Warfare (ASW)

Anti-submarine warfare became one of the cornerstones of national defense after it became known that the Soviet Union was determined to build and deploy a massive number of submarines that would form a series of defensive barriers around Mother Russia. The Soviets planned a 1,200-strong force of blue water and coastal submarines, and with the advent of nuclear power, their undersea fleet would become a formidable weapon. Although the Russian Navy never reached its numerical goal, this did not prevent the United States and NATO from establishing ASW as a top priority in their overall defensive strategy

At first, specialized aircraft were developed that were based on escort and light carriers. Later, these aircraft were based on several Essex-class carriers that had not been upgraded to attack units. Of the early models, the Grumman S-2 Tracker was the most popular and, beginning in 1954, was in service for nearly 20 years. It carried depth charges, ASW torpedoes, and sonobuoys (detector buoys). Dropping sonobuoys around a suspected submarine contact enabled aircraft or nearby surface ships vastly improved detection, and a better opportunity for killing the target. Land-based aircraft such as the P2 Neptune and later, the four-engine P3 Orion, added further more-improved detection coverage off the U.S. and allied nation's coastlines. The MAD, or Magnetic Anomaly Detector, further allowed aircraft to pinpoint possible contacts.

A Sound Surveillance System (SOSUS) was established in key areas where Soviet submarines were known to break out to sea from their homeland

(Greenland, Iceland, and U.K. Gap), as well as off the U.S. coastlines. This was a form of underwater alarm to detect Russian submarines. Hydrophones placed on the ocean floor were linked and emitted a warning when a submarine passed within range. Shore- or carrier-based aircraft and/or surface ships were vectored to target location and could pounce on the submarine. This method of detection and pounce (attack) was so effective that the Soviet Navy began developing longer-range submarine-launched ballistic missiles. These could be fired from within the confines of Soviet-dominated waters.

Beginning in November 1962, many destroyer-type vessels were equipped with the Drone Anti-submarine Helicopter (DASH). These pilotless helicopters were launched from small platforms built onto existing ships and were directed to suspected submarine contacts up to 30 miles from the mother ship. Armed with a sonobuoy and one Mark 46 ASW torpedo or two Mark 44 acoustic homing torpedoes only, the DASH would attack the target with its homing torpedoes. The program, which lasted to January 1971, was deemed an unqualified failure because 416 of the 746 that were delivered crashed. The piloted ASW helicopter came on the tail of this program and in the 1970s became quite effective.

SONAR and ASW weapons aboard destroyer-type ships also improved during the two decades after the Korean War. Supplementing and eventually replacing the depth charge, short-range hedgehog, and Weapon A, was the standoff weapon. Rocket assisted torpedo (RAT) was the first development in the 1950s and was installed aboard selected destroyers. The rocket had a range of 5,000 yards and delivered a homing torpedo (hopefully) near the contact. It was soon replaced by the more reliable and controlled Anti Submarine Rocket (ASROC), which delivered a homing torpedo up to 10,000 yards from its launcher. This system could also be armed with a nuclear warhead. ASROC became the standard ASW weapon on most modernized destroyers, frigates, and guided-missile cruisers.

The Destroyer and ASW

Soon after World War II, the U.S. Navy recognized that its destroyer force would have to defeat the Soviet submarine menace until improved detection and sub-killing technology was developed. The basic strategy was obvious and straightforward: destroy enemy submarines at their base, destroy them en route to their intended targets, and finally, kill them in the target area before they inflict any damage.

The French aircraft carrier *Clemenceau* at sea. The *Clemenceau* and the *Foch* were the first large carriers built after World War II in France. In the early 1950s, the United States loaned the light fast carriers *Belleau Wood CVL-24* (French *Bois Belleau*) and *Langley CVL-27* (French *Lafayette*) to France. France also purchased a light fleet carrier (*HMS Colossus*) from Great Britain in 1951 and renamed it the *Arromanches*. The *Clemenceau* was 869 feet in length and resembled the modernized U.S. Navy Essex class. The 32,780-ton full load *Clemenceau* was commissioned on November 22, 1961, after a six-year building period. These ships were originally designed to carry up to 60 aircraft, but this was reduced to 40 as heavier jets were introduced. The *Clemenceau* and *Foch* were designed to show the naval community that France was still a major maritime power and had a vital national interest in carrier power projection. *TIM*

In 1950, the U.S. Navy and its NATO allies had 1,004 destroyers and destroyer-type warships (destroyer escort, frigate, and corvette) in their naval inventories. The United States Navy had 343 destroyers and 227 destroyer escorts that were even borderline capable of facing Soviet submarines. Of these, the vast majority was in reserve, and the ones that were operational still had the rudimentary ASW weapons of World War II. The Soviet Union had an estimated 360 submarines of varying capability, which meant it would have been unable to mount a campaign against the West. Over the next two decades, both

HMS Leander F-109 was the lead ship of a class of 26 ASW-dedicated ocean escorts built from 1963 to 1967 by Great Britain. The Leander class proved to be quite successful and helped to prop up NATO's anti-submarine warfare campaign against the growing Soviet submarine force. The Leander class was air-conditioned for crew comfort, and was capable of over 30 knots on 30,000 shaft horsepower. Ships in this class were heavily armed with two 4.5-inch dual purpose guns, 20-mm and 40-mm short-range guns, "Seacat" anti-air missiles, Limbo ASW depth charge mortar, and a WASP ASW helicopter that carried homing torpedoes. These escorts also boasted improved submarine detection gear, and were roomy enough to accommodate electronic and weapon upgrades. *TIM*

surface ship ASW and the Soviet submarine became more lethal.

One of the first major developments in Western naval ASW was the introduction of Weapon A or Alfa, installed aboard many destroyers after 1950 as well as the single-ship hunter-killer Norfolk class. Several destroyers and destroyer escorts were also equipped with trainable hedgehogs, and combined with improved detection equipment became more effective. Other destroyers were converted for escort work and redesignated DDE, and many destroyer escorts were also converted.

The fleet received its first new destroyer class since World War II with the 18-ship Forest Sherman class. All of these 4,050-ton full load, 418-foot-long ships entered service between 1955 and 1958. They were general-purpose destroyers armed with the new 5-inch/54-caliber gun and ASW torpedoes.

The first purpose-built ocean escort was the 13-ship Dealey class, which entered fleet service between 1954 and 1957. These were to have been an inexpensive, rapidly built answer to the submarine threat, but many naval officers considered this first offering unsatisfactory. The Dealeys were 1,877 tons full load and 314 feet long. To save topside weight, the superstructure was manufactured out of aluminum. They had a single propeller and could make up to 27 knots. Their armament consisted of four 3-inch/50-caliber guns, six ASW torpedoes, and Weapon A. The immediate successor to the Dealey class was the similarly disliked Claud Jones–class destroyer escort. Its armament differed from the Dealey in that this four-ship class employed the hedgehog rather than Weapon A.

Four more distinct classes of ocean escort followed up through 1974 with the 46-strong Knox class. In the early 1960s, most escorts were armed with the ASROC system, which was likely the most effective method of destroying a fast-moving Soviet submarine. By then, the Russian submarine force included nuclear attack submarines in the November class that were capable of 25+ knots submerged. The increases in underwater speed relegated most of the early ASW ships to immediate obsolescence. Older and slower World War II–converted destroyer escorts were no longer of any value, so a massive program of rebuilding 163 Sumner-, Gearing-, and to a minor extent, Fletcher-class destroyers was inaugurated. All had power plants that could drive them at greater speeds than any Soviet submarine. Many were armed with ASROC and anti-submarine homing torpedoes. Improved sonar and submarine-detection electronics contributed to their effectiveness; however, the Fleet Rehabilitation and Modernization (FRAM) program merely extended the ship's lifespan by another 8 to 10 years.

Coexistent with various programs to improve contemporary destroyers and ocean escorts to combat Soviet submarines was the new construction program that included guided-missile destroyers in the 11-ship Farragut (DLG) class. Primarily designed to defend against aircraft with their Terrier missiles, the Farragut class also carried AS-ROC, as did the Charles F. Adams (DDG) class. The Charles Adams class included 23 units and was so popular that Australia and West Germany ordered ships for their navies. Both of these classes were substantially larger than the conventional World War II destroyer classes. The Farragut class was 4,700 tons full load at 512 feet in length and the Charles Adams was 4,500 tons full load and 437 feet long.

Aside from destroyers and frigates, most new cruisers were equipped with ASROC and detection gear. The trend of all major surface warships being larger and more ASW-capable had begun. Purpose-built ships were a luxury no longer affordable. Even the *USS Long Beach CGN-9* had ASROC.

Other Surface Ships

The amphibious arm of the navy shifted its primary reliance on the Landing Ship Tank and attack transport to a new type that employed the helicopter as well as landing craft. The first of this class were four aircraft carrier conversions. Three were Essex class and one, the *USS Thetis Bay*

LPH-6 (CVE-90), was a former escort carrier. All carried up to 20 helicopters and a full battalion of Marines. These were followed by keel-up purpose-built vessels in the Iwo Jima Class commissioned during the 1960s. They had a similar capability yet displaced 18,300 tons full load and were 598 feet long. Complementing the LPH were a number of successive classes of Dock Landing Ships (LSD) culminating in the five-ship Anchorage class (13,700 tons full load and 561 feet in length). As the Cold War at sea unfolded, it became apparent that a determining factor in winning was the ability to rapidly deploy well-armed troops from ships.

The Korean War reaffirmed the need for minesweepers, and as the World War II classes (Auk and Admirable classes) were phased out, the 750-ton, 172-foot-long Agile class became a standard in the navy. The Agile class was wooden hulled, diesel powered, and capable of 15.5 knots.

The fleet train was modernized with newer stores and replenishment ships being added. The submarine tenders of World War II were insufficient to the task of servicing nuclear attack and Polaris ballistic missile submarines; consequently, the Holland class (18,300 tons full load), Simon Lake class (20,500 tons full load), and L Y Spear class (23,500 tons full load) were built in the 1960s. The *USS Proteus AS-19* was one of the more notable of the submarine tenders as she was commissioned in 1942, yet lengthened and converted to service the first Polaris submarines that operated in the North Atlantic from Holy Loch, Scotland.

Of the stores ships built in the 1950s and 1960s, the Sacramento (AOE) class was the most prominent. These 53,600-ton full load, 792-foot-long replenishment ships had a shaft horsepower of 100,000 and could make 26 knots. They were capable of providing an immense amount of food, spare parts, supplies, and fuel to the fast carrier task forces. These ships carried 20 percent more fuel oil than the largest oilers in existence. They were nearly as long as the Essex-class aircraft carriers and dwarfed all destroyers and most cruisers. The Sacramentos employed helicopters to transfer stores in addition to the high line.

By the end of the 1960s, most of the World War II surface ships had been scrapped or sold off. Those that remained had been temporarily modernized and, in company with those built after the Korean War, made up the U.S. Navy's surface force.

Submarines

The Navy made its greatest strides forward in tactical and strategic importance during the 1950s

HMS Dreadnought S101, Great Britain's prototype nuclear-propelled attack submarine, which was laid down on June 12, 1959, and entered service on April 17, 1963. The *Dreadnought* was built much like her American cousin, the *USS Skipjack*, and it used the same nuclear power plant as the Skipjack class through an arrangement with the U.S. Government. Her whalelike hull enabled great speed (30+ knots) and a high degree of underwater maneuverability. This was necessary, as the *Dreadnought* was designed as a submarine hunter killer. This 4,000-ton (submerged) boat was tasked with locating and destroying Soviet attack and ballistic missile submarines. It mounted six 21-inch torpedo tubes in the bow for this purpose. *TIM*

and 1960s with the development of the nuclear submarine. For the first time, the submarine was able to do what its designers had intended: be an undersea weapon. Until the advent of nuclear energy, the submarine was merely a part-time submersible. Nuclear energy enabled a boat to remain submerged as long as its human crew could withstand being separated from the world above, and as long as foodstuffs lasted.

In 1949, nuclear technology had progressed to the point where the Chief of Naval Operations could set 1955 as the goal of the U.S. Navy having a nuclear-powered submarine. In August 1951, the Electric Boat Company began to build the *USS Nautilus SSN-571*, the world's first nuclear-powered submarine, and the new boat put to sea on schedule on January 17, 1955 (underway on nuclear power). It heralded a quantum leap in U.S.

naval power. The power plant consisted of a single pressurized water reactor (S2W) that generated 15,000 shaft horsepower to its two propellers. Top speed submerged was 20 knots, and 18 knots on the surface. The hull shape was based on the late-war German Type XXI boat, and it was armed with six 21-inch torpedo tubes.

Her performance stunned the international naval community, and the United States made sure that her capability was thoroughly demonstrated, especially to the Soviet Union. In 1957, the *Nautilus* was the first submarine to sail beneath the polar ice cap, thus showing that it could go anywhere and remain submerged for indefinite periods of time.

The Nautilus was followed up with three subsequent classes that closely resembled the Type XXI shape, and the single-boat *USS Triton SSRN-*

Italy was forced to surrender much of its fleet as war booty shortly after World War II, but being a maritime nation, it quickly embarked on a naval expansion and rebuilding program. One surviving cruiser, the pre-war *Giuseppe Garibaldi* was experimentally armed with U.S. "Terrier" anti-air missiles and, interestingly, four tubes for strategic ballistic missiles. In the main, however, the U.S. Navy supplied many excess submarines, destroyers, and minesweepers in the 1950s until the Italian Navy began a concerted effort to design and construct a modern navy. Shown here is the purpose-built guided-missile ocean escort cruiser, *Caio Duilio 554*, which is armed with a twin launcher for Terrier missiles and eight 3-inch/62 AA enclosed mounts. The *Caio Duilio* was multifunctional and carried four ASW helicopters armed with homing torpedoes that operated from a rather broad aft-sited heliport-port. *TIM*

586 class was the largest submarine built to date at 6,770 tons displacement. The Triton was intended to act as radar picket boat, but this role was short-lived.

The nuclear submarine concept was maximized with the use of the Albacore or "tear drop" hull shape. This enabled underwater speeds of 30+ knots, and up until 1969, there were a number of successive classes built that improved progressively as nuclear, hull design, metallurgic, and electronic technology advanced. The most prolific of these were the 14-boat "Thresher or Permit" class and the 37-boat Sturgeon class. The Sturgeons were slightly larger at 4,650 tons, versus the Thresher/Permit class at 4,300 tons. Many of these nuclear attack boats continued to serve well after the end of the Cold War, and were quite successful. They could be employed in any number of attack or reconnaissance modes and more important, kill attack or ballistic missile submarines

as they emerged from Russian- or Communist-controlled havens.

The threat of Soviet nuclear-tipped ballistic missiles being able to strike almost anywhere in the United States was reinforced when the Russians launched their satellite *Sputnik* in 1957. If the Russians could send a rocket into space, then they certainly had the technology to destroy many U.S. cities. The United States hurriedly built protected underground silos that housed its Atlas and Titan ballistic missiles, which served as powerful deterrents to Russian surprise attack. Unfortunately, it was a matter of time before all of these stationary silos were discovered and blanketed with prospective missile hits. Another, more elusive system was required to counter the Soviets in the ever changing "power gap." The U.S. Navy had the answer in its nuclear submarine and fledgling missile development program.

The combination of the guided missile and the nuclear-powered submarine was a marriage of

The Soviet Navy light cruiser, *Sverdlov*, at speed. Of the 24 ships planned, 20 were laid down, and only 14 were commissioned. They were beautiful but obsolete ships at their debut in 1953. In later years, as the Soviet Navy converted from gun to missile ships, SSN-2 Guideline and SAN-4 anti-ship missiles were tested on a *Sverdlov*, yet throughout their lengthy careers, these ships were mainly used as flagships and for cadet training. Most had a large minelaying capacity. With the introduction of more technologically able ships, the Sverdlov class receded into the backwaters of Soviet naval activity. *Navy League*

A Russian Skory or Skori-class gun destroyer. Like the Sverdlov-class light cruisers, the first offering in the destroyer class was based on a pre-war design. This class was armed with four 5.1-inch guns as a main battery and two 3.4-inch guns sited aft. Eight 37-mm guns were designated for anti-air defense. This class also carried 10 21-inch torpedo tubes and an array of ASW weapons. Many were later modernized, and by the latter part of the Cold War, several of the class had been transferred to friendly nations. *Author's collection*

necessity and genius. The first operational attempt was with the nuclear-tipped Regulus cruise missile, which could be launched from surface ships and submersibles. Regulus I was short range, but its successor Regulus II had a 1,600-mile range.

The major disadvantages of the Regulus program was the need for its launching platform to be on the surface, and due to its size, only one missile could be deployed. Although one nuclear submarine was designed for the Regulus missile (*USS Halibut SSGN-587*), the program was phased out in favor of Polaris.

The Polaris program was undoubtedly the finest and most efficient total weapons development program ever undertaken by the navy. In short, a submersible had to be built and able to accurately launch up to 16 nuclear-tipped ballistic missiles while submerged. The program was initiated in 1955, and became the U.S. Navy's highest priority. Before the first successful firing of a missile from a nuclear submarine occurred on July 20, 1960, more than 100,000 people, 30,000 companies, and hundreds of top-level minds worked incessantly to bring the program to its conclusion. The missile that was developed was far smaller than most ballistic missiles of that period. The Polaris A-1 was 28 feet long, had a range of 1,200 miles, and carried a small nuclear warhead (.5 megatons). It had to be fired from below the surface of the water and once it emerged, its rocket engine had to ignite and then, using inertial guidance, had to fly to its target. More than 3,000 test tank firings were made before the missile and its guidance system were perfected. Following this, many launches occurred on the *USS Observation Island EAG-154*, a Polaris test platform.

The launch platform selected was the "Skipjack" class nuclear attack submarine that was made into jumbo size with a 130-foot-long section added. The addition, which was inserted between the forward and aft section of a Skipjack, contained the 16 missile launchers in two rows of eight. The first unit was the *USS George Washington SSBN-598*, commissioned on June 6, 1959. Just over a year later, the first missile was successfully fired from the *George Washington*. The program had fulfilled its expectations, and three years before its deadline!

Eventually, 41 ballistic missile submarines were built up through 1966 and became operational. The Polaris missile was progressively upgraded to its A-3 variant with a range of 2,500 miles and three nuclear warheads of 200 kilotons apiece. By the late 1960s, Polaris submarines roamed the world's oceans waiting to launch at Soviet targets.

A Kotlin-class guided-missile destroyer (DDG). Conversion of nine ships to surface-to-air missile capability was begun in 1962. The Kotlin was armed with one twin arm SAN-1 Goa surface-to-air missile launcher and had a magazine for 20 missiles. The Goa had a 17-mile range and high-explosive warhead. Its speed was estimated at Mach 2. The Kotlin also was armed with a twin 5.1-inch dual-purpose gun mount forward, and substantial ASW weapons. *Navy League*

The creed of this program was simple, "if the missiles are ever launched, the Polaris Program will have failed." By the end of the 1960s the ballistic missile submarine was one of the major deterrents to Soviet attack and remained so throughout the Cold War.

The United Kingdom, France, and Other Western Navies

The other Western navies were progressive in their technological development and built quality warships, but not in the quantity that the U.S. Navy did. The United Kingdom and France operated aircraft carriers during the 1950s and 1960s, but it was obvious that no country other than the United States could expend sufficient resources to build and maintain super carriers. Most European nations were content to allow the U.S. Navy to take the lead in fixed-wing naval aviation, and contented themselves with smaller carriers such as the French Navy 33,000-ton *Clemenseau*, commissioned in 1961. By this time, France had opted

out of NATO and retained an associate role should a general Soviet attack occur. France continued to develop her naval forces with modern cruisers and destroyers and the highly successful Daphne-class diesel-electric attack submarine.

During the 1950s and 1960s Great Britain operated two large carriers (*HMS Ark Royal* and *HMS Eagle*) that each displaced 53,000 tons and carried an air group of 80 to 100 aircraft. Six other carriers of lesser tonnage and capability were kept in service, but tight budgets, competition with the Royal Air Force, and other defense commitments slowly reduced this number.

The Royal Navy was responsible for a number of excellent ocean escort vessels such as the 26-ship Leander class built from 1959–1970. Some of the Leanders were armed with guns or anti-ship missiles (Exocet) and/or Limbo ASW mortars.

With these and other modern destroyer-type ships, Great Britain ensured adequate ASW coverage in the North Sea and the English Channel as a major contribution to containing Communism.

The most prolific of all Soviet submarine classes was the diesel-electric "Whisky," which was ultimately expressed in seven variants for a total of 236 boats. Most were built over a seven-year period from 1951 to 1957, and obviously designed with strong German influence. As the Russian Navy built nuclear attack submarines and better diesel-electric boats, the Whiskys were relegated to lesser roles and many transferred to nations such as Egypt, China, North Korea, and Indonesia. *Navy League*

Following the lead of the U.S. Navy, the Royal Navy built five nuclear-powered attack submarines (Valiant class) and contributed four nuclear ballistic missile boats (Resolution class/ 16 Polaris A-3 missiles) to NATO defenses during the 1960s.

Other NATO members, including the Federal Republic of Germany, built or acquired submarines and destroyers from the United States or Great Britain after the Korean War, which acted as a stepping-stone to the revitalization of their naval forces. Italy was particularly active in rebuilding its fleet and by the 1970s had regained much in terms of a naval posture. Scandinavian nations such as Norway participated in many NATO coastal operations and operated minesweepers and coastal patrol craft that monitored Soviet submarine and surface ship activity.

The period from 1950–1970 was one of research, development, and regeneration for all of the Western navies. It was also a period for facing budgetary realities. Great Britain, France, and Italy would no longer be regarded as major naval powers, but operating within their financial resources they made a valuable contribution to thwarting Communist ambitions at sea.

The Union of Soviet Socialist Republics' Navy

When the Korean War began, the Soviet Navy was an eclectic collection of obsolete warships from the past and from other countries. In the years that followed the end of hostilities, tight security shrouded Russian naval operations and building programs. Western observers knew that the U.S.S.R. would not be content without a blue water navy, and a blueprint for expansion had been decided at the highest levels of the Soviet government. The program was initiated with the mass construction of 6-inch-gunned light cruisers of the Sverdlov class, and all gun destroyers of the Skory class. It was also suspected that copies of Germany's Type XXI submarines were being laid down. The Soviet dictator, Joseph

Stalin, was more determined than ever to build a world-class navy.

Of the planned 24 ships in the Sverdlov class, 14 entered fleet service and 75 of the 80 planned Skorys were commissioned. The Sverdlov class mounted 12 6-inch guns, displaced 18,000 tons full load, and could steam at 34 knots. They were 3,100 tons full load, and their 60,000-shaft horsepower geared turbines could turn up 33 knots. Their armament consisted of four 5.1-inch guns, anti-ship torpedoes, and basic ASW and anti-aircraft weapons. The sleek attractive lines of both the Sverdlov and Skory classes betrayed the obvious influence of Italian designers. They were handsome ships, but obsolete at birth. Like the Sverdlovs, the Skory class was a throwback to the World War II all-gun destroyer.

At this point, the Russian Navy did not pose any real threat to the West, but after the Sverdlov appeared at the 1953 British Coronation Review at Spithead, many naval experts became fearful of the "revitalized" Soviet Navy. For the next few years, much of Great Britain's naval tactics centered on killing Sverdlovs as if they were of similar caliber to Germany's commerce-raiding Bismarck. A major factor in the fascination resulting from the Sverdlov's appearance was the overdone cleanliness of the ship and the professionalism of its crew and officers. Many in the West expected a poorly maintained, out of date, shoddily built ship manned by undisciplined peasants. The beautiful

lines of the Sverdlov and the behavior of her crew shattered this image. Later it became apparent that naval warfare had outdistanced the surface raider, and the irrational fear subsided. Although some ships of the Sverdlov class were rearmed with a twin arm Guideline missile battery, they still remained in local waters and would only have been effective for shore bombardment purposes. Like any surface warship, the Sverdlovs were susceptible to air and submarine attack.

By showing off his finest and most modern heavy warship, Stalin accomplished his objective of putting the world on notice that he was in the process of building the finest navy afloat. It was smoke and mirrors. The Soviet Union was building a large navy, but not for offensive operations. The first task was to defend the homeland from attack.

Submarines

As to the submarine fleet expansion, the Soviet Union had just begun with a smaller copy of the Type XXI submarine—the 1,350-ton "Whisky" class, a medium-range patrol submarine. A total of 236 Whisky-class boats were built and were armed with six 21-inch torpedo tubes and a mine-laying capacity. The Whisky class was the largest single class of submarine ever built by any nation, and it was not surprising that many ended up in satellite state navies. Almost concurrently, the Soviets began building the long-range "Zulu"

Six of the Zulu class, diesel-electric–class patrol submarines were converted to carry ballistic missiles (Zulu V). At first, they were armed with the SSN-1 or Scud, but were later changed over to the SSN-4 Sark missile. The Sark became an operational weapons system in 1961 aboard the Zulu V and although it had a 300-mile range, the mechanics for launching required the boat to surface and be dangerously exposed to Western ASW forces. By the mid-1970s, most of these boats were retired or converted for other duties. Shown is a Zulu IV that closely resembled its ballistic missile cousin. *Navy League*

The *Kresta I* cruiser was armed with anti-ship missiles, anti-air missiles, guns, torpedoes, and the first Russian warship to have a helicopter hangar and flight facilities. The *Kresta I* was assigned a Ka-25 Hormone ASW helicopter, which carried dipping sonar, sonobuoys, depth charges, and homing torpedoes. Its missile suite included the four SSN-3 Shaddock anti-ship guided missiles capable of carrying a nuclear warhead up to 250 miles. Its anti-air defense consisted of two twin SAN-1 Goa missile launchers. When first introduced in the late 1960s, the Kresta I class was primarily designed to kill U.S. and Western carriers. *Navy League*

class. At 1,950 tons the boats in this class could range up to 20,000 miles on their diesel-electric power plant. They were capable of 18 knots on the surface and could make up to 15 knots submerged. They were armed with ten 21-inch torpedo tubes and a mine-laying capability. Of the 28 boats built, six were converted (Zulu V) to be the first ballistic submarines in the Soviet Navy. The Soviet Navy predated the West with the first successful ballistic missile launch in 1955, and shortly thereafter a ballistic missile–armed Zulu-class diesel-electric boat was operational. They carried a maximum of two SSN-4 Sark ballistic missiles with a range of 300 miles. Firing these missiles was a crude affair as the submarine had to surface, and the missiles (housed in an enlarged sail) were then raised above the sail. The nuclear warhead–armed missile was aimed at its target and fired, presumably when the submarine was stable. The range was short and the accuracy was suspect, but the U.S.S.R. was able to do this years before the Western navies.

Subsequent diesel-electric classes of patrol submarines included the Romeo (1958–1961, 18 boats) and the highly regarded Foxtrot (1958–1983, 79 boats). The 2,300-ton (submerged) Foxtrot carried 10 21-inch torpedo tubes and had a 19,000-mile range. This boat was the epitome of the conventional submarine and quite popular with other nations. The Russians stopped a planned 160-unit building program at 62 boats in 1971; however, 17 additional units were built for friendly nations.

In addition to surface and submarine forces, during the early 1950s, more than 4,000 aircraft were assigned to the Soviet navy for coastal defense in concert with coast defense artillery. Most of the aircraft were MiG fighters and highly capable Badger jet bombers. Relatively satisfied that the Soviet Union was prepared to withstand U.S. and NATO carrier and amphibious attacks, Stalin turned his attention to expanding the fleet. He died in March 1953, however, without naming a successor.

Nikita Khrushchev emerged as the new leader, and he was not "naval minded," regarding the Sverdlov as more of a pleasure yacht. He was "nuclear weapon" minded and convinced that the threat of a nuclear holocaust was the proper method of defending the U.S.S.R. as well as spreading Communism under its umbrella. He ordered a halt in many warship building programs and the wholesale eradication of the fleet's larger units. In some respects, this was a wise decision because it allowed human and material resources that were wasted on obsolete ships to be directed to more productive activity.

One of the Soviet Navy's stopgap measures to defend the homeland was the 1958–1960 conversion of five Whisky-class submarines by mounting two outside hull–mounted SSN-3 Shaddock cruise missile launchers (Twin Cylinder). The cylinders were abaft the sail or fin, and could be elevated for firing. The underwater noise, other than when the boat was creeping, could have been heard for miles. Another variant of the Whisky class was the seven-boat Long Bin (SSG) conversion that housed four SSN-3 launchers within an expanded sail. Both boats relied on outside assistance for missile guidance. The Long Bin was slightly more successful than the Twin Cylinder, yet neither would have survived even moderate ASW searches. *Navy League*

In 1956, the most significant event in Soviet naval history occurred with the appointment of Admiral Sergei Georglyevich Gorshkov as commander in chief of the navy. He was ordered to redirect naval thinking to the close defense of the Soviet Union from attacks by U.S. aircraft carrier and surface forces. To this end, he was to build and deploy a large number of small, inexpensive missile-armed ships and patrol boats. The submarine fleet was slated for expansion, and the naval air force was also to be augmented with hundreds of anti-ship missile-armed bombers to deal with the Western carrier task forces.

In compliance with his orders from the Kremlin, Admiral Gorshkov began to scrap older Russian-built ships, war prizes, and all battleships. More than 300 ships were stricken in this purge. Conversely, he initiated a building program that included OSA and Komar missile boats and the four-ship Kynda-class anti-ship missile cruiser. The Kynda, which entered fleet service in 1962

and shocked the naval community by being the first ship whose main battery consisted of anti-ship missiles. It was armed with eight SSN-3 Shaddock surface-to-surface missiles that had an optimum range of 100–300 miles and could be accurately guided with the assistance of a Bear D bomber. The payload could either be nuclear or a 3,000-pound conventional explosive. The reason this 6,000-ton anti-ship missile cruiser was added to the Soviet naval inventory was unmistakable. It was to destroy U.S. and Western carrier battle groups far from the Russian coastline. In what was to become a trademark of Soviet warship layout, the Kynda class was armed to the teeth with anti-air missiles (SAN-1 GOA), 76-mm guns, ASW rockets (MBU), and 21-inch anti-ship torpedoes. At this time, most U.S. and NATO navy cruisers were not nearly as well armed, and their decks looked austere compared to those of their Soviet counterparts. The successor to the Kynda was the Kresta I guided-missile cruiser, which mounted

four SSN-3 Shaddock anti-ship missiles, two twin SAN-1GOA anti-aircraft missile launchers, four 57-mm dual-purpose guns, 10 21-inch torpedo tubes, ASW rockets, and facilities for one Ka-25 Hormone helicopter. The Hormone was ASW capable. The first Kresta I became operational in 1967. These were attractive ships that could make up to 32 knots on steam turbine power. They also reinforced Soviet resolve to combat U.S./NATO aircraft carrier battle groups with potentially nuclear-tipped cruise missiles.

The eight-ship Krupny-class anti-ship missile destroyer was also introduced soon after Gorshkov's appointment. This class carried the SSN-1 Scrubber surface-to-surface missile, which had a range of 130 miles. Its warhead was a conventional high explosive. The Krupny was designed for an anti-ship role. Other destroyer classes followed, such as the 20-ship Kashin and modified version (Kashin MOD) class that emphasized either anti-air or anti-ship capability. The Kashin MOD was armed with the successful Styx SSN-2 anti-ship missile. All had mine-laying ability and anti-ship torpedo armament; moreover, the 4,900-ton full load Kashin class was the first warship to use gas turbine power. This was the wave of the future, and Soviet engineers had solved the turbine blade warpage problem before the Western navies. These ships could make up to 35 knots and could accelerate at a higher rate than steam turbine–powered ships. They also had a

separate helicopter landing pad on their stern. By the mid-1960s, the use of a piloted helicopter aboard destroyers and cruisers was becoming the rule rather than the exception in all navies.

The concern over the Western carrier battle groups was so pervasive in the U.S.S.R. that various submarine classes were examined for their suitability to carry surface-to-surface guided missiles, the way Soviet surface ships and long-range bombers could. Several Whisky-class submarines were converted to fire anti-ship cruise missiles. The most interesting was the Whisky Twin cylinder (1958–1960), which had two long trainable cylinders on its deck that housed SSN-3 Shaddock missiles. Reliance on nearby surface ships or specially equipped aircraft was a must, and the system was ineffective at best. The Soviet Navy did not abandon the submarine-launched cruise missile and eventually perfected the concept with the Juliet (SSG), Echo II (SSGN), and later (in 1968) the Charlie SSGN nuclear variant. The Charlie I displaced a hefty 5,100 tons dived and carried eight SSN-7 anti-ship missiles with a 25–30-mile range. The high speed of this boat (30 knots) meant that it could penetrate a traditional ASW screen and launch its cruise missile at the attacking carriers of the Western navies. There was justifiable anxiety over this new weapons system in the West.

The first Soviet nuclear-powered submarine was the November class, commissioned in 1958. These 4,800-ton (submerged) boats were capable

On July 4, 1958, the first nuclear-powered Soviet submarine became operational. Code-named "N" or "November," this class (SSN) eventually included 13 boats and could dive to a depth of 1,650 feet. For a first effort, the boat was noisy, yet had a dived speed of 25 knots. The November class was armed with six 21-inch torpedo tubes—all forward. In this photo taken on April 10, 1970, the November-class submarine *K-8* is apparently in trouble. On April 12, 1970, it sank, but the crew was rescued. Problems plagued this class throughout their service in the fleet. Over 100 crewmen died and many more were poisoned by radiation in seven separate accidents from 1961 to 1973. The November-class *K-19* was so afflicted with problems that it was dubbed "*Hiroshima*" by its crew. *Navy League*

of diving to 1,650 feet, with a top speed underwater of 25 knots. They were conventionally armed with six 21-inch torpedo tubes, and overall the boat was quite noisy. They were also accident prone due to poor initial construction and maintenance. The November class was followed in 1967 by the much-improved Victor I-class attack boat. It carried eight 21-inch torpedo tubes, and had a top speed of more than 30 knots. The lesson learned from the November class was applied in the Victor I, and it became a formidable opponent. The Soviet Navy was not far behind the U.S. Navy in its development of nuclear power for its submarine force, and it also did not abandon diesel-electric technology and building programs.

The Cuban Missile Crisis caused great embarrassment to the leadership of the Soviet Union. A by-product of this fiasco was the obvious lack of a credible blue water navy. The U.S. Navy had forced Russian submarines to leave the Caribbean and turned back its merchant ships. Added to this was the U.S. Navy and Great Britain's ballistic missile submarine capability. By 1970, there were 41 American SSBNs and four Royal Navy Resolution-class ballistic missile boats. The Russians went on to refit a large number of the Zulus with the 300-mile-range Sark missile, and build the Golf class with three Sark missiles located in a rather large sail structure. In 1958, the Hotel-class nuclear SSBN was brought into service, first with

The Soviet Navy introduced one of the most peculiar classes of warship in naval history with the *Moskva* (1967) and her sister *Leningrad* (1968). Shown here is the *Moskva* being refueled by the fleet oiler, *Boris Chilikin*. These 14,590-ton full load helicopter cruisers were developed to counteract U.S. Navy ballistic missile submarines that were operating in the Mediterranean. Not much better than previous cruiser/battleship aircraft carrier hybrids, they were also not aesthetic to the eye. They were heavily armed with 14 Hormone or the newer model Ka-27 Helix ASW helicopters, two twin SAN-3 Goblet surface-to-air missile launchers, two twin SUW-N-1 ASW launchers, and two twin 57-mm dual-purpose guns. Like most Soviet surface ships, nearly all of their deck space was crowded with weapons. The Moskva class had variable depth and hull-mounted sonar. Experience with this type-vessel proved disappointing, and it was not repeated. The *Leningrad* was decommissioned in the late 1990s and the *Moskva* was scrapped at Alang, India, in late 1997. *Navy League*

the Sark missile, and five years later with the 700-mile-range Serb missile.

In 1968, the successor to the three-missile-capacity Hotel class was the 34-boat Yankee-class ballistic missile submarine. The Yankee displaced 10,000 tons and was 430 feet in length. It carried 16 tubes for the 1,300-mile-range Sawfly missile and was the first boat that approached U.S. and British SSBN capability. The Sawfly was nuclear-weapon capable and later improved with multiple reentry warheads. The first Yankee-class boats completed were assigned to the eastern seaboard of the United States, and their target area extended to the Mississippi River. Later, Yankees deployed off the West Coast could hit any target west of the Rocky Mountains. By 1970, the race for the most powerful submarine-launched ballistic missile capability was tightening up.

A member of this Hormone "B" flight crew is preparing to photograph the U.S. Navy photographers. The Hormone was the first standard shipboard helicopter for Soviet surface vessels. In its "B" variant it was able to provide anti-ship targeting guidance for surface-to-surface missiles. The Ka-25 Hormone was capable of 130 knots with a range of 400 miles. *Navy League*

The Soviet response to the threat of U.S./NATO submarine-launched ballistic missiles was met with a stepped-up ASW campaign that included corvettes of the Grisha class, and two novel hybrid helicopter-cruiser ships of the Moskva class. These ships displaced 17,212 tons full load and carried 18 ASW-armed Hormone-class helicopters. They were also heavily armed with two twin SAN-3 anti-air missile launchers and a twin SUWN-1 ASW missile launcher. Two 12-tube MBU ASW rocket launchers and four 57-mm dual-purpose guns filled out the Moskva's armament. The helicopter had quickly become one of the primary weapons to combat the submarine, and the Moskva class was dedicated to this task.

By 1970, the Soviet Navy had emerged from being an unknown quantity to the rank of the second most powerful in the world. Its achievements from 1950–1970 were almost legendary, and due mainly to Admiral Gorshkov and the Kremlin's unremitting drive to conquer the world.

In the quarter-century since the end of World War II, the Russians had succeeded in building a true blue water navy with bases and safe harbors around the world. It built the first successful ballistic missile submarine and the first operational guided-missile submersible. The Soviets introduced surface ships with anti-ship missiles of proven worth, and were on the verge of expanding into fixed-wing naval aviation. Even more accurate and lethal ASW, anti-ship, and anti-aircraft weapons and their seaborne platforms were on the drawing board. With an unlimited budget and resource sufficiency, the Soviet Navy was racing beyond a defense mind-set and headlong into open ocean confrontation with its adversary of the past 25 years—the American Navy.

CHAPTER 5

THE WAR PEAKS AND SUBSIDES: NAVAL OPERATIONS (1970-1991)

Although it was unknown to the combatants in 1970, the Cold War was at its chronological halfway point. Twenty-one years later it would end, and end in a fashion no one could have predicted. However, in 1970, the Cold War at sea continued unabated.

The Final Agony of the Vietnam War

The war in Vietnam had been raging since

The *USS Higbee DD-806* fought in World War II, the Korean War, and also participated in many surface ship operations off Vietnam. Typical of World War II destroyers that had been converted for ASW work, the *Higbee* found herself fighting in the Battle of Dong Hoi Gulf in April 1972. U.S. destroyers, including the *USS Sterett DLG-31* (later reclassified as a cruiser—CG) and the *Higbee,* were assigned to destroy ground traffic on Highway One on the coastline bordering the Gulf of Tonkin. During the barrage, MiG fighters appeared, and the *Higbee* was damaged by a bomb hit. The *Sterett* shot down one of the attackers with a Terrier SAM. Following the air attack, the North Vietnamese Navy attacked with high-speed patrol boats. These were driven off with heavy damage to the enemy. Both attacks demonstrated the vulnerability of surface ships to low-flying aircraft and anti-ship missiles. *Author's collection*

1964, and there was little hope of victory. By 1970, the United States had experienced a discernible change in attitude about its overall responsibility in the region. The U.S. Navy continued to bombard enemy shore positions from the decks of destroyers such as the *USS Mansfield DD-728* and *USS Orleck DD-886,* but evidence of an organized withdrawal of U.S. forces was unmistakable. In March 1970, the hospital ship *USS Repose AH-16* left the region after four years on station, and just weeks later, it was announced that 150,000 more U.S. service personnel would leave Vietnam within the next year. By the end of the year, all of the 650 river patrol vessels formerly under the control of the U.S. Navy were turned over to the South Vietnamese Navy, and the once 36,000-man U.S. Navy "Riverine" force was reduced to 17,000 advisers. The Navy Department further announced that it intended to deactivate another 58 major warships, making a total of 286 over the prior 18 months.

Of political significance was the repeal of the famous "Tonkin Gulf Resolution." This act, passed in 1964, allowed virtual free rein to the executive branch to conduct war in Southeast Asia. On December 31, 1970, the U.S. Senate revoked the act by a vote of 81 to 10. The United States was not only withdrawing from the war in a military sense, but now politically. This did not end violent and massive demonstrations in the United States against the war; these continued until the last U.S. soldier was removed from Southeast Asia.

In 1971, 45,000 more personnel were brought home. This left a total force of 175,000 U.S. personnel in Vietnam, a number anxiously monitored by the people of the United States. This number was further reduced to 69,000 by May 1, 1972.

The war did not scale down comparatively with the decline in U.S. troop strength, and in late March 1972, the North Vietnamese began a major offensive by sending three divisions of seasoned troops into the Demilitarized Zone that had been established between the warring nations.

One of the methods used to keep the North Vietnamese delegates at the peace talk table was to mine important harbors on their coastline. In May 1972, A-6 Intruders (example shown) sowed mines in a number of critical harbors. Seaborne supplies slowed considerably to the North. The A-6 was a popular bomber and strike aircraft. *TIM*

In response, the U.S. Navy began an intensive naval bombardment (Linebacker Surface Strike) of North Vietnamese positions and stepped up the air campaign. By mid-April, President Nixon ordered a full resumption of strategic bombing of North Vietnam by the U.S. Air Force B-52s. Bombing above the 20th Parallel had ceased four years earlier. Adding to this overall attack, carrier-based A-6 Intruders sowed mines in a number of North Vietnamese deep water ports, including the major traffic center at Haiphong. For years, Soviet ships had been bringing military aid and equipment through this port, which had been attack free. The Soviet and other merchant traders were granted a 72-hour grace period to leave the area, and within hours, seaborne trading was stopped.

Surface ships with a minimum of two screws and two 5-inch guns were needed to help the struggling South Vietnamese Army (ARVN). This meant cruisers and destroyers that had the capability to hit hard and suffer less chance of a fatal propulsion breakdown. Ships including the *USS Lawrence DDG-4* and *USS Sterett CG-31* quickly arrived from other operational areas to join the Linebacker Surface Strike Group and began a series of battles with MiG fighters, torpedo boats, and newly emplaced enemy radar-controlled coast defense guns. By the end of her tour, the Lawrence was undamaged but had been missed by more than 600 enemy rounds hitting close aboard. Other ships were not so fortunate. The *USS*

The *USS Oklahoma City CLG-5* was a former Cleveland-class light cruiser that was converted to carry the Talos long-range anti-air missile. Her twin arm Talos battery, which was nuclear warhead-capable, was sited aft. The *"Okie City"* was often used to bombard shore targets off Vietnam with her forward 6-inch/47-caliber gun battery. In August 1972, the *Oklahoma City* led a group of surface ships that attacked the North Vietnamese Port of Haiphong with guns. Many sailors were relieved when she exited the area as enemy shells were flying between her funnels. Marines manned machine guns on her decks to repel small boats and boarders. *TIM*

111

USS MIDWAY [CVA-41]
RECOMMISSIONED 30 SEPTEMBER 1957

The lead ship of the Midway-class large carrier was the *USS Midway CVA-41*. The *Midway* was not in the same category as the Forrestal-class super carrier, but performed well in the Cold War and beyond. Naval aviators from the *Midway* were responsible for the first and last MiG fighter kill of the Vietnam War. The first was a MiG-17 was shot down on June 17, 1965, and the last, a MiG-21 on January 12, 1973. The *Midway* was also present in late April 1975 as South Vietnamese and American refugees attempting to escape capture by the North Vietnamese Army flew out to her and one of the other 39 ships sitting off the coast. April 1975's Operation Frequent Winds marked the end of the Vietnam War. *TIM —SFCB*

Buchanan DDG-14 was hit by shore battery fire, but the overall damage to the entire force was minimal. One particularly successful attack was led by the missile cruiser *USS Oklahoma City CLG-5* as she and other surface ships shot their way into and out of Haiphong Harbor in a night shore bombardment raid on August 27, 1972. The fast-moving force, reminiscent of surface ship attacks during World War II, also dispatched two North Vietnamese torpedo boats.

By June 1972, the North Vietnamese offensive stalled and was repulsed. Four months later, another cease-fire was initiated in anticipation of

renewed peace talks. Incredibly, on December 18, 1972, the North Vietnamese delegates to the Paris Peace Talks abruptly left the peace table and walked out. The United States then initiated Linebacker II, which was strategic bombing of Haiphong Harbor and Hanoi by the U.S. Air Force, and carriers such as the *USS Oriskany CVA-34* and *USS Ranger CVA-61*. During the Linebacker II operation, 729 B-52 bomber missions were flown, during which 49,000 tons of bombs were dropped on vital installations in North Vietnam. Significantly, the combined U.S. Navy and Air Force assault was met by 200 surface-to-air

An Oskol-class fleet submarine repair ship sits alongside a Soviet Foxtrot submarine. Foxtrot attack boats were often observed in Cuban ports being serviced by one of a number of Russian repair and maintenance ships. The Oskol class displaced 3,000 tons full load and in some instances was armed with twin 57-mm dual-purpose guns in a mount sited forward. The United States was adamantly opposed to any Soviet submarine or forward base activity in Cuba or any other port in the Caribbean. *Navy League*

missiles, and one of the most intense anti-aircraft barrages in history. The losses amounted to 15 bombers, and the intensity of this campaign resulted in the return of the North Vietnamese to the peace negotiations on January 3, 1973. Soviet-made weapon systems were overwhelmed by U.S. determination, skill, and technology.

On January 27, 1973, the Paris Accords that provided for the end of the war for the United States in Vietnam were signed. An element of the arrangement included sweeping hundreds of mines that had been sown in North Vietnamese waters. This effort began on February 24, and continued into the late summer of 1973. For all intents and purposes, U.S. participation in the war ended on March 29, when all remaining U.S. forces departed from South Vietnam.

The U.S. Navy suffered the loss of hundreds of air crew and 300 aircraft and the damage of more than 1,000 aircraft during the war. Naval aviators destroyed 58 MiG attackers, and an unknown number of North Vietnamese aircraft were destroyed by ship-launched Terrier or Talos missiles. Despite the losses, the value of the aircraft carrier was reaffirmed, as was the bombardment capability of surface ships. Much of the ground

An advertisement in the Toronto, Canada, International Airport for leisure travel to Cuba. The U.S. and Western embargo of this Communist state destroyed its already shaky economy. As the Cold War entered its last phase, tourist travel to the island nation began from many nations—except the United States. *Author's collection*

war occurred within gun range of surface ships lying off the coastline.

The cost to U.S. taxpayers for the prosecution of this war was estimated at $108 billion. Aid and assistance to the Socialist Republic of Vietnam by the Soviet Union and China cost approximately $2.3 billion. Naval aid from the Soviet Union continued after the war with the transfer to North Vietnam of five Petya II-class frigates (gun), and a number of SSN-2 (Styx) anti-ship missile armed OSA II fast-attack craft. It was small price to pay for the harvest of U.S. equipment and related technical intelligence.

The bounty reaped by advancing North Vietnamese forces was staggering: fixed- and rotary-wing aircraft, gun systems, and weapons of all types. More than 700 U.S.-built ships and small craft of all types fell into North Vietnamese hands. With the exception of a small number of ships that escaped or were transferred to other nations (i.e., the Philippines), the entire "Riverine" or former "Brown Water Navy" inventory of more than 500 patrol craft was captured. Also captured were a number of modern port facilities capable of servicing large warships (Cam Ranh Bay). This was of particular interest to the Soviet Navy.

The war did not end with the formal withdrawal of U.S. and allied forces, but within months, the North Vietnamese army swept into the south and quickly crushed the dispirited and disorganized South Vietnamese. The final agony occurred over April 29–30, 1975, when the Seventh Fleet provided helicopter transport to more than 9,000 refugees and American citizens who were fleeing the onslaught of the victorious North Vietnamese. They flew out to waiting U.S. aircraft carriers and surface ships lying off the coast. Many rogue South Vietnamese military pilots flew Huey helicopters or anything else that could get off the ground to the waiting fleet, and crashed alongside ships. Boats were then sent to fish out those who survived. The image was a lasting one for all of those who witnessed it. The end had come and with it the knowledge that more than 50,000 Americans had perished in the 11-year war. The U.S. military and its allies had performed superbly throughout the war; however, it would take years before they were fully recognized for their sacrifice.

The war at sea, which began in August 1964 with the North Vietnamese patrol boat attack on the *USS Maddox DD-731* did not end abruptly. U.S. air and surface ship patrols, well into international waters, continued to be harassed by hostile North Vietnamese light surface forces and MiG aircraft. The Cold War at sea off the Vietnamese

A Ropucha-class landing ship tank (LST). Twenty-one units of this class were built in Poland from 1974 to 1986, and were designed to carry up to 225 troops. They were designed as "roll on roll off" amphibious ships and had two twin 57-mm gun mounts for close-in defense and troop support. Two of the Ropucha class were armed with four SAN-5 Grail surface-to-air missile launchers with a 32-missile magazine. This and other efforts by the Soviet Navy to expand its amphibious capability further convinced the West of Soviet global intentions. *Navy League*

coast assumed the same character as that near any other Communist-controlled country.

Global Navy Activity from 1970 Until the End of the Cold War

The United States and its allies fought the Cold War at sea on a worldwide basis, and in the 1970s and 1980s, its primary adversary had embarked on an unprecedented program of naval construction. Although much attention was drawn to Southeast Asia, the naval aspect of the Cold War at sea was no longer primarily confined to roving Soviet submarines and the occasional visit by its surface ships to friendly ports in the Mediterranean, Caribbean, or Indian Ocean.

The message of Communism was being spread through the use of a much-improved merchant fleet and long-legged warships that could steam to any point on the globe. The Russians were learning the value of under-way replenishment, secure anchorages, and friendly ports where supplies and fuel could be secured. The Soviet Union was also using foreign aid and military assistance to struggling Third World countries to its strategic advantage. By 1970, several nations now operated former Soviet warships of all types including a Sverdlov-class cruiser, which was the flagship of the Indonesian Navy. In the main, the Soviet Union sold or leased fast attack craft (OSA missile boats), destroyers (Skori class), and Whisky-class submarines to nations within which they sought a foothold for Communism. The lesson being learned by the

An OSA missile attack boat near its top speed of 36 knots. These 245-ton full load craft were diesel powered and carried four SSN-2 launchers for the infamous Styx anti-ship missiles. They also carried a pair of twin 30-mm enclosed close-in weapons, one each sited forward and aft. Sixteen nations have received more than 100 of these boats (OSA-I and OSA-II) from the Soviet Union and they have seen more war than the majority of the world's warships. *TIM*

In the aftermath of the Mideast War, it became necessary to clear the Suez Canal and adjacent waters of mines that had been laid. The U.S. Navy and the Soviet Navy provided minesweeping forces in this effort. The Yurka #738 minesweeper shown was one of many different classes of Soviet mine warfare ships. Forty-five of the Yurka oceangoing–class were built from 1963 to 1972. They were capable of sweeping magnetic, wire, and acoustic mines. They were armed with two twin 30-mm close-in weapons and could make 18 knots on diesel power. Four of the class were transferred to Egypt prior to the Mideast War. *Navy League*

A Soviet *Tupolev Tu-126* NATO code-named *Moss* photographed from the cockpit of a U.S. Navy aircraft over the North Atlantic in September 1972. The *Moss* resembles a Tu-20 or 95 Bear except that it is a much larger aircraft. The *Moss* was designed to provide early warning and aircraft control. Like the *Bear,* it belongs to the Tupolev lineage of aircraft design. There were few of these four-engine, swept-wing (AWACS) aircraft built and this is a rare view of the *Moss. Navy League*

navies of smaller nations was that surface-to-surface missiles could be deadly to any size vessel, and it was not necessary to have large, costly, and heavily armed warships as the guarantor of regional naval supremacy. A properly aimed barrage of Styx missiles launched from a small, fast, inexpensive craft could defeat a more powerful enemy.

Western nations were also strengthening friendly navies with modern weapons and warships from their inventories of excess vessels. The West emphasized ASW, whereas exported Soviet doctrine was directed more to anti-ship warfare in the littoral (coastal). These individual attitudes were symbolic of their fears of one another. Outfitting sympathetic foreign navies with excess and older ships and weapons was used in an overall effort to contain or extend Communism. Ironically, the Egyptian Navy operated Whisky-class attack submarines, Skori-class destroyers, OSA, and KOMAR fast attack craft, yet the strength of its surface fleet was in its variety of former British destroyers (Z type) and ocean escorts (River, Hunt, and Black Swan classes).

The Arab-Israeli War in June 1967 revealed that the Soviet Navy could rapidly deploy its blue water forces, and in great numbers. Within days, 70 warships of all types, including submarines and replenishment ships, passed through the Turkish straits and were operating in the Mediterranean. At the same time, the U.S. Sixth Fleet consisted of a smaller number of ships, but the firepower of its aircraft carriers and modern surface ships more than compensated. The Soviet Navy was also able to sustain itself abroad with newly established anchorages in the Mediterranean, Indian Ocean, and the Caribbean. By late 1970, it was also operating off the west coast of Africa, and each year seemed to venture farther and with more imposing force. Typically, the surface force was accompanied by long-range submarines, and was continuously changing in composition.

After the conclusion of the 1967 Arab-Israeli conflict, the Soviet Navy opted to retain a permanent presence in the Mediterranean. Approximately 45 ships were at sea at all times and were rotated with ships from the Black Sea and later from the Northern Fleet.

In April 1970, the Soviet Navy made its formal debut into the international naval community by conducting the largest peacetime naval exercise in history. It was coded as *Ocean* or *Okean-70* and consisted of more than 200 Soviet warships demonstrating the capabilities of a naval superpower in many of the world's oceans. The exercise was designed to achieve a number of objectives, determine tactical weaknesses, and then take corrective action. What emerged was the obvious difficulty of exercising a seaborne command from a shore base. The Soviet Navy had been weaned on the concept of littoral defense in which strategic decision making could be ashore, but when diverse forces were in blue water, centralized control from a shore base was cumbersome and counterproductive. The lesson learned was that a number of larger combatants had to be outfitted with enhanced communication systems and designated as flagships. The lesson learned by the West was that the Soviet Navy now had or would soon have a balanced blue water force. Admiral Gorshkov and the Kremlin had a navy that could go anywhere and was openly evolving to strategic parity with the United States.

A key objective was to have a navy that would not allow another shameful withdrawal like that of the 1962 Cuban debacle. In April 1970, a Kresta I missile cruiser, accompanied by a destroyer and two Foxtrot diesel-electric patrol submarines, visited Havana and Cienfuegos, Cuba, in open defiance of U.S. wishes. They were later joined by an Echo II (SSGN) nuclear-powered guided-missile submarine and six Tu-95 Bear bombers. The Echo II and Kresta I carried SSN-3 Shaddock guided missiles that had a 400-mile range with a nuclear warhead. Both the Kresta I and Echo II were relatively modern warships, and although the United States was visibly alarmed at the presence of the Soviet force, there was little protest. By September,

The naval aviator that snapped this shot of the belly of a *Bear* must have been using a telephoto lens. The *Bear* became one of the most common of Soviet weapons seen by the U.S. Navy. As the Soviet Navy gradually left home waters, the *Bear* was in the forefront. They visited Cuba, Vietnam, South Yemen, and on April 14, 1977, two bombers flew down the South Carolina coast near Charleston. The NATO code name "*Bear*" had A – F variants, yet the *Tu-20, Bear D* was most often seen, as it was used for reconnaissance. A fully loaded aircraft was 170 tons and had a range of 7,800 miles. *Navy League*

A U.S. Navy *P-3 Orion* ASW patrol aircraft drops flares. The propeller-driven *Orion* was one of the primary submarine patrol aircraft used by the West and could be found virtually all over the world. The *Orion* carried sonobuoys, ASW torpedoes, and had a range of approximately 5,000 miles. In 1974, a Harpoon missile was successfully test-fired from an *Orion*. This extended its capability to kill surfaced Soviet submarines. In 1976, in an effort to further increase the frequency of maritime air patrols, U.S. Air Force B-52 bombers were assigned to fly anti-submarine missions over the Atlantic Ocean area. The Soviet submarine threat was very real. *U.S. Navy*

A Whisky-class attack submarine (SS) at sea. Although built between 1951 and 1955, many of these boats were kept operational years beyond their designed capability. On October 27, 1981, a Whisky-class boat ran aground in Sweden, unfortunately near a Swedish naval base. There was a larger issue at stake with this incident. It meant that Soviet submarines and in particular, Charlie-type guided-missile boats could be or already were close to U.S. coastlines (inside the 100-fathom curve), and there was little defense available at that time. This innocuous shipwreck served as a wake-up call to the U.S. Navy. *Navy League*

The United States began to deploy warships in the Indian Ocean in the late 1970s in reaction to Communist aggression and general regional unrest. Following a surface squadron of cruisers and destroyers came the carriers, and one of the four that were assigned was the *USS Kitty Hawk CV-63*. All of the major carriers had been redesigned CV/CVN rather than CVA in 1975. U.S. carriers were now considered multi-purpose and could carry fixed wing and helicopters. Gone too was the former role of strategic nuclear strike from the deck of an aircraft carrier—this was the responsibility of the U.S. Air Force. *U.S. Navy*

the United States was sufficiently concerned to register a formal complaint and restate the 1962 crisis terms: "no invasion if there are no missiles." This prevented the Soviet Navy from establishing a permanent forward submarine base at Cienfuegos. By late January 1971, the intended submarine depot ship left the area, yet "saber rattling" by the United States did not completely deter Soviet intentions. For years to come, the Soviet Navy maintained a presence in Cuban waters generally consisting of a support ship, patrol submarine, and one or more destroyers.

For Cuba, the continued support of its government and economy by the Soviet system was vital to its economic survival and its avoidance of starvation. Without foreign trade, the people's revolution was a failure. In order to prop up Cuba's ailing economy, Soviet bloc nations agreed to purchase three quarters of the annual sugar output at $.40 a pound versus the world market price of $.09 a pound!

The Soviet Navy made its presence known in the Arabian and the Red Seas as well as developing anchorages off the Seychelles and the Chagos Archipelago. Major naval units visited all of the nations in the Persian Gulf and often remained for prolonged periods of time.

The Soviet Navy now maintained nuclear ballistic missile submarines in the Pacific as well as the Atlantic. The balance of naval power was rapidly shifting, and surprisingly in June 1971, Leonid Brezhnev, the leader of the Soviet Union, suggested a treaty limiting naval strength between the two superpowers. The United States rejected the offer.

In Icelandic waters, the Soviet Navy was at the same time conducting a major exercise in which the Northern Fleet acted as a NATO carrier battle group and was successfully attacked by other warships. This exercise also demonstrated the ability of the amphibious arm of the Russian Navy. The West watched this operation closely as it clearly indicated that the once "littoral tied" Soviet Navy could also mount a long-distance seaborne land attack. Its naval infantry (similar to the Royal Marines or U.S. Marine Corps) numbered 12,000 strong and was highly trained in shock attack techniques.

While the superpowers were flexing their military muscle at every opportunity, India and Pakistan declared war upon one another on December 4, 1971. In the brief but violent naval engagements, Soviet, British, French, and U.S. naval weapons were employed. In some respects, this was one of many surrogate battles fought between the superpowers, without the use of nuclear weapons.

The Indian Navy took the initiative by attacking Pakistani forces at Kurachi with four Styx-armed OSA-class fast attack craft. The OSAs were towed to the battle site by Soviet-built Petya-class frigates. Six surface-to-surface missiles were fired, and the result was the destruction of a Pakistani destroyer, minesweeper, and merchant ship. This was followed up with a successful gun attack by Indian frigates. Days later, a Pakistani submarine (French Daphne) sank an Indian frigate in revenge for losing one of its own submarines. The Indian Navy had previously caused the former U.S. Tench-class submarine *Ghazi* to be sunk by its own mines.

The war was short-lived but not before a number of fortuitous air strikes were launched from the Indian carrier *Vikrant* (ex *HMS Hercules*) on Pakistani ships and shore targets. Overall the surface-to-surface missile had again proved to be a most lethal weapon, and naval aviation made a heavy contribution to the outcome. Although this was not a war between the superpowers, it was still a part of the Cold War at sea. It allowed the superpowers to visualize combat between themselves in a vicarious way without the loss of their naval assets or dignity. The next test came a few months later with the combined Egyptian and Syrian attack on Israel on October 6, 1973.

The naval battles in the Yom Kippur War pitted new Israeli gun/missile boats (Saar class) assisted by helicopters against former Soviet Komar and Osa fast attack missile boats. The Israelis employed modern electronic countermeasures and target guidance from supporting helicopters to decimate the opposing naval forces. The Styx missile had proved itself against large targets, but was unable to effectively track the fast moving and evasive craft of the Israeli Navy. Electronic warfare and the use of rotary-wing aircraft figured prominently in this contest, in which Israel claimed to have destroyed 38 Syrian and Egyptian craft.

The superpowers were peripherally drawn into this war when it became necessary for the U.S. Government to supply Israel with military aid to maintain parity among the warring nations. The Soviet Navy immediately began to reinforce its Mediterranean squadron with a massive number of ships from the Black Sea Fleet. One hundred vessels of all types steamed through the Strait of Gibraltar to the eastern Mediterranean in early November 1973. Cruisers, destroyers, missile ships, and a fleet train arrived with 25 submarines and intelligence-gathering vessels. The U.S. Sixth Fleet was outnumbered and outgunned; however, its carrier air group strength more than compensated

A squadron of NATO destroyers and frigates operates in formation. Combined NATO operations at sea ironed out many of the difficulties inherent when different types of ships and languages come together. In the early years, they were far less effective, yet this was not so toward the end of the Cold War. *TIM*

The Sverdlov-class gun/missile cruiser *Dzerzhinsky* at speed. On November 17, 1978, this ship carried the commander in chief of the Black Sea Fleet to a state visit to Istanbul, Turkey. This was the first time since 1938 that a Soviet warship had appeared in this port. The Soviet Navy now carried the "Hammer and Sickle" offensively and diplomatically to all areas of the world. The *Dzerzhinsky* had her aft 6-inch turret removed and was retrofitted with a twin surface-to-air SAN-2 missile (Guideline) launcher. *Author's collection*

A Hotel II-class nuclear ballistic missile submarine (SSBN) in trouble 600 miles off the coast of Newfoundland on February 29, 1972. A roving *P-3 Orion* photographed the Soviet submarine uncharacteristically riding on the surface. A Russian fishing trawler and tanker came to the Hotel's rescue before the U.S. Coast Guard arrived. The disabled boat was towed back to the U.S.S.R. It was later learned that several of her crew were killed after the boat lost all power. This was the 10th reported major incident aboard a Russian nuclear submarine since 1961. Overall, it is known that 39 accidents resulting in more than 300 deaths and the loss of five Soviet nuclear boats occurred during the Cold War at sea. *Navy League*

for the numerical difference. A cease-fire, brokered by the Soviet Union and the United States, was agreed upon by Israel and the coalition of Egypt and Syria in late October. The Soviet Union had proved that it could respond with overwhelming naval strength, and the West had done likewise. Like most confrontations at sea, it was a standoff. One of the remnants of this conflict was the need to sweep mines in the Gulf of Suez and the Suez Canal. The U.S. and Soviet Navies participated in these operations. Clearing mines and the hulks of ships sunk in the canal continued until mid-1975.

After the conclusion of the Yom Kippur War, regional hot wars were interspersed with subtle naval engagements worldwide. As the Soviet Navy began to flaunt its power abroad, it interfered with U.S. Naval and NATO naval exercises and was quick to provide assistance to any nation or region that opposed Western interests.

In 1975–1976, rebellion in Angola, which was backed by the Cuban military, was in fact supported by supplies and equipment brought in by the Soviet merchant marine. Units of the Cuban Army were flown in by Soviet troop transports, and soon Bear D reconnaissance aircraft were

An India-class Soviet diesel-powered rescue submarine (SSAG) with two DSRVs submersibles sitting in specially designed wells aft of the sail. Two of this class were built—one assigned to the Pacific Fleet and the other to the Northern Fleet. This photograph was taken in October 1980. The U.S. Navy built two catamaran hull-type vessels as mother ships to its DSRV program. The first was the *USS Pigeon ASR-21*, commissioned on April 28, 1973. *Navy League*

making use of Angolan airfields to patrol much of the South Atlantic.

The Soviet Navy routinely assigned aircraft and intelligence-gathering ships to patrol near U.S. and Western ballistic missile submarine bases in Rota, Spain, Scotland, Guam, and the United States. Surface ships were periodically assisted by long-range submarines that idled near U.S. Navy bases and major Western ports. In the mid-1970s, San Diego harbor was watched continuously by a Foxtrot-class submarine (*Scorpion B-427*) whose task was to record surface ship signatures. Not all operations were successful, as was proved by the "whisky on the rocks" incident on October 27, 1981. A Whisky-class SS U-137 submarine, reportedly armed with nuclear-tipped torpedoes, ran aground on the rocks near the Swedish naval base at Karlskrona and had to be refloated. It was released two weeks later to an embarrassed Soviet Navy. This was not the first time that a suspected Soviet submarine had violated Swedish territorial waters.

This type of activity was a two-way street as U.S. submarines reciprocated by listening in on Soviet naval operations and in particular sought to locate the Soviets' ballistic missile submarines. In 1975 it became public knowledge that specialized U.S. Navy submarines had been eavesdropping on Soviet naval activities within that country's three-mile territorial limits. The operation began in 1960 under the code name of "Holystone."

The boldness of the Soviet Navy was further shown when a powerful surface squadron led by a guided-missile cruiser boldly steamed into the Pacific and to within 25 miles of Honolulu, Hawaii, in the autumn of 1971. After the conclusion of the civil war in Vietnam, the Soviet Navy quickly gained access to the former U.S. naval facilities and airfields. After negotiations that began in 1975, Bear D aircraft flew from former U.S. bases, and surface ships as well as Soviet submarines were welcome in Vietnamese ports and recently captured naval facilities.

Beginning in 1968, the Indian Ocean witnessed the growth of Soviet naval forces with the establishment of a permanent force of one or more major warships, minesweepers, support craft, and two submarines. In addition to protecting the U.S.S.R.'s own interests abroad, it was imperative

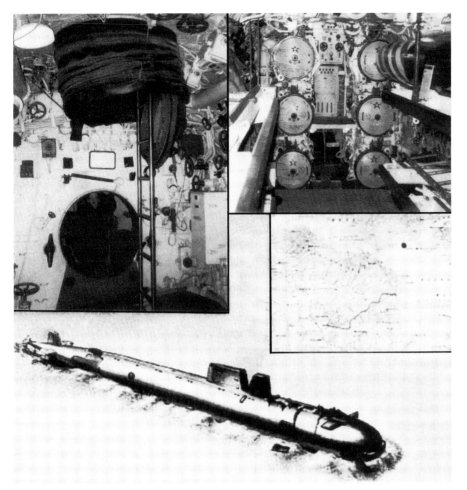

One of the most spectacular Soviet submarine disasters, a Mike-class *K-278* sank off the Norwegian coast. The Mike was designed as a fast deep-diving attack/guided-missile boat and while submerged suffered a serious reactor accident. It surfaced long enough for some of the crew to escape, and as it began to sink, five men escaped using rubberized suits through the escape hatch. Forty-two died and 27 were rescued. The diagram shows an artist's conception of the damaged Mike lying on the bottom, and to the upper right a photo of the interior of a Soviet submarine torpedo room near the forward escape hatch. The photo to the upper left shows the aft escape hatch. It was reported that men could escape through this hatch using specially designed escape suits from a maximum depth of 800 feet. *Author's collection*

that client states and the West recognize the growing power of the Soviet navy. Naval service and repair facilities were built in Somalia, South Yemen, and Ethiopia. Somalia eventually evicted its Russian tenants and the Cuban military mission in November 1977. Egypt did likewise in April 1976 when its President Anwar Sadat denied the Soviet Navy any access to its ports. Victory over Communism was accomplished through diplomatic means and the psychology of fear as much as with guns, missiles, and bombers.

The Indian Ocean escalated as a hot spot for both the West and Soviet navies from the late 1970s into the 1980s. Beginning in 1968, diplomats on several occasions attempted to control regional politics with superpower military intervention, but to little avail. In mid-November 1978, a small surface ship squadron led by the missile cruiser *USS Sterett CG-31* entered the Indian Ocean and began a continuing presence of U.S. Navy in the region. Four months later, in response to the war between South (Communist) and North Yemen, the *Sterett* was joined by the *USS Constellation CV-64*, and subsequently the

USS Kitty Hawk CV-63. The overall regional U.S. naval force was further increased by two more U.S. carriers, the *USS Midway CV-41* and the *USS Nimitz CVN-68.* By mid-January 1980, the U.S. Navy had 25 major combatants and support ships in the region. The Soviet Navy responded in kind and augmented its squadron with guided-missile submarines to counter the U.S. carrier battle groups.

Recognizing that units of the Soviet Navy were continuously present in blue water caused NATO to create various "Standing Naval Commands." By 1973, three had been established: Atlantic, Mediterranean, and the English Channel. Generally, NATO members contributed destroyers, frigates, and mine warfare vessels to these commands that periodically exercised as combined units. This extended the power of the West at sea and caused improved command, communication, and cohesion among NATO navies. It also served notice on the Warsaw Pact that NATO was not a paper tiger at sea.

By 1980, the Cold War at sea had become global. NATO, the United States, and other allied nations played cat and mouse with the Soviet Navy. Wherever and whenever national discord or revolution erupted, the Soviet Navy was present in a support role or an active spectator. The Western powers matched this phenomenon with its own naval power projection to maintain stability between the superpowers and avoid nuclear war.

Accidents, Bumping, Shadowing, and Interference

The war at sea assumed a new and more illuminating character as the Soviet Navy began operations far abroad in the 1970s and into the 1980s. When Russian ships operated in close proximity to the homeland, news of accidents and naval disasters was well hidden from the West. As they ventured farther out to sea and into waters frequented by Western warships, it became increasingly difficult to shroud accidents and shipboard problems from Western eyes. When accidents occurred, the Russians customarily refused assistance from U.S. or other ships, preferring to handle the difficulty with their own resources.

Beginning in July 1961 and up through December 1989, there were 39 known incidents involving Soviet nuclear submarines. Five Russian boats were lost, 300 were known dead, and an unknown number of seamen were injured. Eleven of the incidents involved reactor failures, and nine submarines were damaged by internal fires. By and large, the Echo I and II nuclear attack (SSN) and guided-missile boats (SSGN) experienced the highest number of accidents (14), followed by the November-class SSN (7). A Charlie I (K-429) guided-missile (SSGN) boat sank twice. It first went down on a post-refit test on June 23, 1983, and after being salvaged, sank again at its dock. It then became training hulk. All of these submarine accidents proved quite revealing to the West. It appeared that Soviet nuclear power doctrine/procedure was sloppy, and safety was not a primary concern.

The U.S. Navy and the Central Intelligence Agency (CIA) took advantage of one of the accidents by raising a portion of a Soviet Golf II diesel-electric ballistic missile submarine from its Pacific Ocean grave 15,000 feet down. The boat was lost 750 miles off Hawaii in 1968. In 1974, the CIA-sponsored 63,000-ton *Glomar Explorer* was expressly built to raise the submarine for examination. Shrouded in secrecy, the *Glomar Explorer* raised a portion of the Golf II. The results have never been fully explained, but at the time were deemed of immense value to U.S. Naval intelligence.

The United States had two major nuclear submarine disasters during the Cold War at sea. The

A Golf II conventionally powered ballistic missile submarine slowly running on the surface. These boats carried three SSN-5 tubes in an enlarged sail. The SSN-5 code-named *Serb* could carry a nuclear weapon up to 700 miles. The Golf II had to surface before firing. The boat that was lost in 1968 received very little publicity, yet the CIA was able to determine its location when it sank. Reportedly, six crewmen were brought to the surface by the U.S. salvage ship *Glomar Explorer* and given a proper naval burial. *U.S.N.I.*

The *Hughes Glomar Explorer* moored in the U.S. Naval reserve fleet anchorage at Suisun Bay, California. The 63,000-ton purpose-built salvage ship sat there for decades before being reactivated in 1998 for use in commercial mining minerals from the sea bottom. The center gantry and crane were used to lift the forward section of the *Golf II (SSB)* from the bottom of the Pacific during the covert operation simply known as "Jennifer." *Author's collection*

A Kashin-class guided-missile destroyer (DDG) is shown in this November 1979 photograph. There were 15 of this class built from 1962 to 1967, and it was the first major combatant to employ gas turbine power for main propulsion. The Kashins displaced 4,500 tons full load and were capable of 35 knots. The Kashins were multi-functional and armed with anti-air guided missiles, ASW rockets, and two twin 3-inch guns, and ASW torpedoes. On August 30, 1974, a surface-to-air booster charge ignited in the aft missile magazine of one of the Kashins. An explosion started an unstoppable fire and the ship sank stern first off the Soviet Naval base at Sevastopol. *Navy League*

A Krivak I–class destroyer. The Krivak I, II, and III variants were beautiful and powerful ships that were first built in 1970. A total of 38 units were built and considered to be "guard ships" by the Soviet Navy—capable of independent operations or as battle group escorts. Like most Soviet warships, they were armed for ASW, anti-aircraft, mine warfare, and anti-shipping. At 3,670 tons full load they were capable of 34 knots using gas turbine power. The *Krivak I* (*Storozhevoy*) was seized by a mutinous crew led by the political officer in November 1975. The mutiny was quashed, the leaders later executed, and the destroyer reassigned to the Pacific Fleet. *Navy League*

lost boats were the *USS Thresher SSN-593* on April 10, 1963, and the *USS Scorpion SSN-589* on May 23, 1968. The entire crews of both boats perished. The *USS Guitarro SSN-665* accidentally sank alongside a pier at the Mare Island Naval Shipyard on May 15, 1969—no lives were lost.

Both the West and the U.S.S.R. developed rescue techniques including the DSRV (Deep Submergence Rescue Vessel) and a mother ship. The DSRVs were to be used to rescue survivors from sunken or damaged submarines.

Accidents and incidents were not limited to submarines. On August 30, 1974, a Kashin-class guided-missile destroyer (*Otvazhnyi*) exploded, caught fire, and sank in the Black Sea. Nearly its entire crew of 300 was lost in the conflagration. This was just one of many accidents suffered by both the West and the U.S.S.R.

There were collisions between ships such as the *USS John F Kennedy CV-67* and the missile cruiser *USS Belknap CG-26* on the night of November 22, 1975. Seven men were killed, and the cruiser was burned down to her main deck level. The *Belknap* was later rebuilt at a huge cost. Just days before, the Soviet Navy suffered an enormous embarrassment when the crew of the Krivak I destroyer *Storozhovey* mutinied and attempted to take the ship to Sweden for political asylum. The mutiny occurred due to low pay and harsh treatment (hazing and brutality toward conscripts is commonplace in the Soviet military). The ship and its rebellious crew were quickly intercepted by fighter aircraft and naval vessels with orders to shoot to kill. The ringleaders were tried and executed by firing squad.

The Soviet Navy was not alone in having social problems aboard its ships. Throughout the 1970s, the U.S. Navy suffered riots, illegal drug use, and racial infighting aboard many of its major combatants. On occasion, ships would have return to port as the result of these problems, and in 1978, it was reported that the U.S. Navy had had the highest rate of desertion in its history during the previous year. A total of 14,539 enlisted personnel deserted in 1977 out of a population of 459,857 sailors. Much of the problem was attributed to the lowering of acceptance and sailor retention standards in the American Navy. This was remedied by adjusting performance criteria and discharging all who did not measure up. The desertion rate and turmoil among the sailors gradually dissipated, although the problems with drug use continued.

In May 1981, it was revealed that Soviet agents had been gathering valuable naval intelligence from a U.S. Navy Chief Warrant Officer (CWO) since 1968. The "Walker Family Spy Ring" consisting of John Walker, his wife, son, and a family friend, passed along classified material to the U.S.S.R. on American submarine and communications operations in return for cash. They were tried and convicted of espionage.

Bumping or other interference with Western vessels by Soviet ships became almost commonplace in the 1970s and 1980s. The incidents began in the 1960s and were serious enough to warrant a formal agreement between the Soviet Navy and the U.S. Secretary of the Navy. On May 25, 1972, the "Incidents at Sea Agreement" was signed in Moscow. In the event of future difficulties, the nations could appeal to the provisions on this agreement. Incidents abounded over the next two decades, as the Soviets proved noncompliant. Many agreements with the Soviet Union had this same result. The Russian navy continued a systematic and reckless practice of interfering with Western naval operations and broke many common international rules of the road. As the Soviet Navy began to maintain a squadron of ships in the Mediterranean and other areas where Western ships congregated or were based, they became more outwardly bold. One of the most annoying and dangerous methods of interference was when destroyers, frigates, intelligence gatherers, and even submarines crossed in front of Western carriers during flight operations;this caused radical course changes. While shadowing carrier and other major NATO operations, Russian ships would steam precariously close to Western formations, recording every maneuver and taking thousands of photographs. The only benefit to the West was that they, too, could observe Soviet warships and record changes in weapons and maneuvering qualities.

It was quite probable that Soviet submarines were lurking nearby when any NATO or U.S. Navy exercise was being carried out, and on at least two significant occasions they collided with American nuclear attack boats. On November 15, 1969, November-class SSN (K-19) collided with

A Los Angeles–class nuclear attack submarine (SSN) riding on the surface. The first of this class was commissioned in 1974, and the 6,927-ton submerged displacement boats have proved to be reliable and successful. They were capable of 32+ knots dived, and carried an armament of four 21-inch torpedo tubes, Subroc, Harpoon anti-ship missiles, and Tomahawk cruise missiles. By any account, the Los Angeles class was considered formidable. On October 1, 1986, the *USS Augusta SSN-710* experienced a collision with a Soviet Delta-class nuclear ballistic missile submarine (SSBN) in the North Atlantic. Both boats were submerged and after surfacing they were able to make port safely. Repairs to the *Augusta* cost $2.7 million. *U.S. Navy*

The Delta-class ballistic missile submarine had four variants. The boat shown is a Delta II riding on the surface. The Delta II–class displaced 13,200 tons submerged and carried 16 tubes for launching SSN-8 ballistic missiles. The SSN-8 had a range of 4,200 miles with a nuclear warhead. With this range, the Deltas could operate in home waters or SSBN "bastions" and still hit most U.S. mainland targets. A Delta collided with the *USS Augusta SSN-710* on October 1, 1986. In all probability, the *Augusta* was tracking the Delta—as was the responsibility of any determined Western SSN skipper. *Navy League*

An Echo II guided-missile submarine (SSGN) similar to the one that collided with the U.S. Navy frigate *USS Voge DE-1047* on August 28, 1976. The Echo II carried eight SSN-3 and later SSN-12 cruise missiles and torpedoes for defense. The SSN-3 had a range of 250 miles and carried a high-explosive or nuclear warhead. These boats were designed as carrier or large surface combatant killers. *Navy League*

the *USS Gato SSN-615* near the entrance to the White Sea. No fatalities were reported, and both boats made it back to port. Seven months later, an Echo II (SSGN) K-557 collided with the *USS Tautog SSN-639* in the Pacific, and the Russian submarine was nearly lost. The *Tautog* made it back to port. Western and Soviet submarines played cat and mouse to discover one another's weaknesses. This placed them in close proximity, as did the practice of an attack boat shadowing a missile boat to locate its patrol area. It was not only Soviet submarines that collided with U.S. and Western submarines. A 1969 report given to the U.S. Congress, revealed that U.S. nuclear submarines had collided with or hit Soviet ships no fewer than nine times in the past decade.

Soviet submarines and surface ships also rammed, or were rammed by U.S. Navy surface ships. There were a number of significant incidents that resulted in minor to major damage. On August 28, 1976, the ocean escort *USS Voge DE-1047* literally ran over an Echo II guided-missile submarine. Amazingly, the Soviet submarine reported only minor damage, but the *Voge* required a tow back to Suda Bay, Crete.

The Kara-class missile cruiser *Petropavlovsk* was found guilty of cutting up a large number of Japanese fishing nets off Hokkaido on May 16, 1981. The Soviet cruiser was closely monitoring a combined U.S. and Japanese naval exercise and was inattentive to Japanese fishermen. The Soviets blamed the U.S. Navy, but a later investigation placed the true blame on the Russian intruder.

On a less dangerous but still irritating note, other acts such as the April 2, 1984, firing of flares at the U.S. frigate *USS Harold E Holt FF-1074* by the Soviet cruiser/carrier *Minsk* kept the Cold War at sea interesting. At noon, the *Holt* passed by the *Minsk* more than 300 yards distant, and the Russian hybrid carrier/cruiser launched a number of flares, three of which hit the *Holt*. The American frigate did not respond.

Almost up to the end of the Cold War at sea, incidents still occurred. In 1988, despite the obvious improved relations between the United States and U.S.S.R., Russian vessels still deliberately collided with U.S. Navy surface warships. Old habits and hatreds persisted at sea. Adversaries at sea still fought each other in ways that were noncombatant, but often just as dangerous.

On a more global scale, the dawn of the 1980s portended bad things for the Soviet Union. The U.S.S.R. invaded Afghanistan in December 1979, and by the early 1980s found it to be the same kind of quagmire that U.S. forces found

In this unbelievable photograph, an *Echo II* surfaces after colliding with the frigate *USS Voge* DE-1047 in the Ionian Sea. The frigate ran over the Soviet craft, and the submarine quickly surfaced just aft of the frigate's stern. The *Echo II* suffered damage to its sail, yet was able to make it back to its base. *U.S.N.I.*

themselves in in Vietnam. Freedom fighters (Afghan rebels) stalemated a far superior conventional Soviet army of uninspired conscripts, and by May 1988, Soviet forces began their withdrawal. The Russians lost 15,000 men out of 115,000 committed, and despite their superiority in heavy weapons, were compelled to leave without victory. By February 1989, the last Soviet soldier left Afghanistan. The invasion of Afghanistan coupled with the 1981 Warsaw Pact invasion of Poland to quash a trade union movement quickly dismantled East-West "détente." Much of the diplomatic and social progress that had been made between the West and the Soviet bloc was erased. What followed was a diplomatic roller coaster–like ride in the early to mid-1980s.

In 1982, a real naval war occurred in and around the Falkland Islands in the South Atlantic. This abortive war between Argentina and the

United Kingdom was an incredible and fortuitous warning to all navies who were confident in the capability of surface combatants.

The Falkland Islands War

The Falkland Islands, or Malvinas War, began many years before its violent apex in 1982. Argentina had a century-old claim on the British Crown Colony, but aside from threats and diplomatic action in the United Nations, had done little to enforce its demand. In February 1976, one of its destroyers (*Almirante Storni*—formerly the U.S. Fletcher class-*USS Cowell DD-547*) fired warning shots over the bow of a British research ship near one of the island coastlines. As reported by the British ice patrol ship *Endurance*, this and other forms of harassment had become commonplace. Although negotiations over which nation had sovereignty were proceeding in the United

The Garcia-class frigate *USS Voge DE-1047*. This type of ocean escort was armed with ASROC, two older 5-inch/38-caliber guns, ASW torpedoes, and DASH. It was capable of 27 knots on one propeller. When it hit the Soviet *Echo II*, the damage to its propeller was such that a tow was necessary. Many naval officers argued against the single-propeller type vessel, and this and other incidents proved their case. *Author's collection*

A submerged Victor-class attack submarine was inadvertently rammed by the aircraft carrier *USS Kitty Hawk CV-63* on March 21, 1984, in the Sea of Japan. The Victor was dogging the carrier group and was caught off guard by the fast-moving carrier. Both vessels were damaged, and the Victor had to be towed back to its Vladivostok base. *Navy League*

Nations, there were great domestic difficulties in Argentina. Economically, the country was a shambles, and its leader, General Leopoldo Galtieri, sought to divert public attention to something more dramatic and emotionally captivating—military action against the United Kingdom.

On April 2, 1982, Argentina mounted an amphibious assault on the capital of the Crown Colony, Port Stanley. The assault ships included the British-built Type 42 destroyer (*Santisima Trinidad*), the carrier *Vienticinco de Mayo* (former *HMS Venerable*), and the Guppy converted submarine *Santa Fe* (formerly the *USS Catfish SS-339*). By late in the day, more than 1,500 troops and armor overwhelmed the main island's pitifully small defenses. Rounding out this international mix of weapons, the Argentine military utilized the French-built Super Etendard attack jets and Exocet anti-ship missile. The people of Argentina were ecstatic with this victory over the United Kingdom.

Although a concentrated effort was made at the diplomatic level to resolve the issue without resorting to actual war, it was obviously impossible. The British government then initiated emergency plans to retake the islands militarily. They mounted a counter-assault built around two VS-TOL carriers (*HMS Hermes* and *HMS Invincible*); an amphibious group; surface action force of frigates and destroyers; and nuclear attack submarines. Elements of British force arrived at intervals, and within 10 days of the Argentine invasion, a 200-mile exclusion zone was announced worldwide by the British government. Shipping was forewarned about trespassing in this zone without the permission of the British force commander. The Royal Navy employed its nuclear attack boats as a distant perimeter defense and to track any Argentine naval force that could threaten the main body of the British force.

By April 22, 1982, the carriers *Hermes* and *Invincible* were within range of the Falklands and by May 1 began launching Sea Harrier (VSTOL) strikes on Argentine defense positions near Port Stanley. The combat use of the Sea Harrier vertical takeoff and landing multi-task strike aircraft was new. They proved invaluable in the rough and inhospitable South Atlantic. The Harriers were armed with the Sidewinder AIM-9L air-to-air missile that proved superior to anything being flown by Argentina. This U.S. Air Force/Navy jointly developed missile was designed to kill radically maneuvering, high-speed targets at medium range with much improved infrared seeker. In tandem with the Harrier attacks, long-range RAF Vulcan

The Kara-class missile cruiser (CG) *Petropavlovsk* that was guilty of cutting up Japanese fishing nets while observing U.S. Navy and Japanese warships exercising on May 16, 1981. The Kara class was strongly armed with guns, surface-to-air and anti-ship missiles, ASW rockets (RBU), and facilities for a Ka-25 Hormone helicopter. The Karas were powered by gas turbine and had a top speed of 34 knots. On September 1, 1981, a Kara-class missile cruiser leading three other ships closed to within 230 miles of the Oregon coastline. The Soviet Navy was becoming more brazen each year. *Navy League*

bombers also struck the nearby airfield with 1,000-pound bombs.

First blood was drawn on May 2, 1982, when the Argentine light cruiser *General Belgrano* (ex-*USS Phoenix CL-46*) was sunk by two submarine-launched torpedoes from a shadowing SSN, *HMS Conqueror*. Three hundred twenty-one men were killed or drowned in the freezing dreary waters of the South Atlantic. The *Belgrano's* ASW armed escorts fled the area, and the carrier group led by the light carrier *Vienticinco de Mayo* also returned to the mainland. This marked the end of the surface navy phase of the war, and the beginning of the naval air phase. High-speed aircraft pitted against modern surface ships in this conflict proved to be quite illuminating to naval strategists worldwide.

On May 4, Type 42 destroyer *HMS Sheffield* was attacked by Super Entendard aircraft that launched Exocet anti-ship missiles. A single Exocet hit the *Sheffield* amidships, and its 364-pound high-explosive warhead failed to explode. However, combusting rocket fuel started a major fire that ultimately caused the ship to be lost. Both sides had now lost major surface combatants, and the war at sea was very real.

As the entire world, and in particular, U.S. and Soviet naval leaders, watched, fast-moving attack fighters from the Argentine mainland bore in on British warships and support units. The bravery and tenacity of the Argentine pilots was only matched by the determination of the Royal Navy to defeat them. Former U.S. A-4 Skyhawks attacked British shipping before, during, and after the counter amphibious landing made by the British. The Royal Navy opposed the attacks with Sea Harrier combat air patrol interception, Sea Wolf, Sea Dart, and Sea Cat surface-to-air missiles, and any gun that would fire, including flare pistols.

On February 12, 1988, the *USS Yorktown CG-48*, a Ticonderoga-class missile cruiser, was sailing in company with the destroyer *USS Caron DD-970* in the Black Sea. A Mirka-class frigate and a destroyer (likely based at the nearby Soviet Navy base at Sevastopol), deliberately bumped the U.S. ships. *Author's collection*

A Soviet Mirka I–class frigate. The 18 frigates of this class (Mirka I and II) were built during 1964–1967, and designed for multi-purpose combat with ASW capability. They carry four 3-inch guns in two twin mounts, torpedoes, and ASW rockets (RBU). These vessels were powered by a combination of diesel and gas turbine and have a 4,800-mile range at 10 knots. The Mirkas had a top speed of 30 knots. *Author's collection*

Much of the battle took place in an area known as San Carlos Water ("bomb alley" to the Royal Navy and "death valley" to the Argentine pilots). On May 20, 1982, the invasion by British forces began, and eventually 10,000 men were put ashore to eject the Argentine garrison. After a series of firefights ashore culminating in heavy fighting around Port Stanley, the British ground troops forced the Argentine command to surrender on June 14. The ground war was over and the Falkland Islands back under British control.

During the ground campaign, the Royal Navy suffered the loss of four ships and damage to others due to bombing, and a container ship, the *Atlantic Conveyor*, was attacked and destroyed by Exocet missiles. The ships lost were escort vessels: *HMS Ardent, HMS Coventry, HMS Antelope*, and infantry landing ship *Sir Galahad*. The Argentine pilots flew in low and full speed (600 miles per hour) and launched bombs close to their intended targets. The defending ships fought back with everything possible. But with little room for the ships to maneuver, the resolute Argentines were able to inflict great damage on them as well as sinking four major vessels. For their courage, Argentine aircraft losses were estimated at a staggering 50 percent.

There were a number of lessons learned in this war at sea. Improved detection and multiple high-speed target-tracking electronics were required, as was a "close-in weapons" system. Shooting optically aimed machine guns at inbound jets did not suffice. Anti-ship missile defense became paramount, and the use of aluminum and high-intensity burning materials in ship construction was questioned. For the British, the ability to mount a far-flung amphibious operation within a short time was identified, as was the need to retain an aircraft carrier capability. The successful reclamation of the Falklands was a tribute to British ability, but revealed certain deficiencies in military preparedness.

For the international naval community, the importance of the highly capable nuclear submarine was again demonstrated, as was the destructiveness of the anti-ship missile. Power projection through the use of aircraft carriers was reaffirmed, and the value of the helicopter and VSTOL aircraft confirmed. 250 British service personnel were lost and more than 650 of the Argentine military were killed. Eight years after the war, Great Britain and Argentina finally reestablished diplomatic relations. Argentina has not changed its mind, however, as to who truly owns the Falkland Islands.

This shows the point of impact on the port side aft of the *USS Yorktown CG-48* as the U.S. cruiser is being struck by the *Mirka* in the Black Sea. Minor damage was done to all parties and the U.S. ships withdrew. *U.S.N.I.*

The "Cold War at Sea" Ends, Yet "War at Sea" Continues

The Falkland Islands War diverted the world's attention from the Cold War, but the latter again reared its ugly head. Problems with Third World nations fighting with weapons of Western or Soviet origin became epidemic. The navies of the world, especially that of the United States, were called upon regularly to put out brush fire–type conflicts. Soon after the Argentine surrender, U.S. warships on the other side of the world patrolling in the South China Sea on the night of June 20, 1982, were fired upon by what was certain to be a hostile Vietnamese warship. U.S. warships responded, but the intruder disappeared into the darkness.

There were ongoing problems in the Middle East that necessitated a full-time presence of American naval forces, including carriers in the Indian Ocean and Mediterranean. Lebanon again became a battleground between the Palestine Liberation Army and the Israeli Army. U.S. Marines landed on August 25, 1982, to keep the peace, and within ten days, more than 12,000 refugees were evacuated by elements of the U.S. Sixth Fleet.

Libya began to rattle its sabers in the 1980s and by 1986 sponsored terrorism against Western interests, and actively provoked the Sixth Fleet by firing surface-to-air missiles at aircraft flying from the *USS Coral Sea CV-43*. On March 24, 1986, the Libyan Navy sent out fast attack missile craft from the port of Benghazi to attack U.S. surface

The *USS Phoenix CL-46* (Argentine *AR General Belgrano*) slowly moving through the Panama Canal shortly before World War II. The *Phoenix* was a U.S. Navy 10,000-ton "treaty cruiser" armed with 15 6-inch/47-caliber semi-automatic guns in her main battery. The light cruiser served throughout the war with distinction and was placed in reserve in July 1946. In 1951, she was sold to Argentina with a sister ship, the *USS Boise CL-47*. In the early days of the Falkland Islands War, the *General Belgrano* and her two escorts formed a surface attack group operating near the 200-mile British-ordered exclusion zone. There was some fear that with a speed of more than 30 knots, they could dash toward the British carrier group and with the cruiser's superior speed and firepower, could damage or sink the British force. This rationale caused the rules of engagement to change and the elderly cruiser was torpedoed and sunk. *Author's collection*

ships operating in international waters. Two of the attackers were severely damaged by Harpoon and Rockeye cluster bombs launched by carrier aircraft. A follow-up attack was made on April 15, 1986, when A-6 Intruders from the *USS America CV-66* and the *USS Coral Sea*, accompanied by U.S. Air Force F-111s, bombed a number of selected targets in Libya. The punishment meted out by the navy and air force curtailed any future serious aggression by Libya.

Problems in the Caribbean were becoming increasingly apparent due to Communist insurgency. In July 1983, this led to a naval demonstration by U.S. warships centered around the carrier *USS Ranger CV-61*. Three months later, a 12-ship assault force that included the carrier *USS Independence CV-62* and amphibious helicopter carrier *USS Guam LPH-9* landed troops on the Island of Grenada to oust Cuban and other Marxist forces that had overthrown the local government. On October 27, 1983, two days after the U.S. invasion, the island was secured and evidence was found that a base for nearly 7,000 Cuban soldiers had been planned, and there was a vast stockpile of arms brought in by the Soviets and their client states. More than 1,700 Cuban and other personnel from the Soviet Union or its allies were captured as well.

The remarkable "through deck cruiser" *HMS Invincible* with two Sea Harriers and a Sea King Helicopter near her island structure aft. The British government had determined that there was no further need for fixed-wing aircraft carriers after *HMS Ark Royal* was paid off in December 1978. A "politically correct" effort (entitled the "through deck cruiser") resulted in funds being set aside for the construction of the three-ship Invincible class of VSTOL carriers. The Invincible carried up to twelve rotary-wing aircraft and nine Sea Harrier or jump jets. In combination with the air group of the converted VSTOL carrier, *HMS Hermes*, these ships established air superiority in the Falkland Islands campaign. The Invincible class displaced 19,500 tons full load and was powered by gas turbines with a top speed of 28 knots. After the Falkland Islands experience, they and all other significant surface ships were retrofitted with improved/additional surface-to-air missiles and close-in weapons systems (20-mm Vulcan Phalanx or 30-mm Goalkeeper). *TIM* (Royal Navy)

The *USS Coral Sea CV-43* and other carriers seemed to gravitate to the Persian Gulf, eastern Mediterranean, and Indian Ocean during the 1980s. A new type of naval war was in the offing. Third World nations using Styx or Silkworm (Chinese version of the Styx), Exocets, mines, and U.S.-made hardware were attacking merchant shipping. U.S. warships were not immune—the frigate *USS Stark FFG-31* was struck "accidentally" by two Exocet missiles fired from an Iraqi Mirage F-1 fighter on May 17, 1987. Thirty-seven U.S. seamen lost their lives and the ship nearly sank. To guarantee the flow of oil and other cargoes, the Western navies had to suppress the military activities of these rogue nations. *Author's collection*

Tragically, two months before the Grenada invasion, Soviet fighters shot down a commercial jetliner that had accidentally flown into Russian air space. Two hundred sixty-nine passengers and crew were killed, including a U.S. Congressional representative. The Soviets recovered the Korean Air Lines Boeing 747's flight recorders but failed to notify U.S. authorities.

The mid-1980s proved to be a watershed of strategic one-upmanship between the East and West. President Ronald Reagan initiated plans for a 600-ship navy spearheaded by nuclear carriers, Trident ballistic missile submarines, and the rejuvenation of the four Iowa-class battleships into the most powerful modern gun/missile weapons ever to go to sea. Added to this was the promise of a missile defense system based in space that would defeat any incoming ICBM before it could hit its intended target. Officially titled the "Strategic Defense Initiative"(SDI), it was popularly known as "star wars." To the U.S.S.R., which depended heavily on its ICBM and submarine-launched ballistic

The Sheffield-class Type 42 guided-missile destroyer (DDG) *HMS Coventry* lists to starboard as she begins to sink on May 25, 1982. The 4,100-ton full load ship had just been hit with three 1,000-pound bombs that sealed her fate. In some instances, low-flying Argentine fighter-bombers dropped their bombs before they could arm themselves and they either struck the sea or passed through intended targets without detonating. Those that struck the *Coventry* exploded. The *Coventry* was armed with a twin Sea Dart launcher whose missiles were designed to intercept aircraft or high-speed targets at medium range. Aside from the destroyer 4.5-inch gun and two 20-mm single mounts, the *Coventry* was defenseless against close-in threats. *TIM (Royal Navy)*

The fast frigate *USS Boone FFG-28*, one of 51 Oliver Hazard Perry–class frigates built from 1971–1983. The *Boone* is a sister to the *USS Samuel B Roberts FF-58* and *USS Stark FFG-31*, which were seriously damaged in the Persian Gulf. These "low end" ships were designed as ocean escorts for amphibious groups and convoys. Powered by gas turbines, they were capable of a top speed of 29 knots. Many of the Perry class have also been used successfully in illegal drug–suppression operations in the Caribbean and eastern Pacific. They were armed with a single-arm guided-missile launcher forward (Harpoon and Standard SAM), 3-inch/62-caliber deck gun, ASW torpedoes, and a 20-mm Vulcan Phalanx CAWS. Of particular value are the two ASW helicopters carried by several of the class. *U.S. Navy*

and guided missiles for its military reputation and power, SDI posed an overwhelming problem. In 1980, the Soviet Union was spending more than 14 percent of its gross national product on national defense, and by 1987 this had risen to 17 percent—much of it on naval and allied equipment. By comparison, the United States only spent a fraction of that amount. To keep pace with U.S. naval expansion and SDI, the Soviet Union would have to develop a spectacular matching weapon system or face the probability of economic collapse. The counter to SDI was not forthcoming.

Although the Soviet Navy continued to maintain a presence in nearly all of the world's critical maritime theaters, by the mid-1980s it was evident that the once-feared blue water navy was spending 90 percent of its time swinging at anchor. Only a fraction of the total number of surface combatants were at sea, and many of the 1950s- and early 1960s-built ships were being sold off or retired (Skory-class DD's and Sverdlov-class gun cruisers). Russian Bear and Badger aircraft were still observed worldwide, but not as frequently as in the late 1970s. Soviet warships and land-based naval aircraft were quietly withdrawing from friendly foreign bases. The public line of the Soviet government was that the defense of the homeland was paramount and naval assets were required in home waters. The nuclear attack, ballistic, and guided-missile submarine force remained static and even grew, but overall, the Soviet Navy was downsizing. The momentum that resulted in the design and introduction of newer and more-powerful Soviet warships, (e.g., Kirov nuclear cruisers, Slava guided-missile cruisers and the 64,000-ton full load Kuznetsov-class aircraft carriers) was slowing down as the government announced defense spending cutbacks. By 1989, defense spending was being redirected to the civilian sector, and "guns were being turned into ploughshares."

On December 2, 1989, U.S. President George Bush arrived aboard the missile cruiser *USS Belknap CG-26* at Malta to meet with his opposite number in the Soviet Union—President Mikhail Gorbachev, who was aboard the Russian guided-missile cruiser *Slava*. The meeting took place aboard a Russian ocean liner due to poor weather conditions. The Cold War was thawing quickly, and barriers once held so dear in 1950, 1960, 1970, and 1980 were disappearing in the face of the fall of Communism.

During this same period The U.S. Navy and the West had become gradually committed to keeping the sea lanes open that allowed a free flow of oil from the Middle East to world markets.

The U.S. Navy began to escort tankers in transit within the Persian Gulf to prevent the unprovoked attacks that had begun in the early 1980s by Iraq and Iran, who were at war. The Persian Gulf took center stage in international notoriety throughout the 1980s as U.S. and Western naval resources were poured in to protect tanker traffic. The war between Iraq and Iran resulted in gun, missile, and mine attacks on neutral tankers coming and going in the Persian Gulf (e.g., 179 attacks in 1987). The United States had assumed the role of protector of Western lives, property, and trade in the region, which in turn led to an increased U.S. naval presence in the Gulf. Iraqi or Iranian mines were laid in high-traffic areas, and heavily armed speedboats and missile craft repeatedly damaged merchant ships passing through.

The *USS Belknap CG-26*, on which President George Bush stayed during his meeting with President Gorbachev on December 2, 1989. The frequency of meetings with Soviet leaders increased by the late 1980s, which signaled the end of the Cold War. A month earlier, on November 9, the Berlin Wall had tumbled down and millions of East German citizens began pouring (unhampered) across the border into the West. *Author's collection*

The sea-laid mine was one of the most dangerous obstacles to ships in Middle Eastern waters. The frigate *USS Samuel B Roberts FFG-58* struck an Iranian-laid mine on April 14, 1988, and was nearly lost. In retaliation for this and other mine victims, the U.S. Navy planned and executed Operation Praying Mantis. This operation included surface ship and air attacks on Iranian oil platforms and warships. One of the units assigned was the *USS Lynde McCormick DDG-8*. She and other destroyers and frigates shot up two oil platforms on the morning of April 18, 1988. Throughout the day, Iranian fast-attack craft and other warships responded and were destroyed or damaged by surface-to-surface missiles, gunfire, and aircraft-launched bombs and Harpoon missiles. The scorecard for the American Navy in this operation was impressive. *U.S. Navy*

Escorted by Spruance-class destroyers and Knox-class frigates, a U.S. Iowa-class battleship opens fire. Three of her one-ton projectiles can be seen leaving as they fly toward targets up to 25 miles distant. The "new navy" of the 1980s included the improved Iowa-class battleships that were armed with Harpoon anti-ship missiles, Tomahawk cruise missiles, and Phalanx 20-mm CIWS guns. It was the firing of her 16-inch guns that most impressed observers, and the battleship *USS Missouri BB-63* fired 759 shells at Iraqi targets in support of Operation Desert Storm (1991 Persian Gulf War). Forty-five years earlier, the *Missouri* had been ordered to the Mediterranean as a preventative measure against Communism. *TIM*

The *USS Nimitz CVN-68* with a variety of her potential 90-plane air group on the flight deck. The Nimitz class was better protected than the prototype nuclear carrier *USS Enterprise CVN-65* and its island was smaller. The Nimitz class enabled the U.S. Navy to have prolonged "on station" power projection. *U.S. Navy*

Innocent seamen were dying as a result of these attacks, which often targeted ship's bridges with missiles and gunfire. Diplomatic entreaties failed, and eventually, the United States found itself in a full-fledged naval and air war in the region that ended with a formal clash between Iraq and a U.S.-led coalition of oil-producing and oil-using nations. The invasion of Kuwait by Iraq in the summer of 1990 resulted in the most lopsided victory that had ever occurred in any war when coalition forces defeated the Iraqi military. Iraq had been primarily supplied with Soviet weaponry and technology.

At the end of 1991 the Cold War at sea was formally concluded. The Soviet Navy was dismembered, and many of its combatants either scrapped, sold, or distributed among the newly independent nations that were once part of the U.S.S.R. The units that became part of the Russian Navy still represented a formidable force; however, their primary adversary is no longer the American Navy and its Western allies. Of course, that could change.

Status of the World's Navies 1970–1991
The United States Navy

From 1970 until the official conclusion of the Cold War, the U.S. Navy continued to develop naval aviation, surface, amphibious, and submarine forces. Technological advances in electronics and rotary-wing aircraft dominated in new ship construction. The microchip era had come, and the structure of warships reflected its importance.

Naval Aviation

Of preeminence was the introduction of the Nimitz-class nuclear carrier during the latter half of the Cold War. The age of the fossil fuel super carrier had come to an end, and it was replaced by the first series-built class of nuclear carrier. The namesake of the class, the *USS Nimitz CVN-68*, was laid down in 1968, but took seven years before commissioning. The 97,000-ton full load carriers were built with a 1,040-foot length and a maximum beam of 252 feet. There were four catapults and four deck edge lifts installed. The Nimitz class had two reactors compared to the eight in the nuclear carrier *USS Enterprise CVN-65*, which provides power for approximately 1,000,000 miles of steaming, or the equivalent of 13–15 years.

The carriers were to be primarily defended by nuclear escorts of the California- or Virginia-class nuclear cruisers (CGN); for close-in defense, they had three Vulcan Phalanx 20-mm CIWS guns, and Sea Sparrow surface-to-air missiles. The *Nimitz* and her eight sisters carried a complement of 90 aircraft of varying types and missions. The *Nimitz* entered active service on May 3, 1975, and others of her class have been added every few years.

The Nimitz class provided added credence to the Soviet Navy's doctrine of protecting the homeland from air attack by using submarine- and cruiser-launched anti-ship missiles. The Nimitz class also assured the U.S. Navy of the survival of fixed-wing carrier-borne aircraft well into the twenty-first century.

Surface Navy

In the 1970s, it was the nuclear-powered cruisers that captured the limelight in the surface navy. The *USS California CGN-36* and sister *USS South Carolina CGN-37* entered fleet service in the mid-1970s and were quickly followed by the four-ship Virginia class in the late 1970s. These were handsome and sleek warships that were designed to protect the new Nimitz-class carriers from Soviet air, sea, and undersea threats. In general they were armed with Harpoon anti-ship missiles, Tomahawk cruise missiles (Virginia class), Standard surface-to-air missiles, ASW torpedoes, and two 5-inch/54-caliber deck guns.

They did not have helicopter facilities, nor the AEGIS electronic target detection/tracking system. In a world of constantly evolving electronics, these ships were doomed to early retirement.

The final cruiser-type vessel built for the U.S. Navy during the Cold War was the Ticonderoga AEGIS class. The Ticonderoga class was designed primarily as an anti-air defense escort. This 27-ship class was obviously built to house extensive electronic equipment and new types of radar. The ships had helicopter facilities aft and were powered with gas turbine engines. It was the AEGIS system that set them apart from previous cruisers, and with this system they could locate, track, and assign attack weapons on multiple targets. The

The F-14B Tomcat fighter. First tested in December 1970, it became the hot plane that replaced the F-4 Phantom and F-8 Crusaders made famous over Vietnam. The F-14 had swept wings with a maximum span of 64 feet. Its cruise speed was 576 miles per hour and top speed was 1,544 miles per hour. The Tomcat had a crew of two, and was the primary carrier jet fighter of the last two decades of the Cold War at sea. *U.S. Navy*

An E-2C Hawkeye has just been catapult-launched from the deck of a Nimitz-class carrier. The Hawkeye entered service in 1961 (E-2A), but has been vastly improved over the last 30 years. This aircraft provided carrier-based early warning to the fleet. It is an all-weather aircraft that can track up to 600 targets simultaneously. The Hawkeye was invaluable as the eyes of the fleet. *U.S. Navy*

The nuclear-powered missile cruiser *USS Texas CGN-39* of the Virginia class. These 11,000-ton full load ships were armed with two 5-inch/54-caliber guns, two twin Tartar/Standard/Harpoon missile launchers, ASROC, ASW torpedoes, and two Phalanx 20-mm CIWS (close-in weapon system) Gatling guns. Unfortunately, they had no hangar facilities for ASW helicopters or AEGIS capability. Nuclear cruisers of the California and Virginia class were criticized for not being formidable-looking. Decks were clear of obstructions and there were few weapons. In reality these cruisers represented a continuing trend of protecting weapon systems by keeping most of the associated machinery below deck. Weather and salt are dangerously corrosive to sensitive weapon systems. Eventually, even the missiles would be stored and fired from beneath the deck in vertical launch facilities (e.g., certain Spruance- and Ticonderoga-class surface combatants and all Arleigh Burke–class DDGs). Due to manning and maintenance costs plus limitations in modern electronic upgrading, all of the nuclear cruisers were scrapped by 1999. *Author's collection*

AEGIS created an electronic umbrella to be cast over any of the ships being escorted and could preselect a weapon based on the type of threat. The Soviet tactic of swarm attacking a carrier battle group was checkmated by the AEGIS system.

Destroyers built included the Spruance, Kidd, and at the end of the Cold War, the Arleigh Burke class. All were gas turbine–powered, as was the Oliver Hazard Perry class of ocean escorts.

The Spruance and Kidd classes were alike in most respects and both highly adequate ASW and anti-air platforms. They were 563 feet in length with a 55-foot beam. Powered by gas turbines, these destroyers had a top speed of 33 knots. Both were armed with Harpoon anti-ship missiles and an assortment of anti-air and ASW weapons, including facilities for ASW helicopters aft. It became obvious toward the end of the Cold War at sea that the multiple-type missile vertical launch system (VLS) was the wave of the future. A number of the Spruance class had VLS, as well as the final destroyer class initiated during the Cold War —the Arleigh Burke.

The lead ship, *USS Arleigh Burke DDG-51*, was commissioned on May 6, 1991, just months before the end of the Cold War. Its designed purpose was to defend itself and other ships from airborne attackers, and have an ASW role. They were equipped with AEGIS and essentially a smaller version of the Ticonderoga class. The Burkes had two VLS missile banks capable of firing Tomahawk, Standard (surface-to-air missiles), and ASROC variants. This class also carried one 5-inch/54-caliber gun, two Vulcan Phalanx 20-mm CIWS, ASW torpedoes, and Harpoon anti-ship missiles. They had a top speed of 32 knots.

The lead ship of the Ticonderoga-class AEGIS class guided-missile cruisers: *USS Ticonderoga CG-47*. Her boxlike shape superstructure carried the external SPY-1A phased array radar antenna, a core element of the AEGIS system. At first these ships were condemned for their cost, but after their performance at sea and in dangerous situations, the cruiser and AEGIS system proved themselves. This revolutionary system provided an automatic electronic umbrella against incoming targets, making the Ticonderoga class indispensable as a carrier battle group escort. Powered by gas turbines, this class of cruiser could make over 30 knots on 80,000 shaft horsepower. Gas turbine power enabled this class to accelerate from a standstill to full power within two minutes—vital in ASW operations and for evasive maneuvers. They were armed with two twin Standard missile launchers, Harpoon anti-ship missiles, two 5-inch/54-caliber guns, two 20-mm CIWS mounts, and ASW torpedoes. The Harpoon missile was first designed to destroy Soviet guided-missile submarines (e.g. *Charlie, Echo II*) like a harpoon would kill a whale. The AEGIS-equipped warships provided an effective counter to Soviet submarine, surface- and air-launched high-speed missiles. *Author's collection*

The *USS Spruance DD-963* is moved from her construction site to a launching platform that can be submerged, allowing the new ship to float free after the christening ceremonies. This is the method by which most medium-size warships were built and launched by the Ingalls Shipbuilding Division in Mississippi. It allowed for greater ease in mass production. The *Spruance*, lead ship of a new type of fleet destroyer, was commissioned on September 20, 1975. *TIM*

A SH-3H Sea King helicopter begins landing on the Oliver Hazard Perry–class frigate, *USS Estocin FFG-15*. The Sea King was the workhorse of fleet ASW rotary-wing aircraft, and was commonly assigned to all surface ships with helo facilities. *U.S. Navy*

The last two decades of the Cold War witnessed vast improvements in the U.S. Navy's amphibious ability. Gone was the landing ship tank (LST) of past wars, and in its place came the 39,300-ton full load Tarawa-class LHA helicopter and landing craft amphibious assault ships. Both the Tarawa class (as shown, the *USS Saipan LHA-2*, based at the Norfolk Navy Base) and the 40,500-ton full load Wasp class (LHD) carry up to 42–45 aircraft of a helicopter and VSTOL mix. In particular, the Wasp class can serve as a backup aircraft carrier with fixed-wing Harrier aircraft. The Soviet Navy greatly feared the U.S. Navy's amphibious ability. *Author's collection*

The *USS Arleigh Burke DDG-51*, powered by gas turbines, is making turns for high speed. Although one of the most effective and electronically proficient warships ever built for the U.S. Navy, it was soon discovered that the helicopter had become indispensable to escort ship operations. Later variants of the *Burke* were built with helo facilities that in turn improved their capability as multi-role warfighters. *U.S. Navy*

The 1980s Reagan era of "big navy" expenditures also included the modernization and re-commissioning of all four Iowa-class battleships. Many felt that this was an absurd idea—renovating ships from a bygone era. There was a purpose, however, and that was to counteract a new Soviet threat, the Kirov-class missile cruisers. The Kirovs were huge missile/gun cruisers, designed to escort a battle group in offensive operations or act as the head of a task force. The thin-skinned American ships would not have a chance in a slugging match with a Kirov, but a 59,000-ton modernized Iowa-class battleship would. The Iowas were rearmed with Harpoon, Tomahawk, and Vulcan Phalanx 20-mm CIWS guns. For the latter half of the Cold War and into the Persian Gulf conflict, they served with distinction and effectiveness. All were again retired in the 1990s.

The U.S. Navy also continued to develop and refine its amphibious capability with the Tarawa- and Wasp-class assault ships. Inserting ground assault troops from the sea had been brought to a fine edge with these ships, which employed helicopter and sea transport. They also carried the Marine Corps AV-8B Harrier VSTOL aircraft. To the Wasp and Tarawa classes was added the Whidbey Island class of dock landing ships, and the concept of "prepositioning" came of age. What became known as Maritime Prepositioning Ships were built and assigned to strategic locations worldwide. They were loaded with military supplies sufficient to supply an assault force within a very short time. Much of the U.S. Navy had become dedicated to being able to quickly respond to Communist threats in all parts of the world. As the Cold War at sea diminished, the need to respond like a "super policeman" continued unabated. The tactics used to counteract Soviet aggression were transferable to contest the aggressive acts of rogue nations.

Submarines

The primary additions to the U.S. submarine force were the Los Angeles-class attack boat (SSN) and the Trident intercontinental ballistic missile submarines (SSBN) of the Ohio class.

Attack submarines of the Los Angeles class were activated beginning in 1974 with the lead ship, the *USS Los Angeles SSN-688.* These boats were 6,900 tons submerged and capable of 25+ knots underwater. This class was capable of launching Tomahawk cruise missiles and Mark 48 torpedoes. They were quieter operating and more powerful than previous nuclear attack boats, and were originally designed to counter the Soviet Victor-class attack submarines.

The Ohio class displaced 18,700 tons submerged and had a top speed of 20+ knots submerged. The Ohio class threw a scare into the Soviet military as this SSBN carried 24 Trident (C-4, and later, D-5) ICBMs. Each missile had up to eight MIRVs, with 100-kiloton nuclear warheads. The Trident C-4 had a range of 7,400 miles, and the D-5 variant had a range of up to 12,000 miles. The D-5 had an accuracy of 50 percent of its warheads striking within 90 meters of their intended target. The Soviet Navy did not have a missile system with this capability. Again, numbers and brute force were not as vital as accuracy.

As the Cold War climaxed, the U.S. Navy had taken full advantage of smart weapons and electronic warfare. The cost was enormous, and the Soviet Navy could not keep pace.

Other Western Navies

The U.S. Navy was seconded only by the Soviet Navy from 1970 until the conclusion of the Cold War. The United Kingdom, as a member of NATO, contributed much to the alliance, especially in the area of ocean escort development. The role of Great Britain was to protect the English Channel area and help defeat Soviet submarines that would certainly attempt to interdict merchant traffic. The Royal Navy fielded a number of ASW surface ships that kept pace with Soviet submarine development and would have made a good account of themselves in actual combat. The "through deck cruisers" or VSTOL aircraft carriers of the Invincible class, as they were more appropriately named, revolutionized naval warfare. In many circles, this type of smaller multi-purpose vessel called into question the value of the huge fixed-wing aircraft carrier. The *HMS Invincible* proved her worth during the Falkland Islands war as did her air group of helicopter and Sea Harrier VSTOL aircraft.

The Trident missile ballistic missile submarine *USS Ohio SSBN-726* maneuvers through the Hood Canal near its home base at Bangor, Washington. The Soviet Navy typically employed its nuclear attack boats around the American and Western SSBN havens in order to shadow them to their patrol areas. This game of cat and mouse was normally won by the SSBN. *U.S. Navy*

A Royal Navy Invincible-class, multi-role VSTOL carrier steams in company with a U.S. Navy Nimitz-class aircraft carrier. The difference in size is striking. The Nimitz class displaces 97,000 tons full load and the Invincible class 19,500 tons. The presence of *HMS Invincible* in the Falkland Islands War tipped the balance in favor of the United Kingdom and prevented what might have been one of the most humiliating defeats in English maritime history. There were three Invincible-class carriers built during the later years of the Cold War at sea, the last being the *HMS Ark Royal,* commissioned in November 1985. *U.S. Navy*

The Type 42 guided-missile destroyer *HMS Exeter* seen from the port quarter. Her 4.5-inch dual-purpose gun is readily visible as is her twin arm Sea Dart missile launcher. The *Exeter* performed exceedingly well in the Falkland Islands War by shooting down a large number of attacking Argentine aircraft. The Type 42 destroyers carried the Lynx helicopter, and this destroyer class was primarily designed to provide area air defense for battle groups. *Author's collection*

Great Britain also maintained a credible nuclear attack and ballistic missile submarine (Resolution class SSBN) force throughout the 1970s and 1980s that acted as a great adjunct to the U.S. Naval efforts.

France continued to develop her navy independently from NATO. However, it was fully expected that this country would rejoin NATO in the event of a generalized Soviet attack. The French Navy maintained two fixed-wing aircraft carriers (*Clemenceau* and *Foch*) throughout much of the Cold War. Both were retired in the late 1990s, to be replaced by the 40,000-ton nuclear carrier

Charles de Gaulle. The fascination with nuclear-powered vessels did not begin with this carrier, but had been ongoing with attack and ballistic missile submarines. In 1971, France introduced the five-unit Le Redoubtable SSBN, and in 1983 the nuclear Rubis-class cruise missile submarines.

In tandem with its naval aviation and submarine capability, the French Navy built and deployed a number of guided-missile destroyers and frigates.

Like their larger neighbors, other Western nations gradually reduced the number and types of ships in their naval inventories. Aircraft carriers and cruisers disappeared and went to the

One of the methods by which NATO ships could maintain a lengthy presence at sea was through the use of replenishment ships such as the Canadian Navy's 24,700-ton full load *HMCS Protecteur*. The *Protecteur* is shown here resupplying another NATO asset, the Federal German Republic 3800-ton frigate *Bremen* in this August 30, 1985, photograph. Ships of the West German Navy, such as the Sea Sparrow armed multi-role frigates of the Bremen class, were invaluable. The presence of the Federal Republic of Germany in NATO greatly agitated the Soviet government. *Navy League*

shipbreakers. They were replaced by smaller, yet often more potent, destroyers, frigates, and improved diesel-electric submarines. For many smaller navies, the conventional submarine became so well developed that it slowly became a viable alternative to costly nuclear power.

For most of the West, economics began to drive the size and scope of its navies. The advances in electronic/missile warfare also allowed nations to have powerful, cost-effective ships that were much smaller than in previous decades. The United States ultimately served as the principal defender of the West.

The Union of Soviet Socialist Republics' Navy

The Soviet Navy began the last 20 years of the Cold War at sea with great promise and instilled fear in the minds of most Western naval professionals. From its rudimentary beginning in the early post–World War II years it had come a great distance in only a quarter of a century. With its nuclear attack, guided missile, and ballistic missile submarines, it posed a real threat to the U.S. and NATO's hegemony on the seas. The Russians were not only building what could now be termed a diverse maritime fighting force of surface ships, submarines, and fast attack craft, but were also developing shore- and sea-based naval aviation.

France actively developed its surface navy with such ships as the *De Grasse* shown here moored in Bordeaux. The *De Grasse* was one of three Type F-67 multi-task destroyers built with Exocet surface-to-surface missiles, Crotale SAMs, guns, and ASW rocket and homing torpedo systems. The *De Grasse* and her sisters were also helicopter (Lynx)-equipped like most of the world's modern escort vessels. *Author's collection by Carolyn Bonner*

The "Land Down Under." Australia maintained a professional and well-developed navy committed to the West throughout the Cold War. Many of its ships and aircraft fought with the allies during the Vietnam War. The Sydney Naval Base was the primary naval facility for the Australian Navy and shown are three Charles F. Adams (Perth)—class destroyers and one Oliver Hazard Perry (Sydney)—class frigate (April 1998). All were built and modified for Australian Navy usage. *Author's collection by Carolyn Bonner*

The Danish frigate *Niels Juel* moored in the Norfolk Navy Yard in the United States in the summer of 1997. This frigate and her two sisters were built in the late 1970s as part of NATO's northern defense. They were multi-purpose and were armed with Harpoon, Sea Sparrow SAMs, guns, and ASW weapons. *Author's collection by Carolyn Bonner*

Naval aviation at sea aboard fixed-wing aircraft carriers had been considered the dividing line between a superpower navy and a second-rate one. The U.S. Navy obviously dominated in this form of absolute power projection with Great Britain, France, and other nations playing a comparatively minor role. The Soviet Navy began to challenge this aspect of Western naval power during the latter part of the Cold War.

Naval Aviation

The Soviets built four units of the 43,000-ton Kiev class that were intended as VSTOL aircraft carriers. They were officially referred to as "guided-missile" VSTOL carriers. The namesake of the class, *Kiev* entered service on May 1, 1975. They were 910 feet in length and were the first Soviet carriers that had true fixed-wing aircraft assigned (twelve Yak-38 Forger), and 14–17 Ka-25 Hormone or Ka-27 Helix helicopters. In addition to their air group, the Kievs were very heavily armed with four twin SSN-12 (Sandbox) anti-ship missile launchers, two twin SAN-3 (Goblet) SAM launchers, two twin SAN-4 (Gecho) SAM launchers, a twin SUW-N-1 ASW launcher, and various guns and torpedoes. It was surmised that these ships were designed to guard Soviet SSBN sanctuaries (bastions) against U.S. or NATO attack submarines or aircraft. The helicopters would find and kill SSNs and the Forgers would hunt down and destroy P-3 Orion-type ASW aircraft. These vessels were inactivated after the Cold War, and one, the *Gorshkov*, was reportedly sold to India in 1999 as a replacement for its aging VSTOL carrier *INS Viraat*.

The centerpiece of Russian naval aviation was the three-ship Kuznetsov guided-missile aircraft carrier class. The Soviet Navy finally had a true super carrier at 67,500 tons full load and 975 feet long on the 12 degree angled ski-ramp flight deck. The Kuznetsov was designed to carry an air group of up to 20 Su-27k Flanker D aircraft, which were high-performance fighters similar to American F-15 Eagles. In addition to the fixed-wing contingent, the new ship carried twelve helicopters.

True to Soviet naval policy, the Kuznetsov class was heavily armed with 12 flush-mounted SSN-19 Shipwreck anti-ship missile launchers, 24 SAN-9 short-range SAM launchers, ASW rocket launchers (RBU-12000), and various other short-range missile and gun defense systems. Unlike the Western method of using escorts to defend its carriers, the Soviet Navy made each vessel its own navy. After the end of the Cold War, the Russians retained the Kuznetsov in semi-active state.

The Turkish Navy destroyer *Adatepe*, formerly the FRAM II U.S. Navy destroyer *USS Forrest Royal DD-872*, which guarded NATO's southern flank in the Mediterranean. Many former U.S. Navy Sumner, Gearing, and Fletcher-class destroyers ended up in NATO or other friendly navies. Often these ships were modernized and much more heavily armed than when in U.S. Naval service. The *Adatepe* was armed with ASROC, four 5-inch/38-caliber guns, ASW torpedoes, a twin 40-mm mount forward, and an enclosed twin 35-mm gun on the former DASH flightdeck. A small number of former U.S. World War II–built destroyers were also armed with Harpoon anti-ship missiles. *Author's collection*

To the timeless Bear and Badger long-range bombers of Soviet naval aviation was added the Tu-22M Backfire strike bomber in 1974. These Mach 2–capable bombers could carry the AS-4 Kitchen anti-ship missile, bombs, and mines. The Soviet Navy also began to develop fixed-wing carrier-borne aircraft, and as the Cold War at sea neared its conclusion, the MiG-19 Fulcrum fighter became operational (1984). The Fulcrum was a high-performance aircraft that had a top speed over Mach 2, and approached the U.S. Navy's F-14 Tomcat in potential ability.

Surface Ships

The Soviet surface fleet stunned the world in 1980 when Western observers first saw the guided-missile "battle" cruiser *Kirov*. This class proved that Soviet naval intent was to move from home waters and operate on a worldwide basis. Of course, defense of Mother Russia was not forgotten. As a reinforcement of this doctrine, a surface attack group lead by the *Kirov* demonstrated how this type of force would defeat a hostile Western battle group in an exercise held in 1985. The first nuclear-powered surface ship in the Soviet Navy was also the largest built, at 24,300 tons full load and 814 feet in length. Although primarily powered by nuclear reactor, the Kirovs also utilized a fossil-fuel backup system. The Kirov class was to have five ships, yet only four were built. They were armed (perhaps overarmed) with a variety of sophisticated and diverse weapons that included SSN-19 cruise missiles, SAN-6 and SAN-4 surface-to-air missile launchers, guns, torpedoes, ASW rocket launchers, and helicopters for ASW and anti-ship missile guidance. The SSN-19 had a

The Kiev-class cruiser *Minsk* in a 1979 photograph taken by a NATO reconnaissance aircraft. Visible on her angled flight deck are Forger VSTOL aircraft and five helicopters. The aft lift is in its down position, and the carrier's four twin SSN-12 anti-ship missile launchers can easily be seen forward of the massive island structure. In addition to an ASW role, the Kiev class was considered as a method for projecting Soviet sea power abroad. *Navy League*

300-mile range, and there were 20 angled vertical launch tubes in the forecastle. The SSN-19 could be armed with a nuclear or high-explosive warhead. Ultimately, this type of system was destined to replace the single- and twin-arm missile launchers that have served most navies for the major part of the Cold War.

Other guided-missile cruisers built by the Soviets during the final years of the Cold War included the Slava, Kresta II, and Kara classes. All were armed with anti-ship and surface-to-air missiles. In particular, the Slava class boasted 16 SSN-12 anti-ship launch tubes that crowded her amidships main deck. The Slavas looked menacing and were designed to attack intruding American aircraft carriers.

To the Soviet destroyer force was added the 8,200-ton Udaloy guided-missile destroyer and the Sovremennyy-class anti-ship missile destroyer classes in the 1980s. The Sovremennyy class mounted two

quadruple SSN-22 "Sunburn" anti-ship missile launchers. The Sunburn had a 50-mile range.

One of the most popular surface ship types to join the Soviet fleet was the Krivak, which had three successive variants. Many were used by the Soviet State Police (KGB) for maritime border patrols; however, most were employed as ocean escorts. The Krivaks were armed with a variety of weapons including anti-ship, anti-air, and ASW missiles and rockets. They also carried rails for sowing anti-ship mines.

Rounding out the Soviet surface fleet were upgraded and modern fast attack craft (missile and torpedo) and an emerging amphibious force.

Submarines

The Soviet Navy devoted much of its effort to designing and building faster, quieter, deeper diving, and more powerful attack and missile submarines in the 1970s and on into the late 1980s.

The Soviet aircraft carrier *Kuznetsov* with a helicopter hovering off its stern as it rests in the Mediterranean in January 1996. This type of carrier portended nothing but difficulty for the West when it was first commissioned, but in January 1996 Russian and U.S. Navy leaders met to develop means of exchanging professional information and set up a regular intra-navy dialogue. *U.S. Navy*

In the 1970s, the Soviets built the Victor II and III nuclear attack boats. They were improved versions of the Victor I. The later variants were quieter and displaced greater tonnage under water. Also introduced in the 1970s was the Alfa, one of the fastest underwater boats ever built at 45+ knots. The Alfa was primarily used for testing the use of titanium in hull construction and other innovations. A submarine capable of that speed would have posed a great threat to the West. It was reported that an Alfa did approach and pass beneath a Western task force before sensors or weapons could be brought to bear. The follow-up to early efforts was the Akula, Mike, and Sierra classes built in the 1980s. These boats were larger at 8,000+ tons and faster at 32+ knots submerged. What also set them apart from other designs was the ability to fire state-of-the-art cruise missiles (SSNX-21 "Sampson") with a 1,600-mile range). The Akula was considered by all accounts the best of all Soviet nuclear attack submarines. The Akula and Sierra classes also carried torpedoes and SSN-16 Stallion ASROC for defense.

The Soviet Navy did not drop diesel-electric propulsion as did the U.S. Navy, and it continued to build the Foxtrot, Tango, and finally the highly successful Kilo class attack boats. The Kilo-class

A Kirov-class guided-missile cruiser. Much of its missile armament was forward of the superstructure. The Kirov carried two helicopters aft that could be stored under the deck and brought up by elevator. For close-in defense, this type of large cruiser depended on point defense missiles and eight 30-mm Gatling guns. *TIM*

A Slava missile cruiser whose 16 SSN-12 anti-ship missile tubes dominate the main deck. There were no "reloads," and one of the main criticisms of the Soviet surface fleet was that it was a "one-shot fleet" that had to win on the first salvo. This was based on the concept of winning the war at sea with a decisive first battle. *TIM*

has been exported to many nations and is popular for its quiet operation and listening capability. This capability was valuable when protecting Soviet SSBNs from American or NATO nuclear attack boats.

The Soviet Navy continued to refine its cruise missile program with the Oscar class, first seen in 1983. This was the ultimate in guided-missile submarine development. The Oscar I displaced a hefty 16,700 tons submerged, and its successor, the Oscar II, more than 18,000 tons. Both were armed with surface-to-surface SSN-19 "Shipwreck" cruise missiles that had a range of 300 miles. Six hatches opposite the sail on either side of the upper hull (deck) would open to allow missile firing, and these missiles had either a high-explosive or 300-kiloton nuclear warhead. The

Oscars reportedly carried 24 Shipwreck missiles, 18 torpedoes, and SSN-15 (Starfish) or SSN-16 (Stallion) ASW rocket-delivered nuclear depth bombs or homing torpedoes. The intended target for the Oscar classes was American battle groups and especially those built around super carriers.

The ballistic missile submarine program continued with the Delta - I, II, III, and IV variants. The Delta IV carried 16 SSN-23 "Skiff" ballistic missiles that had a 4,900-mile range and up to four MIRV 100-kiloton warheads. The long range of this missile also meant that the Soviet SSBNs could now patrol within easy protection of air and surface ship protection.

As with the Kirov-class guided-missile cruisers, the U.S.S.R. pushed the envelope with the Typhoon-class ballistic missile submarine. This was

The Sovremennyy class of large destroyer entered fleet service in 1981. These were 7,300-ton full load ships with a 512-foot length and capable of 32 knots on steam turbines. A flight deck and telescopic hanger for a Helix helicopter can easily be seen just aft of the rather large funnel. *Navy League*

A Tango-class diesel electric submarine rides on the surface in this image captured in 1976. The Tango was designed for quiet operation and the ability to remain submerged for extended periods listening for Western SSNs. They displaced 3,900 tons submerged and were armed with standard torpedoes. *Navy League*

The Alfa was a fast underwater boat with an estimated top speed of 45 knots. Six boats were built, the last entering service in 1983. It has also been estimated that an Alfa could dive as deep as 2,500 feet. This photograph was taken in July 1981. *Navy League*

The Typhoon class was to be hidden under the Arctic ice rather than the more traditional SSBN sanctuaries (Bastions) in the Barents Sea and Sea of Okhorst. SSBNs operating in the bastions were protected from Western attack by air, surface, and subsurface assets. The Typhoon was built to sit and wait. In some respects it was a 1980s version of 1960s popular concept of a "doomsday" machine. The only difference was that one was fictional and the Typhoon was real. *Author's collection.*

the absolute weapon of terror. Estimated at more than 25,000 tons submerged, this new type of SSBN was the largest submersible vessel in any navy. It was armed with 20 SSN-20 "Sturgeon" MIRVed missiles that had a range of 4,600 miles with up to 10 100-kiloton independently targeted warheads each. This boat was also armed with SSN-16 Stallion ASROC and torpedoes for defense. The size and armament of this type of vessel was not as sinister as its mission. The Typhoon was designed to remain under the Arctic ice pack for periods extending up to one year. Creature comforts were maximized for the crew of 160. Saunas and a swimming pool were installed to enable the crew to live and work underwater for prolonged deployments. The Typhoon class, of which six were built, was to surface after a nuclear attack had taken place and with its 200 nuclear warheads, interrupt and decimate reconstruction efforts in the West without any warning. It was in response to the U.S. Navy's Trident program, and conveyed the message that even should the West emerge from a nuclear holocaust, the war would continue on Soviet terms.

The last Typhoon entered service in the late 1980s, and reportedly, this class of submarine is so complex that it has been plagued with mechanical and operating problems. Shortly after the conclusion of the Cold War, these boats became

unserviceable and retired. A private foundation has been active in the purchase of a disarmed Typhoon as a public attraction in New York Harbor.

The Cold War for the Soviet Union ended with the dissolution of its government in 1991, yet for the navy it began in the late 1980s. The fleets including SSBNs and attack submarines began to spend more time in harbor or undergoing sporadic maintenance. Funding availability and the infrastructure to support a world-class navy began to break down, and the overall threat of war at sea ended. Weapons, electronic marvels, ship sizes, and numbers in the West did not conquer the Soviet Navy—it was internal economics and social change. The once proud and growing navy dreamed of by Admiral Gorshkov began to die soon after his retirement in 1985, and was but a shadow of its former self by 1991.

EPILOGUE:
WAR WITHOUT BATTLES

As noted earlier, the Cold War at sea formally ended on December 30, 1991, but it had been receding since 1985. Over the period from 1975 to 1985, the Soviet Navy posed the greatest threat to the U.S. Navy since its inception. The Russians designed and built a series of warships that shocked the world with their audacity in size, armament, and capability. Had the proverbial rug not been pulled out from under, the Soviet Navy would have been able to cause the West great distress well beyond the dawn of the twenty-first century.

The question always arises: which side would have been victorious in combat at sea? It cannot be answered in a single sentence, paragraph, or even volumes of analysis. Over a four-decade

period, the Soviet Navy was built from virtually nothing into nearly the most powerful seaborne force in the world. It also made technological strides that were just a step behind Western efforts. Had the West and the Soviet Navy clashed, the result would have been a bloody nose for both parties, with the West likely retaining command of the sea. The sheer size and number of Soviet weapons would not have triumphed over Western technological and electronic defenses. It is conjectured that until the Soviet Navy had been able to achieve parity with the West in its automated systems and electronic weapon and sensor development, it would have come in second best in any combat

In August 1998, a dozen U.S. Navy nuclear submarines await their turn to be scrapped at the Puget Sound Navy Yard in Bremerton, Washington. A long and involved process was devised to remove and safely store nuclear components. The Soviet Navy has been criticized internationally for not ensuring the proper disposal of its nuclear-powered submarines. To the right of the photograph is the now inactivated *USS Triton SSN-586*. The *Triton* circumnavigated the world under water in 1960, and was the largest nuclear boat built to date in 1955. *Author's collection by Carolyn Bonner*

Leahy and *Belknap* cruisers await their fate in this July 1997 photograph taken at the Suisun Bay, California, at the inactive ship's anchorage. Missiles have been removed and the 5-inch/54-caliber gun barrels have been cut in half. The next destination for these once beautiful cruisers is to be used as a target or scrapping. *Author's collection*

at sea. Fortunately, the demise of the Soviet Navy makes this a moot point.

The cost of the Cold War at sea can never be accurately measured. In lives, considering the Korean and Vietnam wars, and other operations over the four-decade war, the West lost more than 150,000 service personnel. An untold number of civilians were killed and injured in the areas where the West and the Communist-controlled states clashed. By contrast, Soviet and Communist-controlled nations suffered losses in the millions. The estimated dead in Vietnam alone was 1,000,000 civilian and military personnel.

The cost in dollars is also immeasurable, and the war depleted the treasuries of the two superpowers. Allied Western and Soviet bloc nations began to reduce their contribution long before the war ended. Their fragile economies and citizenry that were tired of living in fear slowly withdrew support. The United States borrowed heavily from the taxpayers to build and field a powerful, and

very expensive, navy. The Soviet Union irresponsibly expended a huge amount of its assets and all that could be borrowed to compete. In the end, the West endured and recovered from the economic strain, and the Soviet Union collapsed. The war at sea was won by economics.

After the war came to an end, ships and other related weapons were quickly placed in reserve or sent to the shipbreakers. A few of what were once considered formidable warships ended their days as museum and public attractions. They no longer cause fear or foreboding. For those that visit these attractions, it is difficult to explain the presence of so many expensive weapons that were never employed except to prevent the use of opposing weapons.

The Cold War at sea was a war without traditional sea battles, but a vicious and costly war nevertheless. In essence, the war was won by both sides: weapons of mass destruction were never used, and that was the criterion for true victory for mankind.

Soviet destroyers lie partially sunken where they were left moored in Murmansk Harbor. Much of the Soviet Navy went to shipbreakers or was anchored in quiet locations awaiting the inevitable fate of the scrap yard. *Greenpeace*

Former Charles F. Adams—class guided-missile destroyers and guided-missile frigates of the Brooke class moored at the deactivated Mare Island Naval Shipyard in early 1998. These ships are being converted to power barges and are to be sold to Third World nations desiring electric power in various port facilities. A quarter-century before the photograph was taken, ships of these classes were actively shelling North Vietnamese targets and shooting at MiG attackers. *Author's collection*

The shipbreakers at Alang, India, in 1997. Dozens of warships from the ex-Soviet Navy were sailed up on the beach to be sold to the highest bidder and then dismantled. The steel and other metals from these ships have been recycled into consumer products being used worldwide. The shipbreaking facility at Alang is supposedly one of the modern wonders of the world. It is also one of the most despicable. Workers live in squalor and scores die each month as men, women, and children cut up old ships with stone-age tools. *Greenpeace*

The Soviet Navy exported a number of ships to other nations, including Kilo-class diesel-electric submarines. This is another result of the Cold War at sea. Many nations have acquired high-tech warships at bargain prices from the Soviet Union and the West. *Navy League*

The war at sea in the future will likely not be Cold. This artist's conception of the 500-missile-armed "Arsenal Ship" points the way to the next war at sea. Ships armed with smart weapons that can attack any target within thousands of miles will form the nucleus of seaborne battle forces in the future. *Author's collection*

BIBLIOGRAPHY

Primary Materials

Private Papers – Manuscript/Photo Files
 Bonner, Kermit H., Private papers and photo collection.

Special Collections – Manuscripts/Photo Collections
 Call Bulletin Newspaper File, 1994, Treasure Island Museum.
 Greenpeace International
 Treasure Island Museum Photo Files, 1994 – Various.
 United States Naval Institute, 1997, 1998, 1999 – Various.
 United States Navy – CHINFO, Office of Information, 1999 – Various.
 McClellan Air Force Base, PAO – 1999, MiG-17 Fighter Aircraft.
 Mark Peitz, *USS Oklahoma City CL-5*, Vietnam Era.
 Richard Burgess, Navy League Photo Files (Soviet Navy).

Interviews
 Public Affairs Office, Puget Sound Naval Shipyard, Bremerton, Washington, August 1998.
 Interviews with Commander Surface Force – San Diego and CHINFO, Washington D.C., April 1998.
 United States Navy Cruiser Sailors Association, Edward August, Various 1998.
 David Johnson – Center for Defense Information, Washington D.C., February 1999.
 Chris Cavas, Naval Historian and Photojournalist, Various 1999.
 Rick Burgess, Managing Editor, *Sea Power*, Navy League, Various 1998, 1999.
 Naval Inactive Ships Facility, Bremerton Washington, Pete Galassi, August 1998.
 United Defense, LP – Armament Systems Division, Jeff Van Keuren, January 1999.
 Mark Pietz, Remembrances of the *USS Oklahoma City CL-5* in Vietnam, March 1999.

U.S. Government Documents
 U.S. Navy, Chief of Naval Operations, "Understanding Soviet Naval Developments," 1978, 1981, 1991, U.S. Government Printing Office.
 Department of the Navy, "Vision, Presence, Power," 1998.

 Department of Defense, "Soviet Military Power," 1986, U.S. Government Printing Office.
 U.S. Government Printing Office, "Dictionary of American Naval Fighting Ships, Volume V," 1979.
 Puget Sound Naval Shipyard Newsletter, August 1998.
 The White House, "A National Security Strategy for a New Century," 1998.

Secondary Materials

Books, Monographs, Treatises
 Blackman, Paul, *The World's Warships*, Hanover House, 1960.
 Blackman, Raymond, V. B., *Jane's Fighting Ships 1968–1969*, BPC Publishing, Ltd., 1969.
 Bonds, Ray, Editor, *Russian Military Power*, Bonanza Books, 1982.
 Bonner, Kit; Bonner Carolyn, *Great Naval Disasters*, MBI Publishing Company, 1998.
 Bonner, Kit, *Final Voyages*, Turner Publishing, 1996.
 DiCerto, J. J., *Missile Base Beneath the Sea, The Story of Polaris*, St. Martins Press, 1967.
 Durham, Roger C., *Spy Sub*, Penguin Books, 1996.
 English, Adrian, *Armed Forces of Latin America*, Jane's Publishing Co. Ltd., 1984.
 Erkhammar, Bertil and Ohrelius, *The Royal Swedish Navy*, Raben and Sjogren, 1965.
 Faulkner, Keith, *Jane's Warship Recognition Guide*, Harper Collins Publishing, 1996.
 Friedman, Norman, *Modern Warship design and Development*, Mayflower Books, 1979.
 Friedman, Norman, *U.S. Destroyers*, Naval Institute Press, 1982.
 Friedman, Norman, *U.S. Cruisers*, Naval Institute Press, 1984.
 Grove, Eric J., *Vanguard to Trident*, Naval Institute Press, 1981
 Humble, Richard, Submarines, *The Illustrated History*, Basinghall Books Ltd., 1981.
 Jane's Publishing, *Jane's Fighting Ships, 1944–45, 1947–48, 1955–56, 1979–80, 1968–69, 1987–88, 1996–97*
 Jane's Publishing, *Jane's Warship Recognition Guide*, 1996.
 Jordan, John, *Modern U.S. Navy*, Prentice Hall Press, 1986.

Karnow, Stanley, *Vietnam, A History*, The Viking Press, 1983.

Marinha de Guerra Portugesa, *History of the Navy of Portugal*, 1962, Government of Portugal.

McNeil, Jim, "Charleston's Navy Yard," Cokercraft Press, 1985.

Mickel, Peter/Jentschura, Hansgeorg/Jung, Dieter, *Warships of the Imperial Japanese Navy, 1869–1945*, 1977, Naval Institute Press.

Miller, David, *The Cold War, A Military History*, John Murray Publishing, 1998.

Moineville, Hubert, *Naval Warfare Today and Tomorrow*, Basil Blackwell Publishing, 1983.

Moore, Captain John E, *The Soviet Navy Today*, Stein and Day, 1975.

Moore, John Captain R.N., *Jane's American Fighting Ships of the 20th Century*, Mallard Press, 1991.

Morison, Samuel Eliot, *History of the United States Naval Operations in World War II*, Vol. XV, Atlantic-Little Brown, 1962.

Muir, Malcom Jr., *Black Shoes and Blue Water*, Naval Historical Center, 1996.

Palmer, Michael, *On Course to Desert Storm, The United States Navy and the Persian Gulf*, Naval Historical Center, 1992.

Preston, Anthony, *Warships of the World*, Jane's, 1980.

Scott, Harriet and Scott, William F, *The Armed Forces of the U.S.S.R.*, Westview Press, 1979.

Schofield, William G., Captain USNR, *Destroyers–60 Years*, Rand McNally and Company, 1962.

Silverstone, Paul, U.S. *Warships Since 1945*, Naval Institute Press, 1987.

Silverstone, Paul, "U.S. Navy 1945 to the Present," Arms and Armour Press, 1991.

Sommervile, Donald, *World War II Day by Day*, Dorset Press, 1989.

Sultzberger, C. L., *The American Heritage Picture History of World War I*, Crown Publishers, 1966.

Sweetman, Jack, *American Naval History*, Naval Institute Press, 1984.

Tazewell, William, *Newport News Shipbuilding, The First Century*, The Mariners Museum, 1986.

Terzibaschitsch, Stephan, *Aircraft Carriers of the U.S. Navy*, Naval Institute Press, 1978.

Utz, Curtis A., *Cordon of Steel*, Naval Historical Center, 1993.

Various Photojournalists, *A Day in the Life of the Soviet Union*, Collins Publishers Inc., 1987.

Walker, Martin, *The Cold War*, Owl Books, 1993.

Watts, Anthony, *Axis Submarines*, Arco Publishing Co., 1997.

Woodward, Admiral Sandy and Robinson, Patrick, *One Hundred Days: The Memoirs of the Falkland Battle Group Commander*, 1992.

Wright and Logan, *The Royal Navy in Focus 1960–69*, Maritime Books, 1981.

Articles

All Hands, Bureau of Naval Personnel, November 1945.

Atkinson, James D and Yeuell, Donovan P., Colonel United States, "Must We Have World War III?," Naval Institute Proceedings, July 1956.

Beers, Henry P, Warship International, "American Naval Detachment-Turkey 1919–1924," Vol. XIII, No. 3, 1976.

Bonner, Kit, "Tonkin Gulf Incident," Sea Classics, Bonner, Kit, "The End of an Era, The *USS Oklahoma CLG-5* Departs on Her Final Cruise," U.S. Navy Cruiser Sailors Association, Spring 1999.

Buxton, Il, "Breaking Up HM Ships," Warship, 1982.

Carlin, Robert J., Captain USN(Ret), "Strategic Deterrence in the Age of Détente," Naval Institute Proceedings, September 1979.

Eller, E. M., Rear Admiral, USN(Ret), "Soviet Bid for the Sea," Naval Institute Proceedings, June 1955.

Englund, Will and Gary Cohn, "Scrapping Ships, Sacrificing Men," The Sun, December 7, 1997 (Note: Pulitzer Prize Winner, 1997).

Fenlon, Leslie K., Captain USN(Ret), "The Umpteenth Cuban Confrontation," Naval Institute Proceedings, July 1980.

Finney, John W., "Soviets Imperil U.S. Ships," Naval Institute Proceedings, June 1965 (article reprinted from *New York Times* April 4, 1965).

Friedman, Norman, "World Navies in Review," Naval Institute Proceedings, March 1994.

Friedman, Norman, " World Naval Developments," Naval Institute Proceedings, June 1993.

Gruner, William P., Payne, Henry, "Submarine Maneuver Control," Naval Institute Proceedings, July 1992.

Huan, C., Lt. USN, "The Soviet Union and its Submarine Force," Naval Institute Proceedings, July 1957.

Manthorpe, William, Captain USN(Ret), "The Soviet View," Naval Institute Proceedings, July 1991.

Martin, J. M., Captain USNR(Ret), "We Still Haven't Learned," Naval Institute.

Matloff, Maurice, "The Soviet Union and the War in the West," Naval Institute Proceedings, March 1956.

Meister, Jurg, "The Soviet Navy in World War II," Naval Institute Proceedings, August 1957.

Myre, Greg, AP, "Sailor Kills Eight Crew Members on Russian Submarine," September 11, 1998.

Naval Institute Proceedings, July 1955, Reprint of *New York Herald Tribune*, April 10, 1955, "Ocean Radar Post to Rise off Coast."

Noot, Jurien, LCDR, Royal Netherlands Navy, Polmar, Norman, "The First Modern Soviet Submarine," Naval Institute Proceedings, April 1991.

Parke, Everett A., LTCD, USN, "The Unique and Vital DER," Naval Institute Proceedings, February 1960.

Peace to the Oceans Bulletin: "Russian Squadrons in the USA 1863–64," 11-12-97.

Polmar, Norman, "The Republic Navies," Naval Institute Proceedings, November 1992.

Polmar, Norman, "Foreign Aircraft Carrier Redux," Naval Institute Proceedings, July 1991.

Powers, Robert C., Commander, USN, "Linebacker Strike," Naval Institute Proceedings, August 1974.

Sieche, Erwin, "The Type XXI Submarine, Part 2" Warship, April 1981.

Staff Written, Sea Power, 1990,1991, 1992, 1993, 1994, 1995, 1996, 1997, 1998, and 1999 issues, Navy League of the United States.

Staff Written "Farewell to the Foch," Warships International, Spring 1999.

Staff Written, "U.S. Naval Battle Force Changes, January – December 1997" Naval Institute Proceedings, May 1998.

Staff Written, "The Soviet Union Collapses," *Newsweek*, March 8, 1999

Staff Written, Warships International, Spring 1999, A Nation's Flagship."

Staff Written, *Life* Magazine, September 15, 1961, "A Message to you from the President."

Staff Written, "Soviet Ships in the News," Naval Institute Proceedings, February 1973.

Stoessel, Frederic, "The Bite of the Fox," The Tin Can sailor, April–May 1999.

Thompson, Mark, "Star Wars: The Sequel," *Time Magazine*, February 22, 1999.

Watt, Donald C., "Stalin's First Bid for Sea Power, 1933 – 1939," Naval Institute Proceedings, June 1964.

Webber, Mark, Lt. USN, "Kashin Class Missile Frigates," Naval Institute Proceedings, June 1965.

Wheeler, Gerald M., "Naval Aviation in the Jet Age," Naval Institute Proceedings, November 1957.

Winnefeld, James, "The Cold War Power Spectrum," Naval Institute Proceedings, January 1960.

Worth, Richard A., "Defending the 100-Fathom Curve," Naval Institute Proceedings, October 1997.

Newspapers
Los Angeles Times, October 20, 1962.

Web Sites
Internet Sites for U.S. Navy.Mil – Naval Vessel Register.

Other
Grolier Electronic Encyclopedia, 1993, "The Cold War."

Grolier Electronic Encyclopedia, 1993, "Cuban Missile Crisis," Hamby, Alonzo L. /Elie, Abel, "The Missile Crisis," 1966 / Allison, Graham, "Essence of Decision," 1971.

INDEX